SUPPLEMENTS / 7

The Religious Dimension of Socrates' Thought

by James Beckman

Published for the Canadian Corporation for Studies in Religion / Corporation Canadienne des Sciences Religieuses by Wilfrid Laurier University Press

Canadian Cataloguing in Publication Data

Beckman, James, 1943-
The religious dimension of Socrates' thought

(SR supplements ; 7)

Bibliography: p.
Includes index.
ISBN 0-919812-09-0 pa.

1. Socrates – Religion. I. Title. II. Series.

B318.R4B43 183'.1 C79-094072-8

Order from:
Wilfrid Laurier University Press
Wilfrid Laurier University
Waterloo, Ontario, Canada N2L 3C5

ὅσοι δὲ σώζονται νῦν ἐκ φιλοσοφίας,
διὰ τὸν Σωκράτη σώζονται.

All who today find their salvation
through philosophy owe their salvation
to Socrates.

Julian the Apostate, *Letter to Themistius*

To Valerie

Acknowledgements

As always, in a work of this nature, an author accumulates considerable indebtedness for help he has received along the way. I am grateful, then, for the present opportunity to acknowledge publicly the assistance I have received from many quarters: Prof. J.E. Bruns and Prof. F.E. Sparshott, for their critical suggestions and encouragement after reading an earlier form of the present work; Prof. R.E. Allen, under whose tutelage I was introduced to the intricacies of Plato's metaphysics; Fraser Smith, for many hours, over several years, of conversation about Greek philosophy; and Richard Wright, for his admirable work on the index. Above all I would like to express my gratitude to Prof. Leslie Dewart, whose encouragement at a critical time was particularly instrumental in the eventual appearance of this volume. And, too, his close scrutiny of the manuscript has resulted in many of the more glaring literary infelicities being pruned from the work. For any incongruities of style or opinion which remain, in spite of the many helpful suggestions of the readers which have been incorporated in the work, the author alone must bear the responsibility.

The book has been published with the help of a grant from the Humanities Research Council of Canada, using funds provided by the Canada Council.

Note Concerning Text, Translation and Glossary

The Greek text used throughout is John Burnet's Oxford edition, *Platonis Opera* (1900-07), 5 vols. The English translations used throughout, unless otherwise indicated, are from *The Collected Dialogues of Plato*, ed. Edith Hamilton and Huntington Cairns (New York, 1961). Also, to provide a reference to Greek terms for readers without a knowledge of Greek (in addition to the translation given at the first occurrence of a term in the text), a glossary, with English transliteration, is supplied at the end of the work.

TABLE OF CONTENTS

TABLE OF CONTENTS

Introduction

The present work is a study of the religious dimension of Socrates' *thought*, that is, his philosophy; on the other hand rather little is said here on the subject of Socrates' views and attitudes towards what is commonly taken to be the stuff of religion, that is, the gods and their worship and supplication in rites, observances, and prayers. The emphasis on Socrates' philosophical thought is not arbitrary: as we shall see, Socrates forces it upon us. He seldom reveals anything of his attitudes towards the religious concerns of ordinary men. His outlook in this regard is generally characterized by an austere silence, and he seems quite content to ignore religious topics in the conduct of philosophical inquiry —unless, as in the *Euthyphro*, someone else introduces his own convictions and beliefs for scrutiny. But even there, more often than not, his own attitude is somewhat negative and critical. For the most part such concerns would be wholly unnecessary for the philosophical quest of σοφία (wisdom) and ἀρετή (excellence). Now, if this were the extent of the available evidence, it would constitute meager materials indeed for a full-scale study of Socrates' religiousness, for from this point of view there hardly seems to be anything very religious about Socrates at all.

In this light the *Apology* is a surprising revelation. Departing from his habitual attitude, in this work Socrates breaks his silence about his own views. He tells us in ineluctibly clear terms that his philosophy *is* his religion. It is Socrates' conduct of philosophical inquiry among his fellow citizens that constitutes his "service of the God." However faint the indicators of religious piety as popularly understood, Socrates' own testimony makes it decisively clear that profound religious attitudes inform his philosophical career. Yet even if there were no *Apology* we should have suspected it: despite the slender evidence of Socrates' own words there is the evidence of the profound religious *sense* one obtains in observing Socrates in the conduct of his philosophical vocation. In this regard our sensibilities may be a surer guide than the positive, objective evidence. But the fact is that, outside the handful of assertions in the *Apology*, Socrates is a poor guide to our understanding and appreciating the ultimate religious seriousness of his *via philosophiae*. As Kierkegaard fully appreciated, Socrates represents the passionate individual who has arrived, through personal struggle and search, at a comprehensive life-stance, a path of salvation found to be true and authentic for him.

Were we to confine our vision to the positive evidence of religion popularly conceived, we should miss this deeper aspect of Socrates' religiousness. In order to probe the full dimensions of the Socratic way we require a deeper concept of religion to use as a working definition.

The word 'religion', of course, is used in a variety of ways. But in its most common and basic sense it is used to refer to the system of beliefs and practices whereby man relates himself to the unseen superior ("divine") force(s) or being(s) who hold power over him. But the conceptual system which the pantheon represents, and the record of the *acta* of these deities in the mythology, as well as the system of rites, observances, formulae, etc., all realize a deeper function. They constitute the means whereby a people (or group) casts in a determinate conceptual form an answer to the questions, how is life to be lived? what is its meaning and purpose? to what realities or values am I to relate myself in order to comprehend my existence as a whole? In answering these questions religion involves fundamental assumptions about the world and man's place in it. A religion entails a shaping of basic attitudes, valuations, and perceptions of what is real and what is good. Above all, religion entails the ordering and submission of one's total life-experience to certain realities perceived, experienced, and valued (revered, hallowed, recognized as "divine") as transcending all that is merely natural and human. This, it is here proposed, is the appropriate perspective from which to evaluate Socrates' religiousness.

In this light, then, the aim of the present study is to elucidate the full and profound religious proportions of the Socratic philosophical way. The immediate task, however, and the starting point for such a project, must be a critical examination of the positive, direct evidence of Socrates' religious thought. Accordingly, in the first two chapters our attention will be focused on the normal tasks of literary-historical criticism. In the first place we shall discuss the problem of the historical Socrates; next we shall concern ourselves with the use of key religious terms, with the interpretation of explicit statements and arguments (and their implicit assumptions) which have a bearing on religious topics, with the examination of the place of these religious elements in Socratic philosophy at large, and finally, with an interpretation of some of the main features of Socratic dialectic in the light of the positive picture of Socrates' religion emerging from our inquiry.

But in the end this direct path stops short of our goal: too much remains submerged and inexplicit to plumb from his own testimony the depths of Socrates' religious outlook on life. Indeed, one might even say that Socrates himself remained unconscious of the fuller religious dimensions of his conduct of philosophy. To accomplish this end we shall, in the final chapter, turn our attention to those most idiosyncratic and paradoxical features of Socrates' personality—ignorance, irony, and silence. An analysis of their role and significance in the Socratic way will in turn lead us to a consideration of the inner dynamics of ἔρως (love, desire) in the Socratic way. Such an examination of the deep structures of the Socratic way will thus serve as preparation for the final step in our study: to identify in what respects the Socratic way continues, or transmutes, fundamental Greek religious attitudes to life (particularly as they were expressed in the epics of Homer). That is, we shall be in a position to discern some of those deeper resonances of the Socratic philosophical way with the religious, moral, intellectual, and aesthetic facets of the Hellenic experience of life at large.

The Historical Socrates

1. The Problem of the Historical Socrates.

The starting point for any discussion that would claim to speak of the historical Socrates must be a critical evaluation of the sources. This is necessitated in the first place, of course, by the fact that we possess nothing from Socrates' own hand; and in the second place, by the fact that the only documents we do possess were not intended as historical documents as we commonly understand that term today.

The sources for the historical Socrates are four: a fifth-century comedy, Aristophanes' *Clouds*; two groups or families of the literary genre of the Σωκρατικὸς λόγος (Socratic conversation or dialogue), Plato's and Xenophon's depictions of Socrates' discussions with various individuals; and some brief mentions of Socrates in Aristotle.[1] Now, Aristophanes' play is so much bawdy humor, and is, as Guthrie observes, "surely the oddest place in which serious information about a philosopher has ever been sought."[2] Aristotle's presentation of his philosophical predecessors is well known to be "interested"—that is, he sees their views as earlier, inadequate forms of the philosophical opinion he himself is laboring to present.[3] Besides, Aristotle never knew Socrates; he relied on the oral and written testimony of others for his knowledge. The many Σωκρατικοὶ λόγοι, appearing after Socrates' trial and execution in 399 B.C. for crimes of impiety and corruption of youth, constituted a veritable torrent of literary documents ostensibly relating his discussions with various friends and acquaintances. They were, with few exceptions, defenses of Socrates' good name and career by representatives of the various competing Socratic circles. (Polycrates added considerable fuel to the fire by publishing an attack on Socrates in the late 390's.) These λόγοι can hardly have been intended as stenographic reproductions of the actual words of the discussions. Clearly they carry, at best, the historical claim that this is the *kind* of thing Socrates was heard to say. Nowadays scholars are inclined to suspect that such accounts have undergone the influence of personal, subjective bias. "This is the kind of thing Socrates said" may all too often mean "this is what Socrates means to me." And our suspicions are at times confirmed. Plato's and Xenophon's portraits of Socrates clash, though there is enough agreement between them to make the problem of historical criticism real and interesting. Further, we know that Xenophon, at least, was not above putting into Socrates' mouth opinions which were clearly Xenophon's own. In the *Oeconomicus*, for example, Socrates is made to sing the praises of life in the country and the joys and virtues that come from running a farm. The overwhelming preponderance of the tradition confirms what Plato says, first in the *Crito* (52b ff.), where Socrates is depicted as so identifying himself with the life and culture of Athens that he could not begin to think of fleeing her to save his life, and second, in the *Phaedrus* (230d), where it is asserted that trees and open country have nothing to teach Socrates. The conviction of Socrates in the *Oeconomicus*, that the way of the country gentleman was a fine, decent, dignified lot, is clearly Xenophon's own.[4]

In the case of Plato the hand of the literary artist is ever so more apparent than in Xenophon. Speaking of Xenophon's *Symposium* Guthrie comments, "Structurally the composition creaks at every joint."[5] Indeed, in every respect Xenophon's Socratica are literarily commonplace, even drab and dull. Plato, on the other hand, is the consummate artist. Every facet of his dialogues —structure, style, content—is presented with an ease and grace, and an intellectual power, that have no peer in Greek literature. Now, this has appeared to many as all the more reason to suspect the historical veracity of his account of Socrates. Such was the attitude of many nineteenth-century commentators. Xenophon was more historically reliable, they believed, precisely because his commonplace intellectual abilities and his matter-of-fact way of relating things guaranteed that he was interfering little with the hard historical facts. But as Taylor observed, this meant that "[t]he 'historical Socrates', of whom nineteenth-century writers had much to say, meant, in fact, the Socrates of Plato with the genius taken out of him."[6]

It was Taylor and Burnet who, in this century, resisted this tendency to disqualify Plato for his genius. Nonetheless, the historical prejudices that account for this attitude towards Plato still persist and are implicit in commonly held notions of what history is. In his study of Greece, M. Rostovtzeff gives expression to some of these ideas:

> The first duty of history is to *collect facts* about [the] past.
> . . . .
> The facts collected by the historian, when arranged in order of time and definitely assigned to the places and peoples concerned, form only the skeleton of history. These facts, especially such as are recorded in written and oral tradition, require verification. . . . [M]an has not only a strong impulse to learn truth but an equally strong impulse to mutilate it, consciously and unconsciously. Man's tendency to poetic

> creation and the fertility of his imagination cause him often to restate facts till they are unrecognizable; he fills up gaps where he is ignorant and alters what he knows; he mixes up the region of religious and fabulous conceptions with the sphere of actual events. Myth and legend are inseparable from history, and even in our own time grow up round great historical events and, even more, round great historical persons. Together with this process, facts are also deliberately distorted under the influence of various motives—material advantage, or the endeavour to defend the reputation of the narrator or his friend, or the tendency to support a particular point of view or political theory. . . . We must never forget that historical events were not recorded by machinery but by men, distinct personalities with definite characteristics of their own. Few of them have kept free from prejudice while recording historical events which, in one way or another, touched themselves nearly. *Hence the historian, while collecting facts, must at the same time verify them and convince himself that they correspond to reality.*[7]

When such narrow and precise (and, one might even say, ascetic) standards of history are set, it is no wonder that scholars have ended, as Karl Joël did at the turn of the century, with the opinion that with regard to the historical Socrates "we know nothing."[8] Prominent among these extreme skeptics are Olof Gigon and Anton-Hermann Chroust.[9] Gigon, distinguishing sharply between *Dichtung* and *Historie* (or *Biographie*), sees the entire body of Socratic literature without exception or distinction as *Sokratesdichtung*, that is, as a creation of the literary imagination. Each of the Socratics imposed on the name of Socrates his own conception of the ideal philosopher. Thus the various accounts are evidence only of the thought of their authors and have no value towards constructing a picture of the historical Socrates, of whom we know only the barest minimum.[10] Similarly Chroust refers to the Socratic literature as legend, myth, the work of fancy—"from its very inception this tradition was intended to be fiction and nothing else."[11]

In the concept of history enunciated by Rostovtzeff and exemplified in the works of Gigon and Chroust we can detect a kind of positivism: an historical fact is that which can be empirically verified by an historical observer. All that is personal and subjective must be extracted from the historian's raw material. One clears away the interpretive overlay and thus eventually arrives at the hard, bare, objective facts of history. This is, obviously, a minimalist view of history. It is no more and no less superficial and uncritical than the concept of historical events on which it is based. For it will hardly do to conceive the events of history as merely the physical acts or words that leave empirical traces down through the ages after them. The events of history are *human* acts, and thus take on a whole mental or psychological dimension. People say and do things for reasons, and because they hold beliefs and convictions. Their actions proceed from a general outlook on life, as well as from a set of individual attitudes and dispositions. They comprehend their physical acts and those of others as having a certain significance, a significance which does not "show" itself in the physical events. To give an adequate account of human acts it is necessary to reconstruct, at least rudimentarily, the acts in these *full* proportions. It is only by virtue of an unduly and uncritically minimalistic interpretation of the nature of historical events that history can be considered the collecting of historical facts. It is probably a truism to say, as Rostovtzeff does, that the *primary* task of the historian is to ascertain the facts. But this will hardly do as a *full* or *adequate* statement of the task of the historian. It is no doubt equally true that the elucidation of the full proportions of an historical event is a delicate, precarious matter. And it is a safer venture, and one ensuring far greater certainty, to ascertain the hard facts, but we can hardly call it history in the full sense. Indeed, one might well say that knowing the empirical facts of some historical situation one might *understand* next to nothing of what happened. (Or else we might suppose that the child who has studied his history textbook has a good grasp of history—or that the man who has read his newspaper knows what is really going on in the world.) History necessarily entails the attempt to elucidate the ideas and beliefs, as well as their relationships and connections with other ideas and events, that do not "show" in what is empirically evident. Indeed, the actors in an historical situation need not have been explicitly conscious of these factors. Even these real but unconscious factors are fair game for the historian. (For example, it is possible to say true things about the influence of one thinker on another and thus elucidate a non-empirical yet real relationship which even the influenced thinker *need* not have been aware of himself.) In sum, then, although the attempt to reconstruct history is dependent on, and thus limited by, the amount of information the historian has at his disposal, history is the attempt to reconstruct the events in their full *meaning*.

In his *Poetics* Aristotle classified the Σωκρατικοὶ λόγοι as a form of μίμησις (imitation), specifically a form of poetic imitation by language alone, without musical harmony, and in prose (1447a1-b13). Aristotle distinguished poetic imitation from history: "[T]he poet's function is to describe, not the thing that has happened, but a kind of thing that might happen, i.e. what is possible as being probable or necessary" (1451a36-38, trans. Ingram Bywater). Aristotle recognized that is some cases poetic imitation had for its subject an actual historical event: in that case the artist treated the historical event as something that was likely to occur again and again, that is, he attempted to bring out its universal implications (1451b29-32). The poet's aim was, for Aristotle, a higher one than that of the historian: "Hence poetry is something more philosophic and of graver import than history, since its statements are of the nature rather of universals, whereas those of history are singulars" (1451b5-7, trans. Bywater).

Aristotle would thus appear to render his judgment on the side of those who view the Σωκρατικὸς λόγος as a literary fiction without historical value. However, a closer look reveals a more complex truth: poetic μίμησις was in the first place the imitation of actions (1451b29), or more fully, "the imitation of character, actions and things suffered" (1447a28). To interpret Aristotle's elliptical speech, the aim of poetic imitation was to represent human character through depicting the person's actions and responses to the things that befell him (1447a27-28). According to Aristotle (1448b4-17) imitation was natural to man insofar as he naturally took delight in representing the *meaning* of things (ὅτι συμβαίνει θεωροῦντας μανθάνειν καὶ συλλογίζεσθαι τί ἕκαστον, 15-17), particularly with respect to a human character (οἷον ὅτι οὗτος ἐκεῖνος, more literally, "for example, that this man is that," or more loosely, "that a certain man is such-and-such," 17). That is, through the works of the poets (Aristotle has in mind principally the dramatists) men gained insight into human character by seeing how a certain sort of man acted under a given set of circumstances.

With respect to Plato's Socratic dialogues it is at first sight difficult to see the force of Aristotle's words that imitation is a study of character through a depiction of actions and responses, for with the exception of the *Apology* there is no direct focus on Socrates' own character, and Socrates *does* little else than conduct intellectual ἔλεγχος (test, scrutiny) of the views of others. Nonetheless, Aristotle's interpretation holds true if we take Socrates' "doing" (πράξεις, actions) to refer to his conduct of philosophy in general. Accordingly Plato's Socratic dialogues are to be seen as literary representations of the general character of Socrates' conduct of philosophy, as an "imitation" of it designed to give a penetrating insight into the mind of Socrates.

Though Aristotle conceded the poet's artistic liberty to shape actions, circumstances, speeches, etc. towards his end of revealing something about human character, he nonetheless also laid down as a stricture governing the literary genre that it must be like (ὅμοιον, 1454a24) what it imitates. In other words poetic imitation, even though it is not, and is not intended to be, an *historical* account of the facts, is not simply to be opposed to history as "thoroughgoing myth," "pure literary fiction," or "creation of the imagination." In a case such as the Socratic dialogue, where the subject was drawn from actual history, poetic imitation must be a reasonably faithful representation of the person's character (in Socrates' case, his conduct of philosophy).[12] W.D. Ross expresses the essential point: "It is evident that all he [Aristotle] expected in a Socraticos Logos was general *vraisemblance*, not biographical accuracy; and this, I think we may infer, was the general assumption about these works."[13]

In short, while the Socratic discourse was not a work of history in the narrow sense, it nonetheless did have historical value (at least such was its *prima facie* claim), not so much with respect to particular scenes described and words exchanged as with respect to the general delineation of Socrates in action discussing philosophical matters. The Socratic discourse was a literary means free of the confining restrictions and responsibilities of historiography to explore the meaning of Socrates' philosophical career.

These general considerations sufficiently remove the grounds for rejecting Plato's portrait of Socrates as historical testimony. There are no *a priori* grounds for disallowing Plato's witness about Socrates.[14] But this, of course, is not to say that there can be no specific historical, critical arguments brought to bear on his testimony. Such considerations may be of two kinds: Is Plato's account internally consistent and plausible? And, is Plato's account more likely to be true than the other accounts where they conflict?

In the past there have been very few to argue that Plato's account is not internally consistent and plausible, excepting, that is, two problematic points. Plato represents Socrates as developing the full theory of Forms, whereas most scholars today feel confident in assigning that achievement to Plato. However, as we shall argue below, this attribution of the theory of Forms to Socrates does not vitiate the essential consistency of Plato's portrait of his great teacher. The other problem is that Plato seems to contradict himself by asserting simultaneously that Socrates never professed any physical theories (*Apology* 19b-d) and that Socrates was an ardent student of natural science (*Phaedo* 96a ff.). But, as we shall also argue, these statements are not necessarily incompatible. We shall not entertain, then, the internal coherence of Plato's account as open to serious question.

What remains, then, to establish the historical truth of Plato's account of Socrates, is a detailed critical examination of the other, competing accounts in order to arrive at a judgment regarding their internal consistency and plausibility: only when Plato's account has withstood such comparative critical analysis would it be possible to conclude with confidence that Plato's Socrates is more than a literary and philosophical fiction. Yet, however evident the logical propriety of such a detailed historical-critical prolegomenon, it is to be recognized that not all readers will have the same interest, or need, to submit themselves, at this point in the study, to the intricacies and refinements of such a discussion. On the one hand the more general reader, whose interest lies only in the central theme of this study, would find the rigors of such an extended critical prolegomenon to be more of a hindrance and a distraction than a help. On the other hand the scholar already well-acquainted with the problem of the historical Socrates would be obliged to submit to a lengthy treatment of familiar issues. Thus, in the following two sections of this chapter, one will find not the extended, detailed historical-critical discussion mentioned above, but rather brief statements of the positions assumed in the present work with respect to the other principal Socratica: these brief statements represent a summary of results of the detailed studies to be found in the appendices, where, it is hoped, full argument and justification for the position taken may be found.

2. Aristophanes' Portrait of Socrates in the *Clouds*.

In his comic drama, *Clouds*, Aristophanes characterizes Socrates as the foremost sophist (or, as Aristophanes depicts him, "know-it-all") of the day. Socrates runs a φροντιστήριον, or "Thinkery", where disciples are gathered around him to learn about whichever of the intellectual interests of the day suits their fancy. Two branches of learning in particular stand out from Socrates' all-encompassing σοφία: Socrates is portrayed as the foremost exponent of μετεωροσοφία, physical speculation about the nature of the heavens (or more generally, about lofty, abstruse matters, such as the ultimate nature of the physical universe); also, Socrates is portrayed as the foremost expert in verbal sophistry, that is, in the techniques of how to win an argument (particularly in court of law or public debate) regardless of how unlikely or morally reprobate the position one is defending. Now, in Aristophanes' portrayal of Socrates there is a great deal that is beyond the pale of the plausible—such as Socrates' ludicrous theory in which he compares the earth to a type of oven, of which the sky is its hemispherical lid, and its inhabitants the coals; or his practice of being raised aloft in a basket so that his mind can be in closer proximity to the heavenly realities he is contemplating; or his preposterous opinion that gnats hum—indeed blast away, as with a trumpet—through their butt-end; or his at once cynical and absurd advice to his pupils that to learn to think well they must whirl everything around in their minds and mix it all up, or alternatively let their minds run loose and latch on to whatever comes to mind.

If Aristophanes' characterization of Socrates is what it appears to be, a farcical burlesque of every intellectual tendency of the day, then one might fairly wonder why it was ever taken seriously as a historical document. The reason, or reasons, which were clearly pointed out by John Burnet at the beginning of the century, are the following: in the *Phaedo* at 96a ff. Plato assigns to the early Socrates an interest in a number of topics which read like a list of the diverse philosophical and scientific theories at Athens at very nearly the time of the play (423 B.C.).[15] Also, there is a sound, independent historical tradition that Socrates was the pupil of Archelaus, the disciple and successor of the natural philosopher Anaxagoras.[16] These two facts strongly indicate that Socrates did, at least early in his career, belong to the tradition of physical speculation on the nature of the heavens, and indeed of all physical matter, and that by implication Socrates shared their rationalistic, materialistic atheism with respect to the traditional gods. To complicate the matter further, Socrates' "autobiographical" passage at *Phaedo* 96a seems to fly directly in the face of the overall portrait of Socrates in the Platonic dialogues, according to which he never discussed such matters as "things below the earth and in the sky and how to make the weaker, or wrong, argument defeat the stronger, or right, argument" (*Apology* 19).

Since a solution to this problem seems called for in a study of the religious thought of the historical Socrates, we shall state the position assumed in the present study (see Appendix II for a full discussion). First, with respect to the problematic assertions of *Phaedo* 96, Socrates' intellectual biography should not be understood to assert that Socrates was, at one time, an atheistic natural philosopher. Close scrutiny of *Phaedo* 96a ff. reveals that, as Plato relates it, the key elements of Socrates' early philosophical period (Eleatic logical reasoning and an inclination towards explanation in moral, humanistic terms, and particularly towards teleological explanation in terms of the good), were features of his thought from the very first, and that they preceded even his youthful inquiry into natural philosophy. Thus, we may conclude that Socrates was at no time satisfied with the scientific theories of the day, and that he inquired into scientific matters from wholly different premises. He was never in any real sense a natural philosopher, for he never became convinced that the basic enterprise was valid. He must have discussed such theories in the minimal sense entailed by mere acquaintance with and consideration of them. But he did not discuss them in the sense that he participated with other committed and professed natural philosophers on their terms in the search for "scientific" truths about nature.

Second, with regard to the basic features of Aristophanes' Socrates in the *Clouds*, or rather, the basic features of the Socrates caricatured in the *Clouds*, we shall assume for the purposes of our study that, as an independent historical document, Aristophanes' *Clouds* is thoroughly unreliable (see Appendix I for a full discussion). No doubt there is some grain of truth in the portrait of Socrates, but it remains indistinguishable to us now from the "nonsense" (as Plato calls it in the *Apology*[17]). Fact could hardly be differentiated from fiction at all without using control sources such as Plato and Xenophon. But their accounts differ sharply from Aristophanes'. In fact Plato is acquainted with Aristophanes' play and flatly contradicts some of its main allegations (in particular, that Socrates "searches into the things under the earth and the things in the sky, and makes the weaker argument defeat the stronger"[18]). The accounts of Plato and Xenophon make quite clear what Aristophanes' account implies: that there were some very important differences between Socrates' own mode of philosophizing and that of the other intellectuals of the day. In all probability, then, *Clouds* was conceived as an attack on Socrates principally because he was the most conspicuous and notorious intellectual figure of the day. Aristophanes, whether out of ignorance or as a crude polemic, has suppressed the differences and added extraneous elements, all to his own end: the presentation of an uproarious, rollicking comedy.

3. Xenophon's Portrait of Socrates: An Overall Evaluation.

In Xenophon's Socratica (the *Memorabilia*, *Oeconomicus*, *Symposium*, and *Apology*[19]) we have a body of works from which a full and distinctive picture of Socrates may be constructed. And, if we take into account the considerable liberties allowed a Greek historian to embellish his material, we may assume that the general intent of Xenophon's Socratica was to depict Socrates as he knew him, that is, as he perceived and understood him. In Xenophon's Socrates, then, we have a major alternative or competitor to Plato's Socrates (since his account includes a large amount of unique material, handled in a markedly different manner from Plato's). The essential case for Xenophon's account is that because Xenophon was a man of ordinary intellect and had no special interest or ability in philosophical matters we can be fairly certain that his

Socratica are the most accurate and impartial testimony we have. A recent exponent of this general position is Leo Strauss:

> For our precise knowledge of Socrates' thought we depend on Plato's dialogues, Xenophon's Socratic writings, Aristophanes' *Clouds*, and some remarks of Aristotle. Of these four men Xenophon is the only one who, while knowing Socrates himself, showed by deed that he was willing to be a historian. Hence it would appear that the primary source of our knowledge of Socrates should be the Socratic writings of Xenophon.[20]

On the other hand it may be pointed out in Plato's favor that he was in a much better position to know Socrates than Xenophon; that Xenophon's Socratica, for all its considerable volume, nonetheless gives us much less information about Socrates the person than does Plato's; and that—particularly judging from some of Xenophon's other historical works—as an historian Xenophon is no less "interested", no less given to his own biases, than is Plato.

Quite apart from those partisan exponents of Xenophon's Socratica (such as principally, in our day, Leo Strauss[21]), perhaps the greatest number of scholars have tended to look upon the accounts of Plato and Xenophon as roughly compatible, as not seriously contradicting one another (such as principally, in our day, W.K.C. Guthrie[22]). Of this group some would look upon the two accounts as complementary, while many others would look to Plato's account to establish the main lines of Socrates' portrait, to be supplemented or corroborated occasionally in points of detail by Xenophon. In our view, however, to assume such a stance is to be taken in by the superficial likenesses of the two accounts and to ignore fundamental differences of character between the two Socrates they portray (see Appendix III for a full discussion). Xenophon and Plato have depicted radically different personages: a decision between them is forced upon us. Plato's Socrates defends himself against the charge of atheism brought against him, but it never becomes clear precisely how orthodox his own religious views were. And the fact that Socrates consistently claims ignorance in all "higher" matters, and specifically the myths of the gods (in the *Euthyphro*), makes it at least plausible that he was brought to trial and executed for atheism. But Xenophon's Socrates is a model of conventional piety—he in no way falls short in the fulfillment of his religious obligations. He not only believes in the traditional gods, but he even develops theological arguments for a divine Mind who providently guides and directs the course of events in the cosmos at large. So plausible is Xenophon's Socrates that the very thing he would defend Socrates against—the charge of atheism—becomes radically implausible. It can only have been a colossal mistake, a bizarre case of misunderstanding. As Gregory Vlastos forcefully argues, "Plato, and he alone, gives us a Socrates who could have plausibly been indicted for subversion of faith and morals. Xenophon's account of Socrates, apologetic from beginning to end, refutes itself: had the facts been as he tells them, the indictment would not have been made in the first place."[23]

The fundamental discrepancy between Plato's and Xenophon's Socrates is not confined to the question of religion. Xenophon's Socrates is *wise*. He possesses *knowledge* in moral matters and assumes the role of the master instructing his associates in moral right and defining the virtues. He tests and refutes those who err and exhorts them to virtue, nobility, and moral character. The essential features of Plato's Socrates, on the other hand, are familiar. He is ignorant, and for that reason does not teach wisdom or virtue. He only tests the claims of those who think they possess them, and leads his companions on the disinterested and never-ending search for them. He keeps bringing philosophical inquiry back to definitions, but cannot offer successful ones of his own. Further, Plato's Socrates is paradoxical, for he also maintains that virtue is knowledge. And it is clear from the *Apology* and *Crito* that Socrates believes most sincerely that his present stance before the jury and indeed his whole career (wherein rests his defense) are just and righteous. How can he believe he is right without also claiming knowledge? Further, Plato's Socrates is ironic. Xenophon's Socrates glibly, inoffensively expounds his wisdom. Plato's Socrates begins in exaggerated deference to the wisdom of those with whom he converses, and ends with biting, provoking cross-examinations that totally collapse his opponents' alleged wisdom. Can he really have been sincere in assuming the posture of the total ignoramus, anxious to glean a morsel of his companion's wisdom? With Xenophon's Socrates, however, there is never a hint of anything unsettling, or paradoxical, or ironic; never anything which calls into question the comfortable, conventional values of the typical upstanding citizen; and no question of a radical commitment to ἀρετή that transcends all class privilege and party politics. Xenophon's Socrates is virtuous and wise, and instructs others out of his superabundance of wisdom and virtue.

A decision, then, is forced on us—though fortunately it need not be a matter of mere subjective preference. For upon occasion Xenophon, seemingly unwittingly, makes telling admissions against his own characterization of Socrates, and in favor of Plato's: as for instance at *Memorabilia* I.2.3, where he acknowledges that Socrates never professed to teach virtue (although throughout the *Memorabilia* Socrates is made to exhort and instruct in his inoffensive wisdom); and at IV.4.9, where Hippias states that it was

Socrates' practice never to state his own opinions, but continually to put other people to the test by asking them questions (although it is the central feature of Xenophon's Socrates to be a moral teacher and paradigm, to "teach his friends all the good he can," I.6.13-14); and, finally, at IV.5.12-6.1, where Xenophon makes the startling assertion that Socrates never ceased dialectical inquiry into what each thing was—it was Socrates' practice, Xenophon tells us, to make distinctions according to kinds, and to take discussions back to the definition of things (although one may look in vain for any examples of the rigorous logical dialectic, or inquiry into the essential character of a thing, such as we find in Plato's Socratic dialogues—indeed, judging from those few passages in Xenophon which most resemble dialectical inquiry into the essence of a thing, it is not too much to say that logical dialectic is a dark secret to Xenophon's Socrates).

The conclusion may be stated briefly. While all the principal elements of the Platonic Socrates are evidenced in Xenophon's Socrates, in Xenophon they do not form a coherent, self-consistent whole. From an examination of the many points at which Xenophon and Plato at least partially parallel and corroborate each other, it is Xenophon who manifests a relatively superficial grasp of Socrates' life and career. Xenophon, then, can hardly be taken as an alternative or corrective account to Plato's in the respects they diverge, for his account stems from basic misapprehension.

4. Aristotle's Testimony.

Aristotle was, of course, born some fifteen years after Socrates died.[24] He is not, then, a first-hand witness. What he knew of Socrates would have been gleaned from conversations with those in the Academy who had known Socrates, and from reading the various Σωκρατικοὶ λόγοι in circulation.[25] It would be reasonable to suppose that the amount of the written material at his disposal was fairly great, certainly much greater than what has come down to us. And given his scholarly thoroughness and independence of mind, we may also suppose that he did in fact acquaint himself with the majority of it.[26] The fact that what Aristotle tells us of Socrates merely corroborates (in a succinct, summary form) what Plato represents in his dialogues, is not necessarily an indication his testimony has no value. A.R. Lacey observes that a comparison of Aristotle's testimony with other known sources would "show which sources he thought reliable on the point in question, and would suggest that the lost ones were either not among these or did not contradict those we have."[27] He goes on to observe:

Specific evidence for his use of other sources [besides Plato]

> is scanty. Nothing compels us to believe that he had read Xenophon, though some passages suggest a resemblance. . . . But neither need we think that he did not read Xenophon, or that he must have used him if he did. In particular we must beware of assuming that whatever Aristotle says must have some *one* source, as though he were incapable of surveying several sources and exercising his own judgment on them.[28]

The agreement of Aristotle's testimony with Plato's is in itself, then, of some value. It means that in Aristotle's independent, critical opinion the Platonic portrait of Socrates is substantially correct.

Aristotle tells us that "Socrates used to ask questions and not to answer them; for he used to confess that he did not know."[29] Socratic ignorance and elenctic method were in Aristotle's eyes, then, basic features of Socrates' philosophy. Aristotle also testifies to the other term of the Socratic paradox: Socrates held that all virtue was (a form of) knowledge.[30] Aristotle tells us Socrates' inquiry was limited to moral matters.[31] In this Socrates was part of (or inspired?) a general shift of interest in his day: "at this period men gave up inquiry into the works of nature, and philosophers diverted their attention to political science and to the virtues which benefit mankind."[32] The hallmark of Socrates' moral inquiry, as Aristotle sees it, was the attempt to define the objects of moral inquiry, that is, the various virtues. It is this aspect of Socrates' philosophy that especially interests Aristotle, for in thus "fix[ing] thought for the first time on definitions"[33] he made an invaluable contribution to philosophy: Socrates contributed to the emergence of the notion of essence (τὸ τί ἦν εἶναι) and the definition of substance (οὐσία). He further sees Socrates' inductive arguments (evidently Socrates' refutation by examples and argument by analogy) together with universal definition as Socrates' contribution to the enunciation of "the starting-point of science [περὶ ἀρχὴν ἐπιστήμης],"[34] which of course again emerges in its first fully explicit form in Aristotle's philosophy.

In thus interpreting the importance of Socratic dialectic and definition Aristotle is assuming the role of critical historian of philosophy. In this capacity Aristotle tells us something else about Socrates which, apart from its intrinsic importance, guarantees that despite his nearly complete agreement with the Platonic dialogues his judgment is nonetheless independent and critical. It was Plato, he asserts, who (influenced by Heraclitean considerations) separated the Forms (that is, posited them as independent entities existing apart from individual things in the world).[35] Plato, however, has Socrates propound the new theory of

Forms in the middle dialogues; the new theory is put in his mouth. Plato's own attitude in the matter becomes explicit at *Phaedo* 100b, where he has Socrates describe the new method of αἰτία (causal explanation) which posits the separate Forms as "nothing new, but what I have constantly spoken of both in the talk we have been having and at other times too." But Aristotle has made up his own mind and departs decisively from the official Platonic view of Socrates on this fundamental point. (The important point for us here is the *fact* that Aristotle diverges from the official Platonic view. As we shall argue below, the accuracy of his opinion is quite another matter.)

We have discussed all the sources for the historical Socrates —except of course Plato. Where does this leave us with respect to his dialogues? We argued at the beginning that there were no *a priori* considerations which could discredit or diqualify Plato as a source. His dialogues, of course, were not intended to be histories, but rather philosophical dramatizations. His brilliant mastery of the literary form, his splendid dramatic sense, together with his philosophical acumen, have in this regard been used to cast doubt on the historical value of his Socratica. But this, we maintained, was unreasonable grounds to discredit his account. Only *internal* and *comparative* considerations could count in that regard.

We have examined the alternative accounts of Socrates, comparing them at the points where they diverge from Plato, and found them seriously wanting. The only other possible reason to discount Plato's account is internal inconsistency. But given the failure of scholars to find any such serious inconsistency—if, that is, we confine ourselves to a consideration of the early, Socratic dialogues[36]—we shall assume there is none. For it would surely be a pointless undertaking to attempt to demonstrate positively the internal consistency of Plato's account. We may well turn to Plato's early dialogues, then, confident that there we shall find not only an impressive, powerful figure, but that that figure is substantially the kind of man Socrates in reality was, and that the philosophy he is there engaged in is a true picture of the kind of thing the real Socrates could have been found pursuing.

5. Socrates and Plato on the Ψυχή and Death.

As we have noted, in the present study we shall confine our attention to Plato's early dialogues, commonly called the Socratic dialogues, in order to reconstruct Socrates' religious thought (see Appendix IV for a full discussion). Now, in the opinion of many, Plato has too completely identified with Socrates, and too artfully concealed his own mind in portraying his mentor, to allow the distinction of what is Socratic from what is Platonic in the early dialogues. It is widely held, however, that the thinking of Plato may be clearly differentiated from that of Socrates in one respect: there emerges for the first time in the middle dialogues a theory of separate Forms, a theory which is to be ascribed to Plato; Socrates, on the other hand, merely inquired into the definition of the various virtues without positing them as metaphysical entities. (In so differentiating Socratic and Platonic philosophy scholars are, of course, taking their cue from Aristotle, who maintained that it was Plato and not Socrates who first "separated" the Forms.) Yet, as R.E. Allen has shown in his study of the *Euthyphro* and the other early dialogues, this view is not borne out by a close examination of the language of the dialogues (see Appendix IV for an outline of his position).[37] Allen has identified an earlier or Socratic theory of Forms specified in the following way: there are real, objectively existing Forms which are universals, are παραδείγματα (patterns, exemplars), are the οὐσία (being, reality) by which things are what they are, and are objects of real definitions. This constitutes a metaphysical theory of separate Forms, though lacking the full characterization of the theory of Forms to be found in Plato's middle dialogues.[38] Since, then, the theory of separate Forms is not a means to differentiate clearly between Socrates and Plato, we may perhaps be permitted an attempt to find a new perspective, and a new point of departure, to differentiate what is Socratic from what is Platonic. That point of departure, it is suggested, is the concept of the ψυχή (soul).

In the middle dialogues Plato conceived the ψυχή to be the essential person or self, or, more specifically, the immortal, incorporeal *part* of the total living human being. This ψυχή, on separation from the body at death, was virtually equivalent to νοῦς, the intellect which apprehended the Forms. Thus, the essential ψυχή had a fate beyond and independent of the body. For Plato the body was extrinsic and non-necessary to the life or selfhood of the ψυχή. Socrates, however, used the word ψυχή as the virtual equivalent of the whole, living, bodily human person. This is not to say that for Socrates the ψυχή was *identical* with the body or the concrete bodily being, for his usage of the word did not entail its being a substantial entity, while the bodily person is of course such. In Socrates' distinctive usage of the term in the early dialogues ψυχή designated the moral "character" of the person: it was that "part" (or more properly, "aspect", since there is no suggestion in the Socratic dialogues that the ψυχή is separable or autonomous) of the person wherein his ἀρετή, virtue or excellence, could properly be said to reside. Just as we have the option of saying either a person *is* virtuous or a person *has* virtue, so also did Socrates, ψυχή being aligned with the latter form of expression as that in which virtue resided. This alignment of ἀρετή with ψυχή roughly parallels that of intellectual activity with the "mind", emotions with the "heart", or athletics with the "body" in our language. Socrates' usage of the term in the early dialogues no more implied that the ψυχή was a separable part of the whole human being than these other forms of expression commit one to the view that the heart or mind is an autonomous entity within the human person. But by a kind of metonymy this ψυχή was taken to be equivalent to the person, the subject of moral activity, indeed, the subject of all the ordinary experience of life. And this person was no embodied soul or mind: it was the whole concrete, fleshly, "worldly" man. In short, the Socratic conception of the person, and derivatively of the ψυχή, implied a necessary relationship to the body and bodily conditions of being—though in the last analysis it is perhaps truest to say that the Socratic usage was philosophically unanalyzed: it carried no particular implications about the ontological status of the ψυχή, particularly with regard to its status after death. Since this important difference between the Platonic and Socratic concepts of the soul is not often appreciated, we would be well advised to examine their respective usages in more detail.

At *Apology* 29e Socrates admonishes his fellow Athenians: "Are you not ashamed that you give your attention to acquiring as much money as possible, and similarly with reputation and honor, and give no attention or thought to truth and understanding and *the perfection of your soul* [τῆς ψυχῆς ὅπως ὡς βελτίστη ἔσται οὐκ ἐπιμελῇ οὐδὲ φροντίζεις]?" This is, of course, the principal statement of Socrates' teaching of the care or tending of one's soul (θεραπεία ψυχῆς). In this text the ψυχή is that which a man improves or makes more excellent by doing right (or more precisely, by advancing in ἀρετή, which includes intellectual as well as moral virtue), and which he spoils or makes worse by doing wrong. Thus ψυχή here means "character": Socrates is admonishing each of his fellow citizens to make the excellence of his character his prime concern, and not to neglect it in favor of relative "trivialities" like wealth and fame.[39] That Socrates takes ψυχή as the equivalent of "person" is indicated by his substitution of a personal pronoun for ψυχή in a paraphrase of the above statement: "I set myself to do you individually in private what I hold to be the greatest possible service. I tried to persuade each of you not to think more of practical advantages than of his mental and moral well-being [πρὶν ἑαυτοῦ ἐπιμεληθείη ὅπως ὡς βέλτιστος καὶ φρονιμώτατος ἔσοιτο, more literally, "before each took care that *he* (subject of ἔσοιτο, referring back to ἑαυτοῦ) was as excellent and wise as possible"]" (36c5-7).

This easy substitution of "self" and "soul" for one another is frequently evidenced by other Socratic dialogues. The *Laches* takes up a discussion of what form the παιδεία (education) of youth should take. They are convinced that "to take pains with themselves" in order to be trained unto excellence is of supreme importance for youth (179d3, 6-7, e6, 180c1). But it soon appears that this is equivalent to training the ψυχάς of youth, how to make them ἀρίστας (most excellent) (185e1-2, 186a5-6). They hope to find τις τεχνικὸς περὶ ψυχῆς θεραπείαν, "someone skilled (or competent) in the care of souls" (185e4). Similarly, the *Protagoras* begins with Socrates raising the question of what the consequences are of entrusting one's *soul* to the sophists. Here again it is equivalent to putting *oneself* in the hands of the sophists (312c, 313a-e [ψυχή: a2, a7, b2; σαυτὸν: b5, c2]).

In the *Charmides* we find the most revealing of Socrates' discussions of the soul/body relationship. Socrates is relating something he learned from a physician to Zalmoxis, the Thracian king:

> This Thracian told me that in these notions of theirs, which I was just now mentioning, the Greek physicians are quite right as far as they go, but Zalmoxis, he added, our king, who is also a god, says further, 'that as you ought not to attempt to cure the eyes without the head, or the head without the body, so neither ought you to attempt to cure the body without the soul. And this,' he said, 'is the reason why the cure of many diseases is unknown to the physicians of Hellas, because they disregard the whole, which ought to be studied also, for the part can never be well unless the whole is well.' For all good and evil, whether in the body or in the whole man, originates, as he declared, in the soul, and overflows from thence, as if from the head into the eyes. And therefore if the head and body are to be well, you must begin by curing the soul—that is the first and essential thing. And the cure of the soul, my dear youth, has to be effected by the use of certain charms, and these charms are fair words, and by them temperance is implanted in the soul, and where temperance comes and stays, there health is speedily imparted, not only to the head, but to the whole body. And when he taught me the cure and the charm he added, 'Let no one persuade you to cure his head, until he has first given you his soul to be cured by the charm. For this,' he said, 'is the great error of our day in the treatment of human beings, that men try to be physicians of health and temperance [σωφροσύνη] separately'.[40]

It is, of course, the main point of the speech to establish care of the soul as prior in importance and efficacy to care of the body (or any of its parts). In every case prime consideration is to go to the well-being of the soul, whence all good or ill proceeds to the body and its parts. But what is startling at first about this revelation is that it seems to rest on a series of analogies:

soul:body::body:head::head:eyes

and that each one of these analogies is an instance of the analogy

whole:part

The soul thus appears to be the whole man, the πᾶς ὁ ἄνθρωπος mentioned at 156e7-8, and the body only a part.[41]

However, a closer inspection of the statement at 156e-157a reveals a subtler, more complex truth. There it is said that the soul is that *from which* all things good and bad proceed to (the body and to) *the whole man*. In other words, a distinction is maintained between the ψυχή and πᾶς ὁ ἄνθρωπος; they are not perfectly identical. There seems in fact to be an ellipsis in the argument: to care for bodily ills one needs to secure the well-being of *the whole man*, the spiritual-physical totality, and one accomplishes this by securing σωφροσύνη in one's ψυχή. The priority of whole man to body may be in the order of physical being, but the priority of soul to whole man is in the ethical, or perhaps more appropriately, the logical order: by concerning oneself with the acquisition of σωφροσύνη (rational self-control) in one's ψυχή one thereby secures the well-being of the whole man, including his body. The whole man, or the whole personality and all its acts, is *ruled* by the σωφροσύνη in the soul—thus the logical priority of soul to whole man. The excellence and well-being of "character", body, and bodily parts all follow inexorably from a soul in which ἀρετή has been established. The *Charmides* doctrine of the logical priority of soul to whole man does not contradict our findings in the other Socratic dialogues: indeed, it was because Socrates assumed the virtual equivalence of soul and person here in the *Charmides* that the true form of the argument was initially obscured. But the *Charmides* is valuable for the light it can shed on the implicit relationship between soul and person. To summarize our findings in general, Socrates conceptualizes the soul as that *part* of the human person wherein ἀρετή resides, but he commonly uses the word ψυχή in such a fashion that it is virtually equivalent to the whole, bodily man, the concrete human person living in the physical, sensible world. In this connection the word ἀρετή is important. The ἀρετή which resides in the ψυχή, or is predicated of the man, is not the result simply of the activity of the moral-intellectual *part* of the man, but is the result of the moral-intellectual activity of the whole, conscious, "worldly" man. The subject of ἀρετή-behavior is nothing less than the concrete human individual, the conscious, willing, sensing subject of life in the Athenian πόλις (city-state). There is no suggestion in the early dialogues that one could extricate this moral subject (which would then be Plato's "essential man", the ψυχή-νοῦς) from his bodily situation. Thus, for Socrates ψυχή is not conceived as something which functions apart from bodily conditions of being, the conditions of being of an ordinary mortal human being.

In the context of traditional Greek ways of thinking about ψυχή Socrates' conception was a great innovation.[42] In Homer ψυχή principally meant the life-breath, which was conceived to be the animating principle of the body; death was the permanent loss of this life-breath. Derivatively, the ψυχή was imagined to be a ghost-like image or wraith which escaped and went to Hades, the world of shadowy half-realities. But what is most important in the present connection, the ψυχή had little or nothing to do with the normal conscious life of the person (excepting, of course, that it was the necessary condition, the prerequisite, of the life of the person). Thinking, feeling, willing, knowing, etc., were never attributed to ψυχή, in life or in death, but rather to the θυμός, νόος or φρένες (as well as, of course, to the personal pronouns), which were imagined to be dependent on the blood rather than the breath-air. Thus the conscious life of the person was tied physiologically to the body, and the soul had no share in it. A related, but more non-Homeric meaning of ψυχή was the subliminal alter-ego, a kind of unconscious "double" which manifested itself in dreams and like irrational phenomena; but here too there was no connection with the conscious self.

Now, despite the fact that Socrates used ψυχή in contexts where Homer used words like θυμός, νόος and φρένες, there was agreement on one fundamental issue: the *human person* was intimately and essentially bound up with bodily conditions of being. It was the subject of all the ordinary conscious processes, sensation and feeling as well as thought and knowledge. It was at this point that Plato diverged from Socrates and traditional Greek assumptions about the human person by *identifying* the self or person with the ψυχή, that is, with the moral-intellectual part of the human being. The whole human being was thus viewed as a composite, the ψυχή being the essential person and as such taking on ontological status: it was the true subject and substantial entity in the composite human being. In making this move Plato was in part availing himself of Socrates' alignment of ψυχή with the rational thought and moral activity of the person, but he departed from Socrates' conception of the person and the ψυχή insofar as he viewed the body (and its attendant faculties of sensing and feeling) as something extrinsic to the person. In this latter regard Plato's thinking seems to have been influenced in a decisive way by the Orphic myth of the soul. According to Orphic belief the soul was a fragment of the divine imprisoned in the body at birth which the initiate was to purify of the influences of profane, bodily existence by the strict observance of certain rules and regulations.[43] To be sure, Plato sublimated this myth intellectually, substituting ψυχή-νοῦς for the "occult" soul,[44] and the intellectual vision of the Forms for reabsorption into some vague "Divine". Plato saw philosophy as "training [one's self] for dying and being dead" (*Phaedo* 64a). This was accomplished by a process of "purifying" the soul of its polluting contact with, and indeed bondage to, the body and the senses:

> The philosopher's soul utterly despises his body and flees from it, seeking to be alone by itself. (*Phaedo* 65d)
>
> So purification turns out, does it not, to consist in just what we have been discussing for some time past, in separating so far as may be the soul from the body, and habituating it to assemble and gather itself together from every region of the body, so as to dwell alone and apart, so far as possible, both in this present life and in the life to come, released from the body's fetters. (67c)

The relation between body and soul is repeatedly conceived by means of a family of metaphors of bondage and pollution. The soul is infected, befouled, contaminated by the body, thus needing to be purified (*Phaedo* 66b, 67a, 80e, 81b). The soul is dragged down, confused, and dizzied by the body (79c, 81c). It wallows in ignorance (82e, thus recalling the mire in which the soul wallows in the Orphic doctrine of the soul's fate in the afterlife, 69c). It is bound to, fettered by, imprisoned in the body (67d, 82e, 83d). It is permeated and saturated with the corporeal (81c, 83d): indeed, at one point it is even said to *become* corporeal (83d).

The orientation and impetus of philosophy is toward that "other world" free and clear of the bodily condition, toward the direct, beatific vision of the Forms described in the *Symposium*, *Republic*, and *Phaedrus*. The end of the philosophical life is the completely intellectual one of contemplation of the Forms. The only test a soul must pass to gain entry into the other world, the realm of the really real, is whether it has trained itself *to apprehend realities*. In negative terms, the soul must have resisted the power of the senses (the more specific alternative form for "body") which impress on the philosophically untrained that it is objects of sense which are real (or, that reality is what it is construed to be by perception and common sense) (*Phaedo* 81b, 82e-83c).

To be "saved" one must with the utmost and steadfast dedication follow reason (νοῦς, διάνοια).

Though the Forms are simply and absolutely in and by themselves, the soul must be *set* apart so that it is simply in and by itself. Herein resides the practical, moral dimension of Platonic philosophy: one must strive to free oneself from (relative) unreality. One will be judged (as the myth at the end of the *Phaedo* would have it) on the extent to which one has freed oneself, purified oneself of bodily influence. At death the soul will be freed to be itself by itself. But during life the soul is bound by "necessity" (*Phaedo* 64e1, 67a4) to be under the influence of the body. The soul cannot become completely clear of the body in this life. Plato repeatedly and insistently speaks of the freeing, purification, and separation involved in the philosophical life in *relative* terms. One strives to free one's soul from the influence of the body *as much as possible, as much as one can* (ὅτι μάλιστα: *Phaedo* 65a1, 65c7, 65e7, 66a4, 67c6; καθ' ὅσον δύναται: 64e5, 65c8, 83b7; and cf. 67c9). Of course, the soul is by nature akin to the divine, the realm of pure, immutable being (79b16-17, e2-5, 80a-b). But even in this regard the point is repeatedly expressed in relative terms. "The soul is *more* like the invisible than the visible" (79b), "the soul is *more* like the invariable than the variable" (79e), "the soul resembles the divine" (80a), which means that the soul is *more* like the divine, immortal, immutable, etc., than the human, mortal, ever-changing, etc. The moral dimension of Plato's philosophy consists of the obligation to make the soul as much like the divine as possible. In so doing one will overcome the extrinsic influence of the body, which prevents the soul from being what it is properly and in itself. The soul, then, is conceived to belong essentially and properly to the realm of the really real, but as a matter of *fact* resides in this world as well.

Having seen that the Socrates of the early dialogues conceived the soul differently from the Socrates of the middle dialogues, in particular the *Phaedo*, we should hardly be surprised to find that there is a corresponding difference in the conception of the fate of the soul at death.

Basically, Socrates' views on death are to be situated in the context of Socratic "ignorance". At *Apology* 29a-b Socrates says that being afraid of death implies that one knows what is going to happen at death, but no man really knows what happens at death. Socrates claims that the proper attitude is to recognize one's ignorance in this regard and to attend to the only concern of any importance, doing what is right.

But though Socrates here asserts his ignorance he is willing to speculate on the nature of death at the end of the dialogue. "Death is one of two things," he says (40c ff.). Either it is annihilation, οἷον μηδὲν, "no sort of thing at all," the dead having no experience or consciousness (αἴσθησιν) of anything,[45] or it is a migration of the soul from this world to some other. Socrates' point is that either way—and he does not seem to *know* which it will be (in contrast to Plato in the *Phaedo*)—death turns out to be a good thing.

There are several things of importance to be noted here. First of all, Socrates seems to be entertaining popular mythological notions. He is not expounding special views of his own. At 40c7 he adduces the view of death as a transmigration "according to what is said" (κατὰ τὰ λεγόμενα). At 40e5 he says "if what we are told is true" (that is, that all the dead have been transported to some other place).[46] Socrates has merely *supposed* a common mythological view. Accordingly, we ought not expect him to hold views as to *how* the person is transported to another place, for this common view is merely the result of mentally extrapolating the *person* as commonly understood in this life into another place. One simply *imagined* the person having been transported—a simple enough task, however great the philosophical problems connected with it.

Second, Socrates does not conceive of the after-life as some sort of Orphic purified state, *or* as a state of contemplation of divine realities as in Plato. Rather, life in that other world is essentially the same as here. He expects to be taken up with conversation with other notable, noble figures from history. Together they will pursue the philosophical way.

> [A]bove all I should like to spend my time there, as here, in examining and searching people's minds, to find out who is really wise among them, and who only thinks that he is. What would one not give, gentlemen, to be able to question the leader of that great host against Troy, or Odysseus, or Sisyphus, or the thousands of other men and women whom one could mention, to talk and mix and argue with whom would be unimaginable happiness? (41b)

He is inspired by the prospect of examining persons so renowned for their ἀρετή. This way of looking at the matter entails that the ψυχή that Socrates is talking about can be recognized for the earthly personage it was (which it is to be noted was true of the Homeric ψυχή as well). Further, they evidently need to *learn* of their ignorance, to *progress* in wisdom through dialectic (as opposed to Plato's simple beatific vision of divine Forms). We note, too, that at 40c6 Socrates was entertaining the notion of the annihilation of the soul such that it entails the extinguishing of αἴσθησις, ordinary consciousness implying the sensible perception of affairs. The soul, then, even in that hypothetical other world, is the subject of everyday sensible experience. In a word, Socrates conceives of the after-life of the soul as in no essential way different from the human condition here in this life.

One further observation. Against the idea that Socrates like Plato might have held the view that the soul would be judged at death for the moral and intellectual virtue of its earthly life, we note that there is no evidence in the *Apology* that the judges in the after-life judged the deceased's life in the former world. Rather, they are mentioned in the context of judging grievances that arise there in Hades.

It is interesting to note that the new direction of Plato's thought in the middle dialogues is disclosed as early as the *Gorgias*. That dialogue (on the whole a good example of the Socratic dialectical, elenctic style of philosophy) ends with a myth which is an expanded, transformed version of Socrates' speculations at the end of the *Apology*. Socrates relates to Callicles a λόγος which will prove that "to arrive in the other world [literally, Hades] with a soul surcharged with many wicked deeds is the worst of evils" (522e ff.). Socrates no longer displays his characteristic "ignorance", or agnosticism, in higher matters; he is certain that the λόγος is true. Now, this is problematical, for we can hardly suppose that Socrates really believed each detail of the λόγος. From the days of Cronus it was ordained that men who had led godly and righteous lives be sent to live in complete happiness on the Isles of the Blessed, and that ungodly, unrighteous men be sent to Tartarus for punishment. To this end a judgment was set up for each man on the day of his death. He was to be judged by another human being appointed to the task. But for this reason the judgments were not well given and many of the wrong people were sent to the two places. Zeus reasoned that the problem was that the judges could not see the souls of those they judged; they were misled by the fine exterior. Consequently the procedure was to be changed. Each man was to be judged immediately after death and he was then to be *stripped completely, even including his body*. The judges too were to be stripped of their bodies lest "their eyes, their ears, and their whole bodies act as a screen before their eyes" (523d). Thus, a just judgment would be given by *soul scanning naked soul*. The famous figures from the mythical past, Rhadamanthus, Aeacus and Minos were appointed to divide up the duties of judgment.

Socrates insists (524a-b) that he takes this λόγος to be true.

This is certainly a far cry from the "ignorant" mythical conjecture in the *Apology* (we note that Plato mentions the very same mythical figures in the new λόγος here in the *Gorgias*). But in what immediately follows the full import of this shift in opinion becomes clear. Socrates is made to say that he infers something from the λόγος: "Death, in my opinion, is nothing else but the separation from each other of two things, soul and body, and when therefore they are separated from one another, each of them retains pretty much the same condition as when the man was alive . . . ." (524b). But this is the Platonic concept of the soul separable from the body. We have argued that the evidence suggests that Socrates did not hold this view of the soul, and so could not hold this view of death. What was mythical about his concept of soul was that he simply extrapolated the earthly human person into another place. But Plato has a new myth—the myth of the separable soul, the essential person which has a fate after death independent of the body. It is to be noted, however, that this new view of the soul is not yet connected with the theory of Forms. The Forms are not mentioned at all in this part of the *Gorgias*. Later, in the *Phaedo*, Plato enunciates this conviction of the fate of the soul beyond death in connection with the Forms. By virtue of the Forms he will be able to prove this view of the soul's fate. But here all he can do is express his conviction that the λόγος is true. Even so, he does not insist upon it at the end of the dialogue where he sums up the discussion:

> Now perhaps all this seems to you like an old wife's tale and you despise it, and there would be nothing strange in despising it if our searches could discover anywhere a better and truer account, but as it is you see that you three, who are the wisest Greeks of the day, you and Polus and Gorgias, cannot demonstrate that we should live any other life than this, which is plainly of benefit also in the other world. But amid all these arguments, while others were refuted, this alone stands steadfast, that we should be more on our guard against doing than suffering wrong, and that before all things a man should study not to seem but to be good. (*Gorgias* 527a-b)

One set of philosophical arguments stands firm, he thinks. It is a philosophical certainty that virtue is the best path *in life*. He does not rank his true λόγος among the philosophical certainties at the end of the dialogue. Plato is becoming convinced that the soul has a separate fate after death, but that will have to remain only a religious conviction until the *Phaedo*.

The *Meno* too introduces a "true and fine λόγος," and here again Socrates professes to be thoroughly convinced by it (81a,c). He introduces it in order to counter Meno's "trick argument" that one cannot seek what one does not know. The λόγος derives from men and women wise in religious matters (81a). It runs as follows: the soul of man is immortal: at death it merely quits the body to be reborn again in another. Since, then, the soul has lived both here and in the other world and seen all there is to see, it has knowledge of everything that is. Learning in this life, then, is recollection of what one has already learned.

This passage provides us with an invaluable clue to the emergence of the distinctive Platonic outlook of the middle dialogues. For it suggests that the notion of the separable soul only contingently and temporarily residing in a body entered into Plato's thought from without, through the influence of some religious sect.[47] This influence is indicated by the discrepancy between the religious λόγος and the argument to demonstrate it. That argument rests upon the notion of recollection of Forms and professes to "demonstrate" that the soul always possessed knowledge and thus is immortal. But in the end Socrates is made to express his lack of total assurance in his argument:

> I shouldn't like to take my oath on the whole story [λόγος, "argument", as it appears to mean here], but one thing I am ready to fight for as long as I can, in word and act—that is, that we shall be better, braver, and more active men if we believe it right to look for what we don't know than if we believe there is no point in looking because what we don't know we can never discover. (86b-c)

In the end Plato's conviction falters and he ends with an expression of the essential Socratic faith (ignorance in all higher, religious matters and attention only to the proper study of man, the pursuit of ἀρετή in and through knowledge). But his lack of complete satisfaction with the philosophical argument to prove the religious λόγος only stresses that the latter stands as a *terminus* which he is striving, so far unsuccessfully, to reach. Plato is attempting to harness the theory of Forms to a new end, to establish the immortality of the soul which is asserted in the religious λόγος. The argument about which Plato expresses his reservations here in the *Meno* (and merely states as his belief in the *Gorgias*) is precisely what he will establish as a philosophical certainty in the *Phaedo*. The *Gorgias* and the *Meno*, then, evidence the emergence of new quasi-religious convictions about the nature of the soul, and they indicate that these are what impel him to that most sophisticated employment of the theory of Forms in the *Phaedo*. The new view of the soul does not arise simply from speculation on the Socratic theory of Forms, but rather it inspires a new conceptualization and a new use of that theory. This profound religious conviction remains in Plato's thought in the middle period moving behind the scenes, as it were, to manifest itself periodically in the metaphors of purification and separation, and mystical vision of the heavenly Forms.[48]

When Plato interposes this myth, or perhaps better, theoretical metaphor, of the separable soul into the context of Socratic philosophy, there is a resulting shift in orientation and outlook which subtly transforms that project. Let us attempt to characterize this shift, first in philosophical terms, and then more broadly in terms of its implications for the conception of the role philosophy plays in life.

Socratic philosophy was logical and dialectical. Its focus was on fixing thought on what was *really* and *truly* its object, the Form, and forming a λόγος, a definition or *proper and adequate linguistic statement* of the οὐσία (being, reality) of the Form.[49] As Aristotle said, Socrates was the first to fix thought on these λόγοι. And as we have seen, in going about this philosophical quest for the οὐσία Socrates assumed that the object of the quest was different from and independent of particular instances perceived in the everyday world. But the focus of Socrates' intellectual vision stayed on the *what*-it-is, on the intelligible, definable *what-ness* in question, or, as Socrates put it, the particular form (εἶδος) of reality. This entailed the pure, *a priori* logical conception of things. We can see this in Socrates' repeated admonitions in the early dialogues that it was not common-sense perceptible examples he was looking for in asking "What is *X*?", but rather the Form in and by itself. He wanted his partners to conceive the Form purely abstractly: in a word, he was urging them to make the leap to the *a priori* logical level of thought. There is, however, nothing in the *a priori* conception of the Form, for example Equality, which provides grounds for elucidating the relationship between the pure, abstract conception of Equality and particular equal things.

It is, of course, true that Socratic philosophy has a metaphysical moment; it is not adequately described simply as an inquiry into the pure, abstract, logical conception of things. Socratic philosophy asserts (by entailment) that there is a non-reciprocal metaphysical relationship of dependency of the particular on its cognate Form, and that this in turn entails that the Form be a *separate and distinct reality*. But it is to be noted that even this metaphysical assertion is made on an *a priori* basis. From Parmenides Socrates has taken over the central *a priori* insight that whatever is (something or other), is what it is and is not anything else. Or, to put it differently, Socrates has taken over the Parmenidean axiom that whatever really is cannot be qualified by contrary predicates: it is the basic assumption of Socratic ἔλεγχος, it will be observed, that whatever λόγος, or attempted definition, of *X* entails *x* and not-*x* (that is, from which contrary conclusions can be deduced) is not really a λόγος of *X*. And what is most important, the criteria of real being (Parmenides' ἐόν), which Parmenides deduced *a priori* from this initial insight, serve as the crucial premise in positing the Forms: that is, whatever is real must be what it is purely and simply, without admitting change or alteration in any sense, ever the same; it must be what it is in and by itself and not relative to anything else; it must be strictly impossible for it to be qualified by its contrary (or by any contraries). It was *because* particular things in the world did not satisfy these criteria of οὐσία that they needed the Form to account for the (degree of) οὐσία they had. The Form was the αἰτία, or explanatory principle, of the being or reality of particular things. Thus, despite the metaphysical conclusion that the Form was discontinuous with its instances, to the extent of being separate and distinct, there remained implicit the almost paradoxical counter-claim that there was a continuity of form or essence between the Form *X* and particular *x*'s. (This was, of course, indicated by the fact that the particular instances bore the same name as the Form, here represented by the use of the same letter, *X* and *x*, in our notation.) What was irresoluble about the Socratic theory of Forms, then, was the dialectical[50] tension between, on the one hand, the affirmation of *separateness* of Forms from the world, and on the other hand, the affirmation of the *essential continuity* or *isomorphism* between the Forms and their corresponding instances in the world. In the context of his philosophical ignorance Socrates could only accept such a dialectical tension as irresoluble. One could only resign oneself to it as a paradox of *a priori* reasoning—it was not given to mortal intelligence to resolve this ultimate metaphysical mystery.

Plato no more than Socrates was able to resolve this dialectical tension. However, in giving expression to his new, fervent mystical conviction in the middle dialogues that the Forms resided in another world, in a domain separate from the one in which mortals lived out their days, Plato showed a certain willingness to overstep the bounds of Socrates' purely *a priori* dialectical reasoning and thereby to supplant Socrates' resolute "ignorance" with a mythical, or metaphorical, kind of "knowledge". (It should be noted, of course, that Plato qualified the myth of the two separate worlds with the metaphysical theory of degrees of reality.) In his new-found quasi-religious "enthusiasm" for the proposition (be it doctrine or myth) that there was a realm in which the Forms stood as the objects of the deepest intellectual and spiritual aspirations of the human soul, Plato fired man with the prospect of transcending the human condition, of attaining a pure and sublime beholding of these eternal realities. In thus lending positivity to this separate world of the eternal Forms beyond bodily existence, Plato, through his religious excess, had jeopardized Socrates' life-stand on the "ignorant" finitude of the human condition.

But there is a larger contrast to be made between Socratic and Platonic philosophy. The new thrust of Platonic philosophy in the middle dialogues is less towards leading the life of virtue and excellence in this world, and more towards the ardent longing for the vision of realities in another, incorporeal realm. Philosophy, as we have seen, becomes preparation for dying, for entering into that other world. And philosophy constitutes the means of salvation by way of pure intellectual apprehension of transcendent realities. For Socrates, however, philosophy was deeply rooted in, and indeed wholly preoccupied by, the concrete moral life of man in this world. Philosophical inquiry served as the instrument in the quest for "worldly" ἀρετή; it remained subordinate to the attainment of personal excellence in "this" life. The philosophical comprehension of the Forms was not for Socrates, as it was becoming for Plato (at least for a time, until the religious convictions gave way, in the later dialogues, to more sober philosophical criticism), an end in itself—indeed, the highest end in life—but rather was *for* the moral life of mortal man on earth. Socrates began with the actual opinions of men and spurred men on to examine them, to correct them into a consistent whole. The dialectical search for the Forms served as the means of changing men's assumptions and ideas about the various excellences, and thus ultimately of extending and perfecting the personal excellences they already to some degree possessed. However abstract and theoretical Socratic philosophy at times became, its source, permanent roots, and *terminus* were existential and concrete.

It will be seen, of course, that no claim is made here to have penetrated Plato's artistry and laid bare in every respect what is Socratic and what is Platonic in Plato's dialogues—Plato's assimilation of Socrates' philosophy was too complete for that. Yet while there can be no question of unravelling all the strands, a few at least would seem to be distinguishable. For our overall project the above findings mean that a certain ground has been cleared and a certain few reference points have been set up around which we may now proceed to reconstruct a picture of Socrates' religion. The Socratic dialogues, then, may truly be taken, so far as they go, as rough guides to the religious outlook and attitudes of a man distinct from their author, that is, of the man Socrates.

1 We omit discussion of Aeschines. The few fragments of his Socratic dialogues that we possess do not alter our picture of Socrates, though they confirm Plato at a number of points in a dull, uninspiring way. See G.C. Field's reconstruction and discussion of the fragments, *Plato and his Contemporaries* (1930; rpt. London, 1967), 146-52; and J. Burnet's discussion, "Socrates", in Hastings' *Encyclopedia of Religion and Ethics* (Edinburgh, 1920), XI, 667.

2 W.K.C. Guthrie, *A History of Greek Philosophy* (Cambridge, 1969), III, 359.

3 This was established principally by Harold Cherniss in his study, *Aristotle's Criticism of Presocratic Philosophy* (Baltimore, 1935).

4 Xenophon's historiographical foibles—his practice of putting his own views in the mouths of others, his pretense to have first-hand knowledge of events, and his exaggeration of his own role and importance—have been well documented: see G.C. Field, *Plato and his Contemporaries*, 135-45; A.-H. Chroust, *Socrates, Man and Myth: The Two Socratic Apologies of Xenophon* (London, 1957), 1-16.

5 W.K.C. Guthrie, *History*, III, 342.

6 A.E. Taylor, *Socrates* (1933; rpt. Garden City, 1953), 17-18.

7 M. Rostovtzeff, *Greece* (1926; rpt. Oxford, 1963), 4, 7-8 (my emphasis).

8 K. Joël, *Geschichte der antiken Philosophie* (Tübingen, 1921), 7.

9 Olof Gigon, *Sokrates: Sein Bild in Dichtung und Geschichte* (Berne, 1947); Anton-Hermann Chroust, *Socrates, Man and Myth*. Similar in spirit and conclusions is the earlier work of Eugène Dupréel, *La legende socratique et les sources de Platon* (Bruxelles, 1922). However, the argumentation to support Dupréel's skeptical views is considerably less acute than that of Gigon and Chroust.

10 O. Gigon, *Sokrates*, 13-16.

11 A.-H. Chroust, *Socrates, Man and Myth*, xii-xiii.

12 Eric Havelock, speaking of Plato's Socratic conversations, categorically asserts: "The dialogue form, then, is not inspired by any desire to portray character. It was a standard literary method of expressing moral philosophy." "The Evidence for the Teaching of Socrates," *Transactions of the American Philological Association*, 65 (1934), 284-85.

13 "The Problem of Socrates," *Classical Association Proceedings*, 30(1933), 15. For an interpretation similar to Ross's see A.E. Taylor, "On the Alleged Distinction in Aristotle between Σωκράτης and ὁ Σωκράτης," *Varia Socratica* (Oxford, 1911), 52-57. For the contrary view see Eric Havelock, "The Evidence for the Teaching of Socrates," 282-95. V. de Magalhães-Vilhena, in his work, *Le Problème de Socrate* (Paris, 1952), attempts to strike a middle position (see pages 321-53). His interpretation, however, involves a special philosophical view of history: according to Vilhena (see especially pages 1-13, 116-24, 187-93, 453-58) we cannot get behind the various Socratic legends to the real historical Socrates, for the various Σωκρατικοὶ λόγοι, *like all historical documents*, are subjective, intellectual constructs which, while containing varying degrees of truth, fail necessarily to capture the complete, objective historical reality. Thus, the question of the historical value of any particular Socratic document is the question of its relative plausibility in relation to all other Socratic legends. In quasi-Hegelian fashion Vilhena views the quest of the historical Socrates as necessarily renewed by each generation, which evolves its own interpretations, or legends, through dialectical interaction with preceding interpretations. C.J. de Vogel, in her article, "The Present State of the Socratic Problem," *Phronesis* 1(1955), 26-35, seems to accept Vilhena's "middle position" in general outline.

14 Gigon and Chroust show much ingenuity in submitting Xenophon's Socratic works to searching critical analysis: their rejection of Xenophon's Socratica as historical documents, then, is warranted by a battery of detailed critical arguments. This is not the case with respect to Plato's Socratica, however: Plato's portrait of Socrates in the early dialogues, unlike that of Xenophon, is all of a piece; owing to Plato's literary artistry it does not admit of being dissected critically into component elements, motives, influences, etc.—and accordingly Gigon and Chroust do not concern themselves with any such systematic critical undertaking. The Platonic Socrates is rejected rather on *a priori* grounds: because Socrates is wholly mediated by Plato's literary art, because he represents so completely and thoroughly a personal interpretation through Plato's eyes, the Platonic Socratica are to be rejected as historical documents. Indeed, far from viewing Plato's personal interpretation as a *mediation* of the historical Socrates, Gigon and Chroust rather view it as a *screen* or *barrier* which impedes our encounter with the real Socrates: only by separa-

ting off all that can be shown to come from his interpreters does one arrive at the historical Socrates. However, this is to make the philosophically gratuitous assumption that an interpretation from a personal point of view is by its very nature and necessarily an historically false interpretation.

15 J. Burnet, *Plato's Phaedo* (Oxford, 1911), xxxviii-xlii, 99-109.

16 *Ibid.*, 100.

17 φλυαρία, 19c4.

18 *Apology* 19b.

19 Or *Defense*, as we choose to call it in the present work in order to avoid confusion with Plato's *Apology*.

20 *Xenophon's Socratic Discourse: An Interpretation of the Oeconomicus* (Ithaca, 1970), 83.

21 In addition to his *Xenophon's Socratic Discourse*, see his *Xenophon's Socrates* (Ithaca, 1972). Cf. also his interpretation of Xenophon's *Hiero*, *On Tyranny* (New York, 1963).

22 See his *History of Greek Philosophy*, III, 325-48.

23 "The Paradox of Socrates," *The Philosophy of Socrates*, ed. G. Vlastos (Garden City, 1971), 3.

24 The position set forth here can hardly claim to be original; it is substantially the position argued by: W.D. Ross, *Metaphysics* (Oxford, 1924), I, xxxiii-xlv, and "The Problem of Socrates," 16-21; Th. Deman, *Le Témoignage d'Aristote sur Socrate* (Paris, 1942), 5-126; W.K.C. Guthrie, *History*, III, 355-59; and A.R. Lacey, "Our Knowledge of Socrates," *The Philosophy of Socrates*, ed. G. Vlastos, 44-48. Alternatively, it stands in opposition to the views of Taylor and Burnet. Burnet's view simply put is: "Aristotle never says anything about Socrates apart from the doubtful *Eudemian Ethics* and *Magna Moralia* which he might not have derived from works which are still extant" (*Plato's Phaedo*, xxiv; cf. xxiii-xxv). For an acute discussion of Taylor's views see especially W.D. Ross, *Metaphysics* (above).

25 He would also have been acquainted with Aristophanes' play, the *Clouds*.

26 W.K.C. Guthrie remarks (*History*, III, 358):

> Aristotle had no personal interest in Socrates. He weighed his thought as dispassionately as he could. . . . There is no emotional involvement, as there was for Plato and Xenophon,

who were frankly concerned to defend the memory of their friend, "the most righteous man of his time," and as there was for Aristotle himself in his relations with Plato. . . . With Socrates he could always be cool and critical, as in his brief and crushing comment on the doctrine that no one does wrong except through ignorance: it is "in plain contradiction to experience."

27 "Our Knowledge of Socrates," 45.

28 *Ibid.*.

29 *Sophistical Refutations* 183b7. The translations of Aristotle in this section are from *The Basic Works of Aristotle*, ed. Richard McKeon (New York, 1941).

30 *Nicomachean Ethics* 1144b14-21, 28-30; *Eudemian Ethics* 1216b 2-10; 1246b32-36; *Magna Moralia* 1182a15-23; 1183b8-11; 1198a 10-13.

31 *Rhetoric* 1417a20.

32 *De Partibus Animalium* 642a24-31. Cf. also *Metaphysics* 987b 1-2: "Socrates, however, was busying himself about ethical matters and neglecting the world of nature as a whole," and 1078b17-18: "Socrates was occupying himself with the excellences of character."

33 *Metaphysics* 987b3-4.

34 *Metaphysics* 1078b29-30.

35 See *Metaphysics* 987a29-b10; 1078b12-17, 30-32; 1086a37-b5.

36 This does not necessarily mean, however, that there is not historical value in much that we find in the middle and later dialogues. See A.R. Lacey's remarks, "Our Knowledge of Socrates," 41-42.

37 *Plato's 'Euthyphro' and the Earlier Theory of Forms* (London, 1970).

38 That distinctly Platonic theory of Forms, scattered throughout the middle dialogues, may be summarized as follows: the Forms reside in an empyrean realm of eternity, purity and light, utterly separate from the world in which mere mortal souls, weighed down by the dross of their bodies, grope their way amidst shadowy half-realities, in ignorance, error and delusion. The soul's true destiny is to free itself, to separate itself off from its impure condition and rise into the region of divine light, beauty and truth. This two-world ontology is accompanied in the middle dialogues by a theory of degrees of

reality: this world is but a copy, an image, of that transcendent world of "the really real"; things participate in but deficiently realize the realities of which they are the copies.

39 An interesting comparison invites itself with the words of Jesus at *Matthew* 16.26: "What, then, will a man gain if he wins the whole world and ruins his life [ψυχὴν]? Or what has a man to offer in exchange for his life [ψυχῆς]?" (*Jerusalem Bible*).

40 156d–157b. There can be little doubt that this speech of the Thracian physician represents Socrates' own view: in the first place, Socrates represents it as wisdom he has taken over himself, and second, the concept of θεραπεύειν ψυχῆς (care of the soul) (157a1–3, b3–5) which is central to it is also the central doctrine of the Socratic way.

41 Cf. T.M. Robinson's discussion of Socrates' view of the soul in the first chapter of his *Plato's Psychology* (Toronto, 1970), 3–20.

42 There seems to have been a proximate preparation for Socrates' usage of ψυχή in the gradual alignment of thought processes with the ψυχή in the natural philosophers' pursuit of the analogy between ψυχή the life-breath of the body, and air the life-breath of the material cosmos. Still, as Burnet points out, "The Socratic Doctrine of the Soul," *Proceedings of the British Academy*, VII(1916), 251, their preoccupation was with the cosmic and physiological aspects of this view, rather than the individual human soul, in particular as subject of the moral life. For a more extended treatment of the concept of ψυχή in Greek thought see Erwin Rohde, *Psyche*, 2 vols. (Eng. trans. 1925; rpt. New York, 1966), and chapter V, "The Origin of the Doctrine of the Soul's Divinity," in Werner Jaeger's *The Theology of the Early Greek Philosophers* (1947; rpt. Oxford, 1967), 73–89.

43 A comment of Werner Jaeger's takes on special significance in view of our comments above on the (non-)relationship between ψυχή, the life-breath, and the blood: "In particular this [Orphic] βίος required abstention from any form of bloodshed, including even blood-sacrifice and the eating of animal flesh —a prescription that led to a precise ritualistic regulation of diet." *Theology*, 87.

44 The Orphic soul seems to have been conceived after the fashion of the subliminal alter-ego of dream life, etc.; cf. W. Jaeger, *Theology*, 87 and note 47.

45 The term "annihilation", however, is not to be taken to imply that the whole substantial person is snuffed out. Rather, it is only being entertained that the ordinary waking consciousness is snuffed out and that the personal being persists in some sort of dreamless, thoughtless suspended animation.

46 Cf. also 41c7.

47 And of course the candidates most often put forward are the Orphics and Pythagoreans.

48 And perhaps it is precisely this conviction—to raise what is still a highly controversial point among scholars—from whose influence Plato has freed himself in the new directions his philosophy takes in the "later" period.

49 That is, the οὐσία which the Form is—appositional genitive.

50 To use the word for the moment in a more Hegelian sense.

The Religion of Socrates

To extricate from the text of Plato the doctrine of Socrates on any topic is difficult, since the form of Socrates' thought is dialectical. The dialogues do not set forth positive truths. They are open investigations that go wherever the argument takes them; typically they end up largely unresolved. Further, the dialogues test the opinions of those with whom Socrates converses and not, usually, Socrates' own. Since Socrates professes ignorance, he can only test and scrutinize the wisdom of others. He questions others because he has no claim to knowledge of his own. But the difficulty is all the greater with regard to religion, because, to judge from the Platonic dialogues, the gods were, like all "higher" matters, not a frequent topic of Socrates' philosophical discussions. But that is why the *Euthyphro* and the *Apology* are singularly valuable to us. For in the former Socrates discusses τὸ ὅσιον, religious righteousness, or piety, and in the latter defends himself against the charge of atheism. From these two dialogues, we shall argue, one can discern the essentials of Socrates' personal views on the gods and religion (though we shall not for that matter neglect the testimony of the other Socratic dialogues).

1. The *Euthyphro*.

Dramatically the *Euthyphro* was intended to be read before the *Apology*. The former presents Socrates' discussion with Euthyphro on the porch of the King-Archon awaiting his trial; the latter presents Socrates' defense at that trial. The dialogue begins with Euthyphro expressing his surprise at seeing Socrates. Euthyphro finds it impossible to believe that Socrates is prosecuting someone—someone must be prosecuting Socrates, improbable even as that is. Socrates' explanation of the charge being brought against him is riddled with his characteristic irony. He marvels at the knowledge and wisdom of this young unknown, Meletus, who accuses him, for he claims to know that Socrates corrupts the young men of his generation. He seems to know what is in fact the right way to make youth as good as possible. Socrates, in his ignorance, can only admire from afar.

Euthyphro, in obvious sympathy with Socrates, asks to know in what respect he is alleged to corrupt youth.[1] Socrates answers:

> It sounds very queer, my friend, when first you hear it. He says I am a maker of gods; he charges me with making new gods

[καινοὺς ποιοῦντα θεοὺς], and not believing in the old ones
[illegible]' ἀρχαίους οὐ νομίζοντα]. (3b)

Socrates' δαιμόνιον, the peculiar personal divine sign or voice he occasionally receives, seems to be a familiar fact to Euthyphro. He conjectures that this is what the "new gods" of the charge means.[2] It is interesting to note that here as in the *Apology* the charge of atheism is taken to be the specific form of the more general charge of the corruption of youth. It is the precise respect in which Socrates is alleged to corrupt the youth. Euthyphro seems unable to understand what the charge of introducing "new gods" could mean unless it refers to Socrates' δαιμόνιον. We shall see below that the divine sign is not a part of traditional religion; it is unique with Socrates. To anticipate further, we shall see that the δαιμόνιον is indeed at the heart of Socrates' personal religion, but also that Socrates nowhere gives positive unequivocal evidence of orthodox belief in the gods. With these two facts it is possible to see that there was a real *basis* for the religious charges brought against him. It is in this light that the examination of every subtlety and nuance of Socrates' self-defense in the *Apology* (as well as in Xenophon's *Defense* and *Memorabilia*) becomes of paramount importance. But that is to anticipate: that task remains for the next section.

The conversation turns to the case Euthyphro is prosecuting. Socrates is aghast to hear that Euthyphro is bringing his own father to trial for no less a crime than murder. The facts of the case are these: on the estate on Naxos which Euthyphro and his father run, a day-labourer has gotten drunk and murdered one of their slaves. Euthyphro's father bound the man and threw him in a ditch and sent to Athens to find out from the religious exegete what to do in the matter. The man in the ditch, totally neglected by Euthyphro's father, died of cold and hunger. As Euthyphro sees it, his father is responsible for a man's death, and he himself is bound under penalty of religious pollution to submit such a man to prosecution (4b-d). To the popular way of thinking the sanctions guarding the authority and respect due to parents were the most "holy" (or negatively, carried the greatest degree of taboo). The ultimate forms of religious pollution were transgressions against one's parents. There were no grounds conceivable to the conventionally pious mind whereby one could, without blame or fear of incurring a grievous pollution, put one's parents to death.[3]

One might at first glance think that Socrates' shock at Euthyphro's audacity is an expression of orthodox piety. On this view Socrates is repulsed by the pollution incurred by Euthyphro's act. But a closer look reveals that it is really *awe* at the incredible confidence Euthyphro has in his own *knowledge* of religious matters:

> Good Heavens, Euthyphro! Surely the crowd is ignorant [ἀγνοεῖται] of the way things ought to go. I fancy it is not correct for any ordinary person to do that [to persecute his father on this charge], but only for a man already far advanced in point of wisdom [σοφία]. (4a-b)

At the outset of the dialogue Euthyphro displays a sense of affinity for Socrates: he feels they are two wise men who are unappreciated and misunderstood by the ignorant masses (3b-c). But that is not a good description of their true relationship in the dialectic of the dialogue. A contrast is set up between Socrates and Euthyphro: Euthyphro, like Meletus, seems to have *knowledge* in religious matters, whereas Socrates can claim none at all. Euthyphro bases his stance on Homeric myths about the gods Zeus, Kronos and Ouranos (5e-6a). His brand of piety, like Greek piety in general, is based on mythological knowledge. Socrates makes it clear that he does not "know" these mythical things so fundamental to Greek religion:

> There, Euthyphro, you have the reason why the charge is brought against me. It is because, whenever people tell such stories about the gods, I am prone to take it ill [δυσχερῶς πως ἀποδέχομαι, "I find it hard to accept"], and, so it seems, that is why they will maintain that I am sinful. Well, now, if you who are so well versed in matters of the sort entertain the same beliefs, then necessarily, it would seem, I must give in, for what could we urge who admit that, for our own part, we are quite ignorant [μηδὲν εἰδέναι] about these matters? But, in the name of friendship, tell me! Do you actually believe that these things happened so? (6a-b)

This is quite a remarkable passage, for it tells us in no uncertain terms that Socrates belongs to the tradition of rational criticism of the gods of popular religion and that it is this habitual agnosticism of his which is at the root of the charges brought against him. Ever since Xenophanes over a century earlier had attacked the anthropomorphism and immorality of the Homeric gods there had been a strong tradition of religious criticism among the intelligentsia of the day, philosophers, poets and dramatists. Indeed, Socrates is close in attitude to his famous contemporary, the sophist Protagoras. Protagoras had proclaimed his own agnosticism with respect to the gods in these terms: "Concerning the gods I am unable to discover whether they exist or not, or what they are like in form; for there are many hindrances to knowledge, the obscurity of the subject and the brevity of human life."[4] It is probable that Protagoras observed all the religious νόμοι of the πόλις alongside this intellectual critical attitude.[5] As we shall see, the same was true of Socrates. But we note that Socrates' statement here need not be taken to go as far as Protagoras. Unlike Protagoras, who says he is agnostic about both the *existence* of the gods and their *form* or *nature*, Socrates says only that he cannot claim all the things said *about* the gods in the myths as things he knows.[6]

In this agnosticism of Socrates there is a fundamental hermeneutical problem. It amounts, in fact, to a systematic ambiguity running through the entire Socratic corpus. Is Socrates' agnosticism the attitude of the *homo religiosus* or the *homo philosophicus*? Is Socrates' stance a reverent deference to the true nature of deity, a pious acquiescence in the finitude of mortal intelligence? Or is his ignorance of a more radical variety, the expression of a rigorous philosophical rationalism? That is, does his stance imply more than the claim that there are philosophically no grounds for knowledge of any kind about the gods, and that the gods of religion are merely delightful, edifying myths? Does it also imply that there is no legitimate appeal beyond philosophical reason in the matter? In short, are the limits of Socrates' outlook on the world dictated by philosophical reason?[7]

On the answer to these questions hinge two very different portraits of Socrates. What lends weight to the "religious" interpretation are certain conspicuously non-rational features of Socrates' thought, such as his private "god", the δαιμόνιον, the occasional revelations he receives in dreams, and his evidently serious attitude towards the pronouncement of the Oracle at Delphi (which will be discussed at length below). However, anyone inclined to give ultimate weight to the fervent humanism and rigorous rational spirit of Socratic philosophy might well interpret the δαιμόνιον, the dreams, and the Oracle as dramatic irony or as a literary conceit intended for those incapable of grasping the hard, radical truths of Socrates' purely naturalistic philosophical way. Even those inclined to the former view are likely to make an important concession in this regard, conceiving Socrates' religion to form another compartment existing quite comfortably alongside his philosophy. Distinguishing clearly between reason and faith, they would see Socrates the philosopher as also having his religious side.

One can hardly hope for a general, *a priori* and final resolution of these difficulties. In the last analysis the answer must depend on which reading of the data is considered the most plausible and cogent. There is, however, one general consideration which needs to be brought to light here, at the outset of our investigation. Certain attitudes and assumptions not altogether consonant with the

Greek world of the late fourth century tend to obtrude themselves into our thinking in this connection. We tend to conceive the *homo religiosus* and the *homo philosophicus* as mutually exclusive types. Or, at best, we may view them in an uneasy relationship wherein one is decidedly subordinated to the other. What we find difficult to conceive is how religion can be philosophical, or how philosophy can be religious, in an *important*, *direct* and *intrinsic* fashion. The classical definition of the theologian, for instance, is the one who seeks to elucidate by human reason what is already and independently established by religious faith and experience (*fides quaerens intellectum*). In the last analysis religious faith and experience are most commonly taken to be quite "other" than reason. Reason and faith do not depend on one another, nor do they naturally give rise to one another, though at the same time they do not necessarily conflict with or contradict one another. They are simply two quite distinct dispositions of mind. Often religious faith is characterized in terms which make it the contrary of reason: religion is purely personal and subjective, sometimes even an affair of emotion or irrational conviction, whereas logic and reason have by definition to do with what is objectively reasonable to people at large, irrespective of subjective feelings or preconvictions in the matter.

It can hardly be questioned that religious faith and philosophical reason are not identical; some sort of distinction between them is imperative. Yet it may be questioned whether any conceptualization of their relationship which bifurcates them into alien, discontinuous essences is at all appropriate, at least in an interpretation of Socrates. Our purpose here is not to embark on an extended discussion of such a thorny matter, but simply to raise the question on a theoretical level. For we shall find below that the results of our investigations clash with these prevailing assumptions. We shall find that the apparently "non-rational" and "supernatural" features of Socrates' thought are fully *integrated* into the Socratic philosophical way—though this is not to say that they may be reduced to a purely naturalistic world-view. In short, Socrates' philosophical way is (what is almost a paradox to the western mind) a *fundamentally religious*, though rational and non-supernatural, experience of the world. We shall find ourselves forced to steer between the Scylla of interpreting Socrates in a manner which bifurcates him into religious and philosophical compartments, and the Charybdis of interpreting him as the exponent of a reductionistic world-view wholly uninformed by religion.

Returning now to the *Euthyphro*, it is important to realize just what Socrates' partner represents. Though he appeals to the Homeric myths, which were the common basis for Greek religiosity, he is not a typical pious soul. Thus, the dialogue is not simply and straightforwardly a refutation, a showing of ignorance, of the forces of orthodoxy that eventually executed Socrates.[8] Euthyphro is a peculiar breed of religious specialist. He is at once a μάντις, a seer, and a theologian of somewhat fundamentalist proclivity. He seems to come from a family scrupulous in religious affairs. His father, as we have noted, went to the extraordinary length of sending from Naxos to Athens to see what should be done about the pollution from the initial homicide. The pollution he was concerned about was not a matter of legal guilt; he was not seeking legal advice about what to do with the apprehended murderer. He wanted to know what to do about the religious pollution (μίασμα), the quantum of religious guilt, conceived as a kind of holy infection, which one incurred automatically by the very act of killing another human being. This could be expunged only by the right religious powers and formulae. In this regard Euthyphro is of like mind to his father.

Now, this religious sense of pollution was orthodox enough. However, what made Euthyphro's such a strange case in Socrates' eyes was his claim to possess special knowledge in the matter that was so certain and assured as to prompt him to scrupulosity to a shocking degree. The sanctions of religious pollution were built solidly as a system of taboos around the family, both immediate and extended. To suppose that one could plead avoidance of religious pollution as the justification for having one's father prosecuted was just too much for the typical pious Greek to accept. Euthyphro must be very "wise" indeed, "quite far gone in wisdom,"[9] to tread so self-confidently on orthodox sensibilities. He scorns the ignorance and inconsistency of what the masses think about the gods (4e-5a). In one limited respect, at least, Socrates must have admired Euthyphro's stand. Euthyphro refuses to be a respecter of persons, and in particular of blood ties, when it comes to questions of justice (δίκη, 4b). Socrates too refuses to be a respecter of persons with regard to what is just and right. However, as we shall see, the rationale behind their respective stances is very different. Euthyphro stands on the religious authority of myth: he adduces a single passage from Homer as a proof-text. But Socrates assumes an unconditional attitude towards justice and right simply because they are what they are in and by themselves, absolutely and unqualifiedly, without reference to anything or anyone else.

The main part of the dialogue is of course the attempt to define τὸ ὅσιον, the holy or religious right.[10] Τὸ εὐσεβές, the pious, stands as a synonym (see 5c9-d5, where they are used interchangeably). Both τὸ ὅσιον and τὸ εὐσεβές imply some relationship to the gods; thus the holy, or the pious, is that part of "the right" which receives religious sanctions; it is the part of justice which is upheld by the gods. Indeed, the duty to do that which is ὅσιον or εὐσεβές is imposed and sanctioned by the gods.[11] Thus the dialogue would at first appear to be of little value (beyond what we have already learned from it) in discerning the outlines of Socrates' own religion. The discussion consists of a philosophical scrutiny of Euthyphro's various attempts to define τὸ ὅσιον, in which Socrates does not set forth his own views. He concerns himself solely with showing the confusion and self-contradiction in Euthyphro's attempted definitions and consequently his ignorance in religious matters, since he quite literally does not know the first thing about religion: as Socrates observes at the end, the argument was circular—it got nowhere. The *Euthyphro* thus appears to be a good example of Socrates' negative, destructive philosophical techinque, and accordingly, it could not be used as a source of Socratic doctrine.

The foregoing is perhaps a good statement of the *dramatic* dialectic of the dialogue. It correctly construes the way the actual exchanges between Euthyphro and Socrates go. At the outset of the dialogue Euthyphro is supremely self-confident that he knows what the holy is. But Socrates remarks after Euthyphro's final attempt:

> After that, will you be amazed to find your statements walking off, and not staying where you put them? And will you accuse me as the Daedalus who makes them move, when you are yourself far more expert than Daedalus, and make them go round in a circle? Don't you see that our argument has come full circle to the point where it began? Surely you have not forgotten how in what was said before we found that holiness and what is pleasing to the gods were not the same, but different from each other. Do you not remember? (15b-c)

Socrates, whose irony is particularly thick in this dialogue, continues to press his colleague and friend for the truth of the matter, for surely Euthyphro knows, if anyone does:

> And so we must go back again, and start from the beginning to find out what the holy is. As for me, I never will give up until I know. Ah! Do not spurn me, but give your mind with all your might now at length to tell me the absolute truth, for if anybody knows, of all mankind, it is you, and one must not let go of you, you Proteus, until you tell. . . .

> But now I am sure that you think you know exactly what is holy and what is not. So tell me, peerless Euthyphro, and do not hide from me what you judge it to be. (15c-e)

But it has already been made abundantly clear that Euthyphro does not know, and the question is apparently left unanswered when they part company.

There are, however, hints that Socrates' answer lies hidden, or at any rate, implicit, in the arguments that were pursued by him in the dialogue. If we return to 11e we may note that it is *Socrates* who initiates as the line of argument the relationship between the holy and the just. Then at 13a, after coddling an answer out of Euthyphro, Socrates seems to be genuinely pleased with the answer, though he presses on to correct a weakness in it. The line of argument continues to 14b-c where Socrates comments:

> Surely, Euthyphro, if you had wished, you could have summed up what I asked for much more briefly. But the fact is that you are not eager to instruct me. That is clear. *But a moment since, you were on the very point of telling me—and you slipped away. Had you given the answer*, I would now have learned from you what holiness is, and would be content. As it is—for perforce the lover must follow the loved one wherever he leads the way—once more, how do you define the holy, and what is holiness?

Here Socrates suggests that if only Euthyphro ("Straight-thinker") had been able to follow through the line of the argument they might have uncovered the answer. But alas, Euthyphro's statements wander about (see 11b ff.). Socrates dutifully follows where Euthyphro takes him, for there is one thing the Platonic Socrates may never do: to supply the answer to the argument. It is true that he might steer the argument (and certainly here he has done as much as he possibly could); but in the last analysis the actual discovery of the answer must be made by the one he is questioning. It is essential then that Euthyphro see his own way through to the proper conclusion: Socrates is quite prepared to leave him in his confusion until he does. But perhaps the reader of the dialogue might be a better pupil than Euthyphro; that is, if he studies the dialogue examining this suggestion hypothetically in order to discover the implicit conclusions missed by Euthyphro, he may allow Socrates' teaching to come to light. Let us, therefore, follow this procedure.

Socrates has declared his intent to become Euthyphro's pupil and learn what the holy is. Though Euthyphro offers only a proof in the particular instance (that his father must be prosecuted for transgressing the holy, 5d-6a), he professes to know "many other things about religion that will amaze you." He is easily persuaded then to address himself to the general question, "What is the holy?" The question as Socrates is careful to define it seems a matter of common sense to him (5d). He is expected to define the holy "itself by itself" (αὐτὸ αὑτῷ), "the same in every action" (ταὐτόν ἐν πάσῃ πράξει), the holy which is "like itself" (αὑτῷ ὅμοιον), which has "a certain single character" (μίαν τινὰ ἰδέαν).[12] This holiness is the single character (εἶδος) by which holy things are holy. Thus it may be used as a standard (παράδειγμα) to determine whether particular things or actions are indeed holy (6d-e). All this is quite acceptable to Euthyphro and he proceeds to enlighten Socrates as to what it is.

Euthyphro's first attempt at a definition indicates that this wise seer is not always his true brilliant self. After Socrates' careful specification as to the kind of answer he wants, Euthyphro leaps into the fray with the definition that the holy is just the sort of thing he is doing. So Socrates is very appreciative when Euthyphro finally submits a candidate fit for scrutiny: the holy is what is dear to the gods (τὸ μὲν τοῖς θεοῖς προσφιλὲς, 6e10, "that which the gods love"). But Socrates is able to make fairly short shrift of this definition. Euthyphro had already agreed to the proposition that the gods quarrel and disagree about "the just and the unjust, beautiful and ugly, good and evil" (7d)—for such is the concept of the Homeric gods. This means that different things please the gods. The holy, then, is different things and not one thing. Socrates patiently but ironically explains,

> In that case, admirable friend, you have not answered what I asked you. I did not ask you to tell me what at once is holy and unholy, but it seems that what is pleasing to the gods is also hateful to them. Thus, Euthyphro, it would not be strange at all if what you now are doing in punishing your father were pleasing to Zeus, but hateful to Cronus and Uranus, and welcome to Hephaestus, but odious to Hera, and if any other of the gods disagree about the matter, satisfactory to some of them, and odious to others. (8a-b)

Socrates here shows that one cannot simultaneously hold (1) that there is some one thing, τὸ ὅσιον, common to all holy things and acts, (2) an anthropomorphic concept of the gods such that they have only incomplete and imperfect knowledge and thus disagree and quarrel over things, and (3) a theological voluntaristic theory of the οὐσία of religious right (that is, right-ness being logically consequent to the gods willing or taking pleasure in it).

Now, we certainly know that Socrates holds the first proposition, but we cannot be sure from the negative dialectical form of his argument that his refutation means non-acceptance of either or both of the latter. Socrates, however, *insinuates* that he does not personally believe the gods disagree, as the popular myths would have us believe.

> It is the individual act, I fancy, Euthyphro, that the disputants dispute about, both men and gods, *if gods ever do dispute* [εἴπερ ἀμφισβητοῦσιν θεοί]. They differ on a certain act; some hold that it was rightly done, the others that it was wrong. Isn't it so? (8e)

The very fact that Socrates questions in passing whether the gods do disagree, when the point is logically irrelevant to his argument, suggests his own doubts about the matter. Still, this must remain only an "insinuation", a "suggestion".

Socrates, in any event, drops the matter and goes on to tackle the third supposition (that it is the gods willing or wanting it which makes things holy). Thus he is willing to grant to Euthyphro for purposes of argument that all the gods do agree about what is holy and pious (9c-d).

The first and essential step of this most subtle, complex and ingenious of Socratic arguments is to introduce (10a ff.) the distinction between an action and its own proper πάθος[13] on the object on which the action is performed: carrying/being carried, leading/being led, seeing/being seen, loving/being loved.[14] It is not the *grammatical* distinction between active and passive voice that Socrates is concerned to make here. True, in the initial examples Socrates distinguishes between *active* and *passive* participles (φέρον/τι φερόμενον, ἄγον/ἀγόμενον, ὁρῶν/ὁρώμενον). But Socrates is not interested in a grammatical distinction: this becomes apparent at 10b where the distinction he is driving at is put in terms of *two passives* (φέρεται/φερόμενον, 10b1). He is rather intent on pointing out that a thing's *being carried* accounts for it being a *carried thing*. This distinction between a thing's being acted upon and the resulting state of a thing from its being acted upon does not turn on the distinction between active and passive verb forms. The action being performed and its πάθος are precisely obverse, that is, opposite sides of the same coin. In any action performed on an object there are two aspects: the action being performed on the thing and the *a*ffect (not *e*ffect), or more properly, *affection* produced in the thing. To perform action x on an object may of course result in *effects* a, b, c, etc. (which may be either necessary or contingent). But whatever *effects* an action x may have on the object, it is simply a *formal* truth that the object is in the state of 'having been *x*-ed'.[15] R.E. Allen stresses that it is not a *logical* or *linguistic* distinction, but a "priority in the structure of facts."[16] It is true that it is not a linguistic (grammatical) distinction, and that it is a distinction about the structure of reality. But that does not prevent it from being a purely *formal*, *logical* truth. It is not empirically or contingently true. *Whenever* (necessary truth) an action is performed on an object there is a *real* distinction between the action and its πάθος such that there is a non-reversible logical priority of action to πάθος.

Next Socrates makes Euthyphro admit that the holy is loved because it is holy (10d). The admission is readily made; it seems a matter of common sense to Euthyphro. But this is the crucial admission. Euthyphro is now firmly clamped in the jaws of the vise, and they now begin to close. We know from the distinctions just made that the holy is (what is) loved by the gods *because* of their loving. That means that the gods' loving is the explanation of the holy. On the other hand, Euthyphro has admitted that the holy in itself must be the explanation of love of the holy. Thus, if Euthyphro's holy is something that can be explained by the god's loving it, then it must be something different from the holy in itself. What Euthyphro has defined and the holy itself must be different things. This means in turn that once again Euthyphro has not answered the question, what is the holy in itself?

From the point of view of the dramatic dialectic of the dialogue there are no positive results. Socrates has simply laid Euthyphro's attempted definition by the wayside. However, there is a negative point at least to be recognized—Socrates has shown that one cannot maintain Euthyphro's theological voluntarism along with the conviction that the holy is one thing in and by itself. Nor can one define religious right in terms of the gods, if one maintains this belief in the essential Form. But we know Socrates did hold that belief, so we can safely conclude that he rejects both those theological positions. However, there is more to be gleaned from the argument.

Euthyphro has failed because he attempted to define the holy in terms of the gods. Conversely, he failed because he did not realize the implications of Socrates' conception of the εἶδος or ἰδέα, the holy in and by itself. The holy, as indeed every Form of a virtue, is what it is absolutely, without qualification. They do not depend on any other *thing* or *person* for what they are (which is not to settle the question as to whether one Form is defined in terms of another Form). Their οὐσία does not depend on any existent thing for its being what it is. They are from this point of view logical simples, or logical ultimates. The discussion in the *Euthyphro* has helped to make clear what is implicit in the Socratic first principles. The holy, and all the Forms, are *logically prior* to the gods. We know further that the only thing of ultimate importance to Socrates was the moral life. The pursuit of ἀρετή was his consuming interest. To become virtuous entailed knowledge as a necessary, and perhaps even sufficient condition (though this remains a moot point in the interpretation of Socrates' philosophy)—this is, of course, why Socrates engages in the pursuit of definitions of the virtues. But to know about the gods was *logically irrelevant* to the definition of the Forms. Socrates may have held that *if* there were gods (or, more positively, *whatever* gods there were) they were paradigms of virtue. Not in the sense that the Forms were paradigms, however. The Forms were the ultimate criteria of the virtue of an act or person. The gods were understood to be paradigms in the sense of personal models, perfect personal exemplifications of the virtues. But, along with the rationalist tradition generally, Socrates no doubt rejected the traditional mythological gods precisely because they failed to satisfy even ordinary human criteria of virtue. Often they committed acts which were despicable and repulsive on human moral standards. But even if one were to extend one's theological search for true gods one would need criteria of virtue to judge whether such and such a candidate for deity was true and authentic. For Socrates these were of course the Forms of the virtues. But this means that, should one consider the possibility of higher, critical theology, one would still need to have philosophical knowledge of the Forms. For Socrates this philosophical knowledge and the consequent virtue, was quite enough. But what we can see in the *Euthyphro* is an elucidation of *why* it was enough, and *why* the question of the gods was peripheral to his life's project. It is, in sum, an explanation of the fact that Deity was not a topic to be investigated in Socratic philosophy.[17]

But Socrates does not yet allow Euthyphro out of his grasp. He chides him for being lazy and soft in his surfeit of wisdom and goads him on to a further, hopefully more astute, display of his wisdom. Socrates offers to come to his aid and help him teach what the holy is; he introduces a new line of investigation: the relationship of holiness to justice. He wants to know from Euthyphro whether the two are co-extensive or whether holiness is less extensive than justice. Agreeing that holiness is part of justice, Socrates urges Euthyphro to specify what part of justice it is. Euthyphro responds with what is no doubt a sound statement of orthodox worship of the gods:

> Well then, Socrates, I think that the part of justice which is religious [εὐσεβές] and is holy [ὅσιον] is the part that has to do with the service [θεραπείαν] of the gods; the remainder is the part of justice that has to do with the service of mankind. (12e)

Socrates is pleased with the response, but says that there is nevertheless one "small" thing wrong with it, namely, what the key word in it means (12e-13a). Euthyphro of course fails to see the point right away, so Socrates has to make it clear step by step. Essentially it is this: if holiness is service (θεραπεία) of the gods, in the sense of ministering to their needs and wants, then it is men who give to the gods what the gods need for their own good and for their own improvement. But this is hardly thinkable according to the orthodox notion of the relationship of gods to men. The gods were deemed to be wholly self-sufficient in their own sphere and gave to men out of their abundance and benevolence. So on these theological grounds the first meaning of θεραπεία is to be rejected.

Euthyphro tries another: we serve the gods in the sense that we assist them in the work which they do, we help them produce the product they are aiming at. Ὑπηρετική is introduced to mark the change in nuance: "service" now means assisting in the work the gods do, though of course in the role of servant. Socrates presses Euthyphro further: "Now tell me, best of friends, about the service of the gods. What result will this art serve to produce? You obviously know, since you profess to be the best informed among mankind on things divine!"(13e). But Euthyphro does not know. Instead he reverts to the old type of answer: he reasserts in general terms some things he is convinced are holy. Socrates is annoyed that Euthyphro avoids what he feels is the unavoidable conclusion from the line of argument. But there is no direct refutation of Euthyphro's attempted definition. The matter is left hanging. Socrates seems to feel something very important would be achieved if it were answered—what *is* the work of the gods?

Socrates resigns himself to the materials at hand and takes up a consideration of Euthyphro's next attempt: holiness is knowing how to say and do right things in prayer and sacrifice. Sacrifice, they agree, is giving to the gods, and praying is asking. This raises the time-worn question: what could there be that the gods lack, and which could be given to them to their pleasure and benefit? In other words, in what commodity could men deal with the gods? Euthyphro keeps gravitating towards a view of religion as a commerce (ἐμπορική, 14e) between gods and men (and in doing so he is surely orthodox). But he fails to identify what the commodity in this heavenly intercourse may be.

But even after this failure Euthyphro remains confident that he has the answer—it is the praise and honour and worship that we give the gods. Socrates shows how this is but another example of the complete circularity of Euthyphro's argument, for then the holy would be giving the gods things they love (and desire, and take pleasure in, and find useful), which was already proven to be an invalid definition.

The circularity of Euthyphro's arguments reflects not just his own confused concept of holiness and piety. The premises to which he assents are either plain common sense or the prevailing orthodox presuppositions about the gods and religion. Showing that Euthyphro's concept of religion is circular, Socrates shows that the orthodox concept is likewise. (This is a different claim from saying that the refutation of Euthyphro is a refutation of an orthodox pious soul, which we have already claimed the dialogue is not. His own piety is non-typical, but the views of his that Socrates tests are quite typical.) But precisely what is the focus of his critique?

The key to that question lies in the answer to another question raised in the dialogue—what is service of the gods? The conclusion which Euthyphro evaded was that, since there *was* nothing to give to the gods, then there was no reason to differentiate piety from justice. The gods were of course involved in the work of meting out justice in the world—*that* was the product to which men should contribute their services. But piety was identified as a distinct part of justice only because it was supposed that there were things to be given to the gods. If the only concern of the gods was justice, and not at all receiving something from men, then the whole traditional idea of religion as a commerce between gods and men had to be jettisoned. Indeed, a further reason is given to show why the view that man was holy because of his relationship to these heavenly beings was mistaken. The only pertinent relationship was the direct one to holiness itself: as Socrates showed, the gods were irrelevant to the definition of holiness. Whatever this holiness was, it could not be discovered by looking to the gods, for essentially the same problem would arise. There was no need to take the gods into account in defining holiness, and so presumably there was no need to take them into account in the attempt to acquire it (especially considering the close relationship between knowing and being virtuous for Socrates). But once the logical priority and autonomy of holiness is seen, the very reason for distinguishing religion from justice vanishes. *Real* holiness, or *real* piety, Socrates implicitly argues, is justice. To seek justice is the way of true religious righteousness. But that is a perfect summary of the Socratic philosophical way. The *Euthyphro* says in effect that it was Socrates, and not the practitioners and defenders of orthodoxy, who was the *true* pious citizen.[18]

Before terminating our discussion of the *Euthyphro* we might consider some of the more important opinions of other scholars on this point. R.E. Allen resists the attempt to discern Socrates' own views on the matter on the perfectly reasonable grounds that it is negative dialectic we have in the *Euthyphro*, not positive doctrine.[19] Thus he criticizes two famous opinions. J. Adam saw that Socrates' questioning Euthyphro as to the noble products the gods produce did not end in refutation. Following Bonitz's Principle ("Whatever remains unrefuted in a Platonic dialogue contains the key to its positive teaching") Adam concluded that there *are* noble products which the gods produce and which men therefore might assist in producing. Allen rightly points out that there is no thesis left unproved by the discussion because the discussion only inquired whether there were such noble products.[20]

Burnet understood, contrary to Adam, that the dialogue is not meant to affirm that holiness is service of the gods in producing noble products; he supposed instead that the dialogue is meant to deny it. Burnet's opinion is interesting and well worth quoting:

> If there were any definite ἔργον which the gods produce with our help, it must indeed be something 'mighty fine'. But in fact there is none, since ὁσιότης is no specialized art but a condition of the soul (ἕξις ψυχῆς). That is the positive result which the *Euthyphro* is meant to suggest to those who know the true Socratic doctrine, though it is nowhere explicitly stated.[21]

Allen aptly comments:

> But surely, if the *Euthyphro* were meant to suggest that holiness is not an art with a product, but a condition of soul, it would have suggested it. In fact, neither Adam nor Burnet are right, for the dialogue takes no stand on the issue over which they disagree. It is, perhaps one virtue of attending to dialectic rather than doctrine that one need not invent what one does not find.[22]

However, to criticize Burnet for reading his concept of ἕξις ψυχῆς into the text is not to discredit his main point: there *is* no virtue, piety, separate and distinct from justice—"it is our *whole* duty to care for our *own* souls" to bring about justice and wisdom in them. Indeed, Allen later grants that there is no product of holiness or piety,[23] but fails to see that this negative fact is a significant one.[24] True, there is no cryptic, positive and successful definition of piety in the dialogue.

Nonetheless, the argument does seem to point to some definite (however negative) conclusions. Vlastos has realized this in his recent essay on the paradox of Socrates, though he stops short of concluding that there really is no such virtue, piety, which fulfills a separate duty to the gods:

> [S]ince the gods are great and powerful past all imagining, they surely don't need our services to improve *their* estate; and since they are also good and benevolent, they do desire what is best for us—and what can this be, but the improvement of our souls? Isn't this then the object of piety, this the discharge of the highest obligation we owe the gods?[25]

2. The *Apology*.

The *Apology* is the prime source for ascertaining the religious element in Socrates' thought.[26] In the first place it presents his argument against the charge that he does not believe in the traditional gods of Athens—and in so doing provides us with as much of a testament of his religious views as can be found anywhere in the Socratic dialogues. In fact the *Apology* is unique in this respect—it is the only place where Socrates provides a *positive* explanation of his philosophical way. Most of the time he is occupied in questioning those who know in order that he might become wise, for he does not profess to know anything. The typical outcome, of course, is not a gain in wisdom for him, but rather his interlocutor is confronted with his own ignorance. So Socrates here departs from his normal practice of the negative method (though as we shall see, not completely) and explains what he is doing in the conduct of philosophical inquiry. Socrates proclaims that his philosophical way is a religious duty: it is nothing less than service to the deity; it is obedience to a divine command. But the *Euthyphro*, as we have seen, shows what true service of the gods is—it is seeking to further justice, both in oneself and in one's fellow citizens. The *Gorgias* shows that Socrates is the only true practitioner of the political art, which is defined (at 515b-c) as making citizens as good as possible:

> (Socrates:) I think that I am one of very few Athenians, not to say the only one, engaged in the true political art, and that of the men of today I alone practiced statesmanship. (521d)

These two truths find their unified expression in the *Apology*. But this is to anticipate the conclusion—let us attend now to the dialectical intricacies of the dialogue.

> The *Apology* is Socrates' defense against the following charge: Socrates is guilty of refusing to recognize the gods recognized by the state, and of introducing other new divinities. He is also guilty of corrupting the youth. The penalty demanded is

death.[27]

We can be fairly sure this is substantially historically accurate, since Diogenes Laërtius' statement reports Favorinus, who claimed to have consulted the Athenian archives in the Metroön. The differences of wording between this and Plato's rendering (24b8-c1) are minor. (Actually Xenophon's is even closer, the only exception being a single word, εἰσφέρων for εἰσηγούμενος, a substitution that does not alter the sense.) So Socrates on all accounts is accused of two things: (1) (a) not accepting the gods of the city, but (b) accepting, (or, according to Xenophon, introducing) novel divinities; and (2) corrupting youth.

There is nothing controversial about the rendering of (2), but justification of the rendering of both parts of (1) is in order. First, the key phrase θεοὺς οὐ νομίζοντα (Xenophon: θεοὺς οὐ νομίζων) is translated as "not accepting the gods" because it reflects the ambiguity of νομίζειν. As many have pointed out, νομίζειν is related to νόμος, customary law or usage. Νομίζειν can mean to observe such a νόμος, that is, to practice it, or it can mean to hold it, to recognize it, to *accept* it. Now if someone is said not to accept the gods of the religious νόμοι of the city, it is *a priori* unclear whether they are referring to practice or to intellectual recognition and acceptance. Of course if someone did not observe the νόμοι by his conduct it would be implied at least that he did not intellectually accept them. But the difficult case, and the case that applies to Socrates, is that in which the person observes the νόμοι but whose intellectual credence is in doubt.

Some, of course, have denied this ambiguity in sense of νομίζειν here. Burnet and Taylor, and more recently Reginald Allen, take the accusation brought against Socrates to mean that Socrates did not *worship* the gods of the city. Νομίζειν θεούς, says Burnet, "refers primarily to religious 'practice' (τὰ νομιζόμενα) rather than to religious belief." "The charge is one of non-conformity in religious practice, not of unorthodoxy in religious belief."[28] But the arguments of Hackforth, Tate and Guthrie have been more than sufficient to lay such a view to rest.[29] J. Tate has adduced instances from Herodotus, Lysias, Aristophanes, Euripides where νομίζειν θεούς is used in the sense of νομίζειν θεοὺς εἶναι (which of course can never mean "worship the gods"). This is to establish that οὐ νομίζειν θεούς in the indictment *can* mean that Socrates did not believe in the existence of the gods. The *Apology* itself makes it clear that this is in fact the sense the words are meant to bear. At 26b-c Socrates begins interrogating Meletus as to the precise meaning of his charges. Does he wish to say that Socrates believes in *some* (τινας) gods, or that he doesn't believe in *any at all* (παντάπασι . . . οὔτε. . . .)? In the first half of the question Socrates uses νομίζειν εἶναι θεούς; in the second he uses simply νομίζειν θεούς. Clearly the latter is being used synonymously with the former. At 29a Socrates paraphrases the initial charge using οὐ νομίζω θεοὺς εἶναι, showing that he took the charge to be an imputation of atheism, at least in a restricted sense: with respect to the traditional gods. This is proved in the wider context of the argument of the *Apology* as well, for the initial part of Socrates' defense is to dissociate himself from the atheistic natural philosophers like Anaxagoras. At 35d Socrates points out that if he were to urge the jurors to go against their oath he would in effect be teaching them to disbelieve in the gods (θεοὺς . . . μὴ ἡγεῖσθαι . . . εἶναι) and thus would show by inference that he himself does not believe in the gods (θεοὺς οὐ νομίζω). Again, θεοὺς νομίζειν is equivalent to believing in the gods. To this proof Tate adds examples from Plato's *Laws* where νομίζειν θεούς is repeatedly used interchangeably with νομίζειν θεοὺς εἶναι. All these arguments then not only establish our initial rendering of (1)(a), but actually warrant a further disambiguation of it: the weight of the charge is that Socrates did not "accept" the gods of the πόλις in the sense that he did not believe in their existence. Socrates then is being tried for his intellectual beliefs.[30] Hackforth was no doubt right in saying that a man could not be tried for things he did not say, that is, personal opinions he had not given utterance to.[31] Nor was it likely that his criticism of the mythological conception of the gods was sufficient for his prosecution. But we shall see that his habitual *silence* about the gods, his professed *agnosticism* with respect to the traditional gods of mythology, and the notorious δαιμόνιον, the object of his own personal belief, when taken together were quite enough to account for the charges having been brought against him. (That is not to say that it was justified; only that it is plausible that he was thus brought to trial.)

The δαιμόνια καινά of (1)(b) has caused a lot of trouble to interpreters. What does it mean? What does it refer to? Burnet rightly emphasizes its vagueness. And he points out that there is no noun-substantive usage of δαιμόνιον in classical Greek;[32] thus he is sure it does *not* mean "strange divinities". Hackforth is inclined to see the accusers coining the usage here for the first time.[33] Thus he accepts Euthyphro's interpretation (*Euthyphro* 3b) that the accusers had Socrates' δαιμόνιον in mind when they accused him of introducing "new gods" (καινοὶ θεοί).[34] (This was Xenophon's interpretation as well, *Defense* 12; *Memorabilia* I.1.2) We shall not quarrel with the traditional interpretation that Socrates' divine sign was the principal object of the charge:

in the minds of his accusers the δαιμόνιον was a "god". Socrates, however, does not say it was, and indeed the unusual way of referring to it seems to reflect a definite intention to *avoid* calling it a god. Burnet is sensitive to this point in translating it "the divine something". The vagueness of the term seems to be an authentic Socratic touch. By admitting he was informed by his δαιμόνιον Socrates was only saying that he heard a voice from some divine spirit (δαίμων) or other; Socrates seems to want deliberately to emphasize the indeterminacy of his spiritual communication.

The charge is in the plural: Socrates introduces some new spirits of his own personal belief. Burnet takes the δαιμόνια καινά to refer to πράγματα, as at 27c1, which thus accords with his interpretation that it is religious practices that are in question.[35] What seems more likely in light of our argument above is that the plural δαιμόνια stands for the δαιμόνιον plus the Clouds, Air, Ether, etc., that were insinuated as his own personal deities by his "early accusers" referred to at *Apology* 18-19, and in particular Aristophanes. The plural form then represents the accusers' shrewd conflation of Socrates' well-known δαιμόνιον with the other "new-fangled" divinities of the *Clouds* which he was commonly but mistakenly understood to recognize: by a cunning insinuation he was really on trial, as Socrates realized all too clearly, not simply for his private sign (which, as Xenophon argues at *Memorabilia* I.1.3 ff., was hardly different in principle from all the many other orthodox forms of divination), but for the kind of impious skeptical rationalism of the general sophist type.[36] And it is to be observed too that the *Apology* recognizes that he has received revelations in dreams. The *Apology*, then, is Socrates' self-defense against the charge of atheism with respect to the traditional gods of Athens and of introducing new divinities of his own.

The fact that Socrates argues very carefully against the popular misconception of him as a natural philosopher is significant. It suggests that Socrates was defending himself against the kind of law against ἀσέβεια (impiety) brought down by Diopeithes in 431 B.C. According to Plutarch that law was against "those who did not accept religious practices [τὰ θεῖα, or perhaps "the religion (of the πόλις)"] and teach doctrines about lofty, heavenly things [περὶ τῶν μεταρσίων]."[37] But although the law was posed in terms of orthodox *practice*, it is nonetheless clear that the legislators were after those with unorthodox beliefs as well. For that was the point of making teaching about the nature of the heavens a crime of ἀσέβεια. Whether one agrees with the interpretation of Burnet that the natural philosophy of the early Greeks was thoroughly rationalistic and naturalistic, or with that of Jaeger that these natural philosophies were actually theologies since the ultimate material ἀρχή was considered divine, it nonetheless must be granted that these systems were atheistic with respect to the traditional gods. It was their implied atheism that made these physical theories impious. It is true we have no records of the laws of impiety among the Greeks, as indeed we have no knowledge of the law in 399 B.C. when Socrates was brought to trial. There is probably good reason for our lack of knowledge, for it seems to have been the case that the offenses that constituted ἀσέβεια were never clearly or systematically spelled out. Indeed, in some cases unwritten law was used as the criterion for ἀσέβεια.[38] Impiety was whatever offended the religious sensibilities of the orthodoxy of the day.[39] Clearly on those terms the new philosophical teachings were decidedly impious. (It is also significant in this light that Socrates makes a point of dissociating himself from Anaxagoras, who was one of the first to be snared by Diopeithes' legislation; see 26d.)

Socrates could, of course, in good conscience dissociate himself from the atheistic natural philosophers. We have discussed above (and below, in Appendix II) the nature of his early acquaintance with them; Socrates was no atheist in that sense. And unlike the foreigner Anaxagoras, who could perhaps justifiably be accused of non-observance of the gods of Athens, Socrates was, on all the evidence, scrupulously "orthoprax". That cannot have been the issue at the trial. Indeed, if it were, his defense would have been a simple matter. He would need only to call witnesses to the fact of his habitual practice. Xenophon states categorically that Socrates offered public and private sacrifices: "He offered sacrifices constantly, and made no secret of it, now in his home, now at the altars of the state temple. . . ."(*Memorabilia* I.1.2). According to Xenophon Socrates dutifully observed all the sacrificial observances of the πόλις (*Memorabilia* I.3.1). On this point of fact there is no good reason to doubt Xenophon, and Plato corroborates it as far as he goes. In the *Euthydemus* Socrates says "I have my own altars and my own religion and family prayers and all that sort of thing, as much as any other Athenian" (302c). This is private, family religion, but when taken together with Socrates' scrupulous respect for all the laws and observances of the πόλις which he expresses elsewhere, there is no reason to doubt that Socrates was "pious" with respect to the religious νόμοι.[40] In the *Crito* Socrates remains adamant in refusing to break the laws and constitutions of the πόλις even when he is certain that he is being sentenced to death unjustly by them. Crito has urged Socrates to escape; Socrates puts this argument in the mouth of "the laws":

> Now, Socrates, what are you proposing to do? Can you deny that by this act which you are contemplating you intend, so far as you have the power, to destroy us, the laws, and the whole state as well? Do you imagine that a city can continue to exist and not be turned upside down, if the legal judgments which are pronounced in it have no force but are nullified and destroyed by private persons? (50a-b; cf. also 49b, 51a-b)

And in the *Apology* Socrates says:

> I . . . made it clear not by my words but by my actions that death did not matter to me at all—if that is not too strong an expression—but that it mattered all the world to me that I should do nothing wrong or wicked. (32c-d)

So Socrates' orthopraxy is not in question at his trial, and accordingly Plato does not mention it in his account.

But, as we have argued, orthopraxy was not the only concern of the laws of impiety. True, orthodox religion was just that section of the νόμοι, the customs and observances of the state, that had to do with worship and sacrifice to the gods. But by the time of Socrates there was a well developed tradition of rational, and indeed skeptical, criticism of the gods of traditional religion. The various σοφοί or σοφισταί had gained a powerful influence on the cultured mind of the day and had begun to have an eroding influence on the religious piety of the state at large. The defenders of the πόλις could no longer be satisfied with mere external compliance with public ritual. They were shrewd enough to perceive the radical implications for the political establishment of the new critical attitude toward the gods. To undermine the unquestioning acceptance of the traditional mythically conceived gods was ultimately to undermine the unquestioning acceptance of the form of the πόλις—for the gods were a basic element in the official ideology, i.e. self-understanding of the state. Theoretically, at least, it was through the gods that the contingent social-political order was grounded in the timeless holy. The values instituted in laws were sanctioned as more than arbitrary determinations of human lawgivers. It was for this reason that, on Plutarch's account, trials were instituted in Athens just before the Peloponnesian War for three related offenses: impiety, atheism, and teaching about celestial phenomena. The trials were attempts to defend the state's sacred credentials, so to speak, by attacking the new thinkers for their *intellectual beliefs*, and indeed ultimately for their *way of thinking itself*. This means, in short, that Socrates would have to give positive, unequivocal evidence of intellectual orthodoxy in order to persuade the jury that the charges were false and unjust. Nothing short of that would constitute a *legal* refutation of the charges. For any of the intelligentsia this would certainly be an exceedingly hard thing to prove. Once in court the defendant was clearly at the advantage of his accusers. Fortunately the law of ἀσέβεια was not often invoked.[41] Yet it obviously could be brought up, with telling results, against any of the new intellectuals should anyone be either conscientious or devious enough to lay charges. Socrates was vulnerable inasmuch as he was critical of the popular mythically conceived gods and spoke only of vague divine forces operative in his psyche alone.

Once we understand exactly what would have constituted a frontal refutation of the charges, it becomes clear why Socrates did not as much as attempt such a defense.[42] And it was clear, as Socrates himself suspected (36a), that his own line of defense was not likely to be successful. For instead of giving positive evidence of orthodox belief, Socrates, with consummate fidelity to his philosophical method, attempted an elenctic refutation. He tested his accusers and showed them to be ignorant, confused and mistaken: they did not know what they were talking about. In form, then, his refutation was negative. True, he elucidated aspects of his own religion—the devotion to the god of Delphi, his δαιμόνιον, and dreams. But though the former was orthodox, it was not a god of Athens—it was a pan-Hellenic form of religious piety. And the charges demanded that he prove acceptance of the gods of Athens. The latter two are private forms of religious piety and similarly would be useless to satisfy the jurors of Socrates' orthodoxy. Socrates stood by these elements of his personal religion and completely failed to argue what he had to argue to win acquittal: that he accepted intellectually the form of religion current in the state. This is clear in Socrates' refutation of the immediate charges brought against him.

The man bringing the charges against Socrates is one Meletus, described in the *Euthyphro* as "a young man, and unknown" (2b).[43] Socrates makes his estimate of Meletus plain in the *Apology*: Meletus is merely posturing as the conscientious citizen deeply concerned about the moral and religious education of youth:

> First [the charge] says that I am guilty of corrupting the young. But I say, gentlemen, that Meletus is guilty of treating a serious matter with levity, since he summons people to stand their trial on frivolous grounds, and professes concern and keen anxiety in matters about which he has never had the slightest interest. (24c)

One may imagine Meletus as a young man intent on making a name for himself as the man who convicted Socrates of atheism. He seems to have been especially concerned with the religious law of the city, for he spoke against Andocides on another ἀσέβεια charge that same year.[44] He complacently trusts in the goodness and rightness of all the values of the πόλις, and equally complacently assumes that the popular estimate of Socrates as an atheist σοφός is true. He is ignorant of Socrates to the point of attributing to him the view "that the sun is a stone and the moon a mass of earth," thus confusing him with physical speculators like Anaxagoras. As far as philosophical ἔλεγχος goes, Socrates has an easy time of it.

It is important to realize that Socrates' defense against the charges in *this* part of the dialogue is generally of the form of philosophical ἔλεγχος. Socrates proceeds on the assumption that not he, but Meletus, is the one who has knowledge. Socrates questions Meletus to find out his meaning and to see if it stands up. Do you mean, Socrates asks, that I believe in some gods, only not those of the state, or none at all? Meletus, forgetting that his formal statement of the charge recognizes Socrates' personal gods, stumbles over himself in the headlong attempt to seize upon the more incriminating alternative—Socrates, he says, is a complete atheist. As a result Meletus entraps himself in contradiction and so is dismissed by Socrates as one who does not know (specifically, what he is saying). But Meletus' headlong leap to his own defeat is not simply due to ignorant confusion on his part; nor is Socrates' destructive ἔλεγχος merely a point of logical debate. Meletus *naturally* leapt to that alternative because it was the real, operative element in the accusation. Behind the key phrase δαιμόνια καινά stand the unorthodox divinities of the *Clouds*: Meletus and company wanted to impute to Socrates the kind of atheistic rationalistic sophistry caricatured in the *Clouds* —perhaps they even ignorantly believed in the truth of their accusation. Thus the self-contradiction of the charges reflects the inherent self-contradiction of Aristophanes' popular caricature of Socrates (which of course would have been a matter of little concern to the great comic dramatist)—for there too Socrates does away with the gods, yet introduces strange divinities of his own. Thus by engineering Meletus' dialectical embarrassment Socrates shows what was really in his accusers' mind—as well as the complete rightness of defending himself against his "early accusers".

The form of Socrates' parry is illuminating: it is, he says, *the general belief of all mankind,* Anaxagoras and such being the exceptions, that the sun and moon are gods. I am not to be confused with the likes of Anaxagoras—which would seem to imply the contrary of what you charge me with.

Probably the jury were too dull-witted to perceive that Socrates' argument does not logically yield the conclusion that *he* holds that the sun and moon were gods. Socrates merely *assumes* the common belief of men: what needs to be proved is that *he* holds it. At any rate the jury was not likely to be impressed with Socrates' argument on other grounds. The religion of the πόλις was not founded on a sun or moon cult; they were not the principal deities in the Athenian pantheon. Socrates must show that he believes in the gods of the πόλις. Indeed, one might find many members of the rationalizing intelligentsia who were inclined to accept the heavenly bodies as divine. His main argument addresses itself to this question of the relationship of his personal god to the traditional gods. Socrates begins by announcing the conclusion his argument will arrive at:

> It certainly seems to me that he is contradicting himself in this indictment, which might just as well run: Socrates is guilty of not believing in the gods, but believing in the gods. And this is pure flippancy.
>
> I ask you to examine with me, gentlemen, the line of reasoning which leads me to this conclusion. You, Meletus, will oblige us by answering my questions. (27a4-b2)

The argument essentially is this: You grant that I am the recipient of divine actions (δαιμόνια πράγματα). (Socrates is evidently referring here to his δαιμόνιον, his divine voice.) Now, no one thinks that there are actions performed without beings to perform them. Thus there are δαίμονες. But we all take δαίμονες to be gods or children of the gods. Thus my claim to be the recipient of an authentic δαιμόνιον entails the acceptance of the existence of the gods. But the former was granted by Meletus in the very charges. This yields the desired conclusion: Meletus asserts that I believe in the gods and that I do not believe in the gods.

This part, too, of Socrates' argument is elenctic in form. Instead of setting out what he knows (for he professes not to know anything), Socrates attacks what his opponent self-confidently professes to know: in this case that Socrates does not believe in the gods. Socrates uses premises fully acceptable to his opponent: first, the common-sense truth that where there is an action there must be a being to perform it, and second, the popular mythical belief that δαίμονες are the offspring of the gods. And he uses these premises to conclude that one cannot look upon his gods as "strange new gods" (ἕτερα δαιμόνια καινά, 26b). One *must* suppose, on the theological principles, as it were, of popular mythology itself, that Socrates' gods belong to the traditional pantheon. The technique is familiar: Socrates once more has confounded his opponent by showing that he contradicts himself.

It is likely that the men of the jury were somewhat dazzled by what must have seemed to them Socrates' display of philosophical wizardry—how remarkable so simply to derive contradictory assertions from Meletus' initial statement! It certainly did not *look* so confused! they must have thought to themselves. But nonetheless, being the unphilosophical men they were, they must have felt that the connection Socrates had drawn between his gods and the traditional gods was a trifle tenuous. Socrates no doubt failed to *persuade* them—to do that he would have to have been more the orator and less the philosopher. What they wanted evidence of was, in effect, that Socrates accepted for himself the traditional ways of conceptualizing the gods. They wanted positive, unequivocal evidence of his habitual way of thinking of the gods. On that score Socrates' arguments must have failed miserably, for in the context of the jury's requirements Socrates' apology must have appeared as guarded, elliptical and ambiguous.

In the course of the above arguments Socrates repeatedly insinuates himself among those who accept the popular understanding of the gods. At 26d he says: "Do you suggest that I do not believe that the sun and moon are gods, *as is the general belief of all mankind*?" At 27c: "*Is there anyone* who believes in supernatural activities and not in supernatural beings?" At 27c-d: "*Do we not hold* that supernatural beings are either gods or the children of gods?" And at 27d: "If . . . these supernatural beings are bastard children of the gods by nymphs or other mothers, *as they are reputed to be*, who in the world would believe in the children of the gods and not in the gods themselves?" Socrates in short argues from the popular mythological understanding of the gods. But the *Euthyphro* demonstrates that in a number of respects it is quite clear that Socrates believes that certain facets of the popular understanding are mistaken and misconceived. In this regard he belongs to the tradition of rational criticism of the gods—just the sort of people at whom the religious laws were directed. Socrates, of course, does not profess to know positive things about God or the gods such as other demythologizers did. But nonetheless he does not accept the gods as they are popularly understood, and is thus legally an atheist. Socrates' defense against his "earliest accusers" is of the same form. People believe, he says, that I am just another σοφὸς ἀνήρ, one of the σοφισταί wise in heavenly matters and the nature of the earth and how to defeat one's opponent in logical argument. But what these early accusers say, as did Aristophanes, who foisted this misrepresentation on the public, is simply untrue. There is not a bit of truth in these accusations (17a,b, 19d). His defense, here again, is a flat denial of the charges.

This is, of course, not all there is to Socrates' defense—if it were, it would hardly have merited the fascination and admiration it has commanded down through the ages. There is a positive side to Socrates' defense as well. Indeed, he claims to tell the whole truth (17b, 20d). "Perhaps some of you will think that I am not being serious, but I assure you that I am going to tell you the whole truth [πᾶσαν τὴν ἀλήθειαν]"(20d5). And the revelation is that he has conducted his philosophy out of nothing less than utter devotion to a *religious* duty. But it is significant that this is not presented as an attempt to demonstrate his orthodoxy —he is not deluded enough to think that such a procedure would work. Rather, in the context it is presented simply as the explanation of why he was misconstrued by the public as an atheistic philosopher. The reason, he says, is that he was searching out the Oracle's response. He *knew* that he had no claim to wisdom, but the God at Delphi had said that there was none wiser than he. What could this mean? It was no doubt a riddle. Socrates seems to have accepted the Oracle's response with scrupulous respect. He took it as a divinely imposed duty to search out the meaning (21e). After deliberating for some time he decided that the Oracle must be tested by thoroughly questioning men with a reputation for their wisdom. He discovered that those most famous for their wisdom were really profoundly ignorant. He systematically tested politicians, poets, and skilled craftsmen. He came to realize that the Oracle's meaning was this: Socrates was wiser than all these because he knew that he knew nothing.

The introduction of this theme—Socrates' religious vocation and duty to the God of Delphi—establishes the profound dramatic pathos of the dialogue. Socrates is being tried for impiety, yet it is precisely his complete dedication to his God, even to death, which has offended his accusers and brought him to trial. The deepest conflict is that between the religion of the πόλις and Socrates' own religion. The *Apology*, when taken together with the *Euthyphro* (and the *Gorgias*), is intent on showing that Socrates is the only true pious citizen, the religious citizen *par excellence*, and that he is being tried precisely for this reason. The presentation is tragic in the sense that it is not designed as an argument of Socrates' innocence before the law, but that though he was *legally* an atheist, truly and actually (that is, in terms of a philosophical understanding of the matter) he was the furthest thing from it. He stands in judgment of the current orthodox interpretation of what constituted religion in the πόλις. But this is to anticipate; let us first attend to the details of Plato's dramatic presentation.

When Socrates heard the deliverance of the Oracle, he explains, he took it so seriously that he deliberated for some time. He finally decided that the pronouncement should be subjected to a test: he would go about and interrogate those who professed wisdom of some kind or other. He took the pronouncement of the Oracle as a permanent obligation to continue this sort of philosophical scrutiny of individuals. At 21e Socrates says it seemed necessary to him to make that which pertained to the god (the Oracle) the thing of greatest importance. He felt compelled to put the god before the opinions of men. That is, he must continue to examine men philosophically despite the antipathies this aroused. At 23b Socrates says this inquiring and searching was κατὰ τὸν θεὸν, according to the god. "And when someone seems to me not to be wise I assist the god [τῷ θεῷ βοηθῶν] and show that they are not wise" (23b6-7). This he calls his service (λατρεία) to the god. (At 30a Socrates says his philosophical way is god's command, κελεύει ὁ θεός, and that his obedience is his *service* to the god, τὴν ἐμὴν τῷ θεῷ ὑπηρεσίαν.)

Socrates continues his stand on his divine mission after his interrogation of Meletus. Socrates did his best to explain to the jury that the charges were unjust, and why, though he had no hopes that he would actually succeed. Yet, accommodate himself he would never do. A passage in the *Crito* sums up his attitude:

> You must not give way or retreat or abandon your position. Both in war and in the law courts and everywhere else you must do whatever your city and your country command, or else persuade them in accordance with universal justice, but violence is a sin even against your parents, and it is a far greater sin against your country. (51c)

The section of Socrates' defense immediately following his refutation of the charges develops just this theme: just as Socrates took his stand in the battlefield like a hero, and just as he took his stand on justice against the opinion of the many when he served in the Assembly, so he takes now his heroic stand in obedience to God. However, an immense problem confronts us: there is a mysterious discrepancy between the way his jurors use the word θεός and the way he uses it. And at every turn he seems to be deliberately evasive and cryptic. In accordance with his philosophical method generally he does not want to tell us the answer, he invites us to search for it. Socrates again introduces the new phase of his defense by raising a possible objection to his own case: "But perhaps someone will say, Do you feel no compunction, Socrates, at having followed a line of action which puts you in danger of the death penalty?" (28b). He is maintaining some semblance of dialectical method: he will not resort to the kind of persuasive rhetoric and heartrending ploys, (such as parading in one's family and relatives, etc.) which defendants frequently resorted to in order to win their acquittal. Socrates meets the objection: no one who makes any claim to virtue can allow considerations of life or death to interfere with carrying out his moral duty. He likens himself to the heroes who died at

Troy, and especially Achilles, the greatest hero of all. The moral code of the Achaean warriors obliged Achilles to avenge the death of his friend Patroclus. But Thetis, his goddess-mother, warned him that this would result in his death. "Then die I must," was his reply. Socrates was not being presumptuous in making such a comparison. For, as he recalls to the jury's mind, some years earlier he had made celebrated heroic stands in the battles at Potidaea, Amphipolis and Delium. Now, he insists, it should be no different. He has been assigned his post by God and he must stand firm:

> This being so, it would be shocking inconsistency on my part, gentlemen, if, when the officers whom you chose to command me assigned me my position at Potidaea and Amphipolis and Delium, I remained at my post like anyone else and faced death, and yet afterward, when God appointed me, as I supposed and believed, to the duty of leading the philosophical life, examining myself and others, I were then through fear of death or of any other danger to desert my post. That would indeed by shocking, and then I might really with justice be summoned into court for not believing in the gods, and disobeying the oracle, and being afraid of death, and thinking that I am wise when I am not. (28d-29a)

The injustice of the charges here becomes brilliantly clear: it is precisely because of his pious obedience and submission to the will of God that he will be put to death.

At the beginning of his *Defense* Xenophon mentions the μεγαληγορία of Socrates' defense. This word seems to carry all of the following connotations: loftiness, with resounding words, with great courage and boldness, but perhaps also shades of the less flattering "big-talk". Xenophon, of course, is offended by it—he thinks such a tack was, to say the least, indiscreet. And so he attempts to show how this was really quite "reasonable" on the part of Socrates—it was, he says, because he realized he was going to die in a short time anyway that he assumed such an ill-advised stance. The resulting portrait of Socrates is an annoying, self-righteous, "big-talker," someone who is puffed up with his own good opinion of himself. His defense consists of a parade of all the good gentlemanly virtues he possesses.

Certainly Xenophon was offended by the μεγαληγορία of Plato's account, if it is to be included in his mention of "the many who have written on the subject." So far Socrates has defended himself, he has stood his ground. But the remaining part of his defense turns into an almost abrasive, strident counter-attack. Even if you offered me acquittal, he says (29c-d), should I stop this philosophical gad-flying, I would never accept it.

> Well, supposing, as I said, that you should offer to acquit me

> on these terms, I should reply, Gentlemen, I am your grateful and devoted servant, but I owe a greater obedience to God than to you, and so long as I draw breath and have my faculties, I shall never stop practicing philosophy and exhorting you and elucidating the truth for everyone that I meet. (29d)[45]

But this is precisely one of the principal targets of the new religious laws. Socrates is an individual who stands over against the religio-political orthodoxy. As far as the defenders of the πόλις were concerned, Socrates was one with the σοφισταί, those who criticized the religious-political synthesis from the standpoint of individual rational criticism.[46] Further, his relation to his own personal "god" was not mediated by the πόλις. From their point of view it is easy to see how Socrates would appear a subversive. The dictates of his own conscience came before the claims of the πόλις. He judged *them*. They did not realize what was good for the πόλις. Neither did Socrates profess to *know* such a thing, but he sought it and urged his fellow citizens to seek it:

> I shall go on saying, in my usual way, My very good friend, you are an Athenian and belong to a city which is the greatest and most famous in the world for its wisdom and strength. Are you not ashamed that you give your attention to acquiring as much money as possible, and similarly with reputation and honour, and give no attention or thought to truth and understanding and the perfection of your soul? (29d-e)

He goes so far as to assert, "it is my belief that no greater good has ever befallen you in this city than my service to my God" (30a).

Socrates' boldness seems to evoke a tumultuous reaction from the jury (30c). But far from easing up, he hurls the ultimate insult in their faces:

> It is [my δαιμόνιον] that debars me from entering public life, and a very good thing too, in my opinion, because you may be quite sure, gentlemen, that if I had tried long ago to engage in politics, I should long ago have lost my life, without doing any good either to you or to myself. Please do not be offended if I tell you the truth. No man on earth who conscientiously opposes either you or any other organized democracy, and flatly prevents a great many wrongs and illegalities from taking place in the state to which he belongs, can possibly escape with his life. The true champion of justice, if he intends to survive even for a short time, must necessarily confine himself to private life and leave politics alone. (31d-32a)

Truly it is not surprising, as Socrates himself says at 36a, that the jury brings in the guilty verdict. But still Socrates will not relent from his "ill-considered" tack. He is asked to suggest a penalty. This is an invitation to persuade the jury of a more lenient punishment than death. His response is instructive in pointing out just how far Plato's Socrates is from Xenophon's "average Athenian citizen" Socrates. He claims, "I have never lived an ordinary life—I did not care for the things that most people care about" (36b). Perceiving that my strictness with regard to personal principles would have brought about my end before long, he says, I set myself instead the course which I thought the most beneficial to you and me: to work outside the public sphere and try to persuade you individually, face to face in conversation to concern yourselves first and foremost with the excellence of your souls, both moral and intellectual. The only fitting "penalty" for this service is free maintenance at the state's expense.[47] You give this of course to the athletes who return to the πόλις wearing the laurels of victory—how much more deserving for me to win such a prize. "These people give you the semblance of success, but I give you the reality" (36d-e).

One *caveat* must be entered here. Although Socrates represents an individual conscience who stands resolutely against the state, this is not the same thing as the Christian's recognition that God's claim over him comes before the state's claim. The Christian looks to God first and the state second. But from the *Euthyphro* we have seen that the work of the gods is justice. For Socrates there is no separate religious domain for man apart from his life as a πολίτης. And Socrates' duty is wholly oriented to the πόλις. Furthering the goodness, virtue, justice of citizens in the πόλις is his only motivation. The Christian, however, may be motivated for the good of the state, but ultimately it is for the love of God.

The *Apology* presents the Socratic philosophical way as having a religious foundation. Or, to put it differently, Socrates' religion is his philosophy. This raises an important question. Is the philosophical way ultimately religious? Is it based on *irrational beliefs*?—first of all, the Oracle, and secondarily, the δαιμόνιον and dreams? Are these the ultimate grounds for the Socratic philosophical way? Certainly this is the construction which is usually put on these religious features of his thought. Guthrie speaks of "the irrational side to Socrates."[48] This view that Socrates possesses quite irrational beliefs *alongside* his philosophy is probably the common view. It is evident in Burnet's attitude towards the δαιμόνιον:

> It belonged to the 'irrational part' of his soul, even more than dreams (cf. *Crito* 44a6), which sometimes did give positive instructions (*Phaed.* 60el sqq.) as the 'divine sign' never did (*Ap.* 31d3). That being so, it is obviously futile to rationalize it. We must simply accept the fact that it was a perfectly real experience to Socrates, though not apparently of paramount importance.[49]

And it is evident in Hackforth's opinion that Socrates was "content and wisely content not to attempt an explicit reconciliation of reason with faith."[50] Matters of faith, he urges, were beyond human reason so far as Socrates was concerned. (This is implicit in Allen's opinion that Socrates was both conventional and sincere in observances *and* religious attitudes, *Plato's 'Euthyphro'*, p.62. There was on the one hand his philosophy, and on the other his religion.) To say, then, that Socrates' philosophy is rooted in an irrational belief, a supernatural revelation of a divine being, is to break up the naturalism, the insistence that Socrates possesses only human wisdom, fundamental to his philosophical outlook: it is to insinuate a profound inconsistency in it. Far from being the resolute insistence that he knows nothing in higher matters, in all that surpasses the everyday concerns of human life, it becomes in its very foundations an irrational view of life derived from that which is beyond *human* ken. Now, it is always possible that Socrates was thus inconsistent, but the point ought not be granted without further examination. In what follows we shall submit to scrutiny what Socrates related about the two aspects of his religion, the Oracle and the δαιμόνιον.[51]

3. The Oracle.

At 20d-e Socrates explains how he became known as a man wise in higher matters like the natural philosophers, and one skilled in the tricks of argument like the sophists, even though he possessed no such wisdom. The reason, he says, is a certain human wisdom (ἀνθρωπίνη σοφία). He is referring, as becomes clear at 21d6-7, to his awareness of his ignorance: "At any rate it seems that I am wiser than [they] to this small extent, that I do not think that I know what I do not know." He introduces the god of Delphi as a "worthy witness" (ἀξιόχρεων, 20e6, μάρτυρα, e7) to this *human* wisdom of his: as we shall see, whatever the Oracle may contribute to Socrates' self-understanding, it is not the source or cause of the limited, human wisdom he possesses.

At 21a Socrates relates how his close friend and associate Chaerephon approached the Oracle with the question whether there was anyone wiser than Socrates. H.W. Parke has advanced persuasive arguments for taking Chaerephon's consultation of the Oracle to have been in the form of lots and not the more uncommon and dramatic prophetic utterance of the Pythia while in a trance-state.[52] According to Parke the occasions of the more elaborate consultation of the Pythia were severely limited: originally once a year on the feast of Apollo, by the fifth century B.C. they were conducted monthly for nine months of the year. The method of lots (the chance drawing by the Pythia of a white or black bean) was a fairly recent innovation in response to demands on the Pythia's powers. Thus Chaerephon's question must have been in a form which could receive a "yes" or "no" answer: "Is there anyone wiser than Socrates?"[53] Socrates characterizes Chaerephon as σφοδρός, overly zealous, impetuous. The word connotes an excess.[54] One can perceive Socrates' natural awe and distaste at his friend's unthinking rashness, as well as, of course, his sense of embarrassment, given his habitual posture of disclaiming any wisdom for himself. At any rate, the tale seemed to cause a furor among his audience as Socrates tried to tell it—"as I said before, gentlemen, please do not interrupt." Perhaps, as Burnet suggests, it was because the Oracle was out of favor, as it had undermined the Athenian cause in the struggle against the Persians through its policy of appeasement and had supported the Spartan side in the Peloponnesian war.[55] But this simply highlights the character of the Oracle's pronouncements in general. H.W. Parke speaks of the general decline in the reputation of the Oracle among those of intelligence and acumen:

> The stories of how Lysander attempted to manipulate the oracles show the extent to which the prestige of oracles was beginning to dwindle. It was still useful to obtain their support for special projects, but no one would be greatly surprised or shocked if they were in some instances the product of chicanery.[56]

The truth is that the kind of simple-minded piety evidenced by Socrates with respect to the Oracle is somewhat naive. It had become obvious to most intelligent men that the "supernatural" character of the Oracle's divination was not as pure and free from political sway, nor from monetary and other mundane interests as the orthodox piety of the day might like to believe. It is difficult to take Socrates' apparently serious response to the Oracle without a grain of suspicion. But let us examine his words further to see what it was the Oracle revealed to Socrates.

Socrates explains he was taken aback by the Oracle: "what could it mean? Surely it could not mean just what it said, for I am only too conscious that I have no claim to wisdom, great or small."[57] This makes it amply clear that the Oracle did not teach him his philosophical ignorance—he was *already* convinced of it. It was precisely *because* he was sure he had no wisdom that the pronouncement was a paradox to him. As Socrates represents it he first puzzled over the matter (ἠπόρουν), then decided on a course of investigation. He would go to someone who was looked upon as a wise man and thus attempt to test, indeed even to refute (ἐλέγξων), the Oracle and show (ἀποφανῶν) that he was not in fact the wisest man of all (21c). To some this is hardly an attitude indicative of piety—for it seems to show downright disrespect for the

Oracles's pronouncement. But, as Guthrie and Parke have pointed out, this was an exactly appropriate response inasmuch as the Oracle *usually* spoke in a riddle.[58] This of course would apply in the first instance to those occasions when the Oracle gave a lengthier reply, but even in the case of a "yes" or "no" answer it was not out of the ordinary to suppose that its real meaning was not open to plain view. It had to be pored over carefully, and this Socrates did. Nevertheless, it must be admitted that Socrates has expressed what he was doing in especially strong, supremely confident terms. He is so sure of his conviction he has no wisdom that he supposes he might refute the Oracle and show it up to be wrong. Socrates' pious acceptance of the Oracle is not without a suspicious trace of ὕβρις (pride).

The results of Socrates' test, or rather series of tests, systematically examining each category of wise men, is of course well known. In Socrates' own words in the *Apology*:

> From that time on I interviewed one person after another. I realized with distress and alarm that I was making myself unpopular, but I felt compelled to put my religious duty first. Since I was trying to find out the meaning of the oracle, I was bound to interview everyone who had a reputation for knowledge. And by dog, gentlemen, for I must be frank with you, my honest impression was this. It seemed to me, as I pursued my investigation at the god's command, that the people with the greatest reputations were almost entirely deficient, while others who were supposed to be their inferiors were much better qualified in practical intelligence. (21e-22a)

Socrates says that as a result of his attempt to find the meaning of the Oracle he realized that he was arousing the resentment of many. But since he represents the realization as a new one we must suppose that his elenctic questioning of the wise, which was the cause of the resentment, must also have been new. In other words, Socrates' peculiar and characteristic question and answer method emerged out of his reflection on the Oracle's pronouncement.

If this were all Socrates said about the Oracle the matter would remain hopelessly ambiguous. On the one hand there is Socrates' utterly serious sense of duty to the Oracle to question those who were wise—at least we must suppose it was such if he was willing to carry out this philosophical duty no matter what the personal loss in the esteem of his fellow citizens, and indeed, if he was willing to carry it out even under pain of death. So we seem to be left on the one hand, then, with no alternative than to suppose that Socrates felt an intense personal devotion to the God of Delphi, a devotion belonging to the sphere of irrational religious conviction, outside the pale of rational philosophical discussion. Yet on the other hand there is the curious and typical irony that pervades the passage. It is hardly thinkable that Socrates seriously set out, convinced that *he* had nothing one could really call "knowledge", to see *if* others really were wise as they thought themselves to be. This is simply another instance of the irony so characteristic of his philosophy. He always represents himself as the deferential ignoramus attempting to test another's wisdom in the hopes that he might come to share some modest portion of it. But his pose is transparent; it is clear he is all too aware of the other's ignorance from the very start. He expresses his surprise that the wise opinions of his opponent have ended in such confusion—but it is clear that he was intent on bringing about this result from the very outset of the discussion. Yet if the testing of the Oracle is ironic then it casts suspicion on the whole account. How do we know that the sense of duty Socrates feels is not also part of the dramatic representation of the matter, a kind of fictional dressing of some less picturesque truth?

In this light Socrates' comment at 23a-b comes as a remarkable revelation of his own view of the Oracle episode.

> But the truth of the matter, gentlemen, is pretty certainly this, that real wisdom is the property of God [τῷ ὄντι ὁ θεὸς σοφὸς εἶναι, 23a5-6], and this oracle is his way of telling us that human wisdom has little or no value. It seems to me that he is not referring literally to Socrates, but has merely taken my name as an example, as if he would say to us, The wisest of you men is he who has realized, like Socrates, that in respect of wisdom he is really worthless.

Socrates is here relating his conclusion as to the truth of the riddle. *This* is why, he explains, I go about inquiring and searching according to the God, trying to assist the God by showing individuals they are not really wise. What is especially striking about this explanation of his vocation is that there is nothing individual or particular about it. He serves "the God" who speaks through this oracular pronouncement. It is not the localized, particularized Delphic Apollo that he is serving, but "the God who is in truth wise." Since the wisdom in question is not particular matters of oracular pronouncements, but the wisdom involved in how to lead a good, virtuous life, a life of moral, physical and intellectual excellence (ἀρετή), it is clear that Socrates is speaking of some high deity to whom can be attributed the wisdom-virtue he is seeking philosophically. But what is further striking about this religious service of the God is that the divine term of the relationship lacks all determination. Nothing at all is revealed about "the God" (or "the Godhead," or "the divinity," as we might also have translated it); the notion is not in the least filled out.

Yet what *is* manifest is that Socrates' philosophical way is service of the abstract truth he has just stated. Socrates' mission is to bring home to men the realization that the wisdom they possess is no real wisdom, that nonetheless there is a transcendent, "divine" wisdom which is indeed the very standard by which the radical limitedness of human wisdom is judged. Socrates is intent on making men aware of this divine standard. We note in this connection that as Socrates interprets the true meaning of the Oracle there is no reference to him individually and personally. He is only the occasion for the pronouncement of a general truth—a truth that is quite traditional among the Greeks. Socrates' insistence that he has only limited, *human* wisdom recalls that most famous saying of the Delphic Oracle, "Know thyself," that fundamental principle of classical Greek religiosity.[59] It means, of course (in part), "Man, know thy place and keep it. Beware of ὕβρις[60] and do not transgress on the divine." In this light the Socratic way is a concerted effort on the philosophical plane to reinforce and extend the traditional Greek religious sense of the discrepancy between the human and the divine. Socrates' destructive method is meant to reinstate the sense of limitedness in the sphere of human thought. But philosophy is not entirely negative even though no wisdom is attained, for implicit in that very mode of philosophizing is the supposition that there *is* a real wisdom-virtue. This wisdom is divine—that is, it transcends man's grasp of it. There are absolute, objective norms of wisdom and virtue independent of man's full comprehension or attainment. Men may found their νόμοι, their customs, laws and conventions on them or they may not—divine ἀρετή remains. It transcends the arbitrary changes of fashion in the human sphere. Socrates is the servant of these divine realities. His philosophical method is religious inasmuch as it conveys implicitly the concept and sense of absolute truth and wisdom of which we men fall so very far short.

But what of "the God"? After all, Socrates said (23a5-6), "in reality it is God who is wise"—not, "wisdom is God." The latter usage would of course be the familiar predicative usage of θεός without the article, and would accordingly mean "wisdom is divine."[61] Socrates seems to want to talk of an evidently personal "God". But however much this might be true, it remains that the concept of "the God", except for two logical functions, is empty of all determination. "The God" is the bearer of divine σοφία and is the "whence" the Oracle's pronouncement came. Nothing of the God shows itself to Socrates except the truth he has gleaned from the Oracle. Now, in the general context of the *Euthyphro* and the *Apology* this silence is *significant*. The *Euthyphro* makes it clear that Socrates viewed the divine excellences as the primary criteria of divinity—the gods were divine in relationship to them.

The *Apology* emphasizes the thorough-going "ignorance" of Socrates' philosophical world-view and his consequent agnosticism in "higher" matters. His attitude with regard to death is particularly instructive in this regard:

> [L]et me tell you, gentlemen, that to be afraid of death is only another form of thinking that one is wise when one is not; it is to think that one knows what one does not know. No one knows with regard to death whether it is not really the greatest blessing that can happen to a man, but people dread it as though they were certain that it is the greatest evil, and this ignorance, which thinks that it knows what it does not, must surely be ignorance most culpable. This, I take it, gentlemen, is the degree, and this the nature of my advantage over the rest of mankind, and if I were to claim to be wiser than my neighbour in any respect, it would be in this—that not possessing any real knowledge of what comes after death, I am also conscious that I do not possess it. (29a-b)

Socrates' attitude towards the afterlife (40a ff.) parallels his attitude towards "the God". He reasons that death *may* be *either* annihilation *or* a migration to some other place. On *either* count he thinks death would be a good.[62] And *if* it is the latter he suggests that there will be just judges there (as opposed to his present judges) and other fine men to converse with. Yet the possibility of an after-life is in no way something he *knows*, and it does not provide the foundation or motivation for the conduct of life.[63] On the contrary, it is clear that he faces death with confidence because of his moral view that "nothing can harm a good man either in life or after death" (41d; cf. also 30d).[64] Thus his views about the after-life are tentative conjectures, mere plausibilities.[65] The same would appear to be true of his attitude to the divinity speaking through the Oracle. He perceived the truth of the Oracle and took it to be divine. The God whence this truth came was the bearer of divine wisdom. To paraphrase Socrates' attitude, "There may indeed be a personal God such as the myths have maintained for as long as we can remember. This is not something I know, but I know that the non-existence of such a God is also something I don't know. And though I cannot pretend to know anything about such a God I may nonetheless plausibly, conjecturally posit such a divine being. But in any case, however much I might recognize such a being I must not lose sight of the primary objects of religious piety, the wisdom and virtue which the God possesses."

The episode of the Delphic Oracle did not mark Socrates' first realization of his ignorance; much less did it mark the beginning of his love of wisdom or ἀρετή; neither did it mark the emergence of his characteristic care of souls or his turning from scientific interests to ethical and human concerns; neither, finally, did it represent the inclusion of a new irrational and religious element in his conduct of philosophy. Nonetheless, the episode of the Oracle may be said to mark the emergence of the Socratic philosophical way as such. Through his own personal reflection in the mirror, provided by Chaerephon's fortuitous act of exuberance, of his own philosophical stance *vis-à-vis* the other σοφισταί of the day, his own various intellectual interests, convictions and tendencies coalesced into a single, unified vision of the philosophical life. What were formerly Socrates' differences of opinion, outlook and philosophical style as an individual member in that circle dedicated to the pursuit of σοφία and the παιδεία of youth, became crystallized after the Oracle's pronouncement into a distinctive form of philosophy in concerted and self-conscious opposition to the prevailing σοφία of the day. Indeed, in this regard Socrates was almost *compelled* to reflect on the Oracle's meaning and make a public response to it, for it threatened to lump him in the minds of the general populace with all those other σοφισταί of the day as the most accomplished and wise of them all. In this respect the Oracle represented as much a danger to his career of philosophy as his "earliest accusers." Socrates knew for himself there were important differences between himself and the σοφισταί. Lest his life in philosophy be fundamentally compromised and subverted he had to differentiate himself radically in the public mind from the other σοφισταί of the day. The process of testing the Oracle signified the emergence of the Socratic philosophical way. Those most distinctive features of the Socratic philosophical way had become fused together for the first time *precisely in order to respond to the Oracle*: the question and answer method, founded on the cornerstone of ignorance and pervaded by irony. Indeed, his entire life from that point on was determined by the Oracle's pronouncement: he assumed the public character or *persona* of one without knowledge of his own, submerged his own individuality behind the mask of irony and assumed the role of the gadfly subject to the enmity and misapprehension of his fellow citizens —all this, he says, in the service of the truth pronounced by the Deity, which was of course at the same time his own life's truth. His life became a witness not to himself or his own wisdom but to the transcendent values on which his life stood, a witness to a vision of life, at least for those with eyes to see. Because his service of the God was to witness with his own life to something beyond himself, his own historical individuality was to remain hidden behind the veil of irony. Thus it is an historical irony that that most remarkable individual, who stepped out on to the stage of history as a result of Chaerephon's felicitous enthusiasm, never to be erased from the living memory of the human race, remains himself an enigma, a riddle and a paradox in his own historical individuality.

4. The Socratic Δαιμόνιον.

The key passage for attaining an understanding of Socrates' δαιμόνιον is *Apology* 31c-d:

> The reason [for not entering public life] is what you have often heard me say before on many other occasions—that I am subject to a divine or supernatural experience, which Meletus saw fit to travesty in his indictment. It began in my early childhood—a sort of voice which comes to me, and when it comes it always dissuades me from what I am proposing to do, and never urges me on. (31c-d)

The δαιμόνιον is a familiar fact to the jury. It is something divine (θεῖόν τι, 31c8) and something that has to do with a spirit or spirits (δαιμόνιον [τι], 31d1).[66] Again the vagueness of Socrates' conceptualization is apparent. It is some sort of voice (φωνή) that comes to him. The notion appears similar to ours of the "voice" of conscience. But Zeller has pointed out that Socrates does not talk of the divine voice in the same contexts as our notion.[67] It is confined to future contingencies (as opposed to pangs of conscience after the act) and does not always have to do with judgments of moral value; it is rather concerned with practical consequences of a course of action. It warns him that such and such a course of action will turn out ill. It is thus always negative in form. Socrates' δαιμόνιον does not even have a positive message, as it were—it only acts as a warning or indicator when he is doing something which will not ultimately turn out for the good. Nor does it seem to confine itself to religious matters. In the *Phaedrus* (242c) it prevents him from leaving after his speech until he has delivered another which compensates for the irreverent tone of the first one. In the *Euthydemus* (272e) it prevents him from leaving the place where a group of handsome youths are soon to appear for a discussion. In *Alcibiades* I (103a) it prevents him from speaking with Alcibiades for many years. In the *Theaetetus* (151a) it sometimes prevents Socrates from accepting back pupils who too quickly assumed that they had learned all they could of Socrates only eventually to discover their lack of understanding.[68] These are all quite mundane, even trivial instances.

Those who see the δαιμόνιον as a species of irrational religious belief would tend to assume that something is hidden here. Certainly, it looks like a purely natural psychological process—a simple intuition of "hunch"—familiar enough in everyday life. But, it is felt, Socrates sees *much more* in it than this. The vagueness of his description of it necessitates its remaining opaque to us. However, if one assumes that the vagueness of Socrates' conceptualization of the voice is not the vagueness of that which cannot be expressed in rational discourse, but rather purposive vagueness due to the strictness and consistency of his philosophical agnosticism, quite another result is obtained. Socrates' description of the δαιμόνιον reveals nothing about any god or δαίμων precisely because no such thing is revealed to him. *All there is* is the voice, the intuition, which "comes" to him. This "divine action" is nothing "supernatural" in the sense that its meaning is hidden to natural thought processes. It is not some self-authenticating revelation of truth not comprehensible to human nature. It is just what it appears to be: a hunch or intuition, but neither is it, as it might be viewed today, an event solely and entirely in the history of the individual's own psyche. Socrates recognizes the fact that the hunch just "comes" to him. It does not proceed from the narrow circle of his conscious, willed activity; it does not proceed from his ego. This constitutes its "divine" character. It comes from some transcendent "beyond", that is, from some source or dimension which is beyond the grasp of his merely human consciousness of the world. Thus he says it is "some divine action, the action of some divine spirit or other." The ambiguity of the reference to the δαιμόνιον is the measure of its preciseness as a description. Like the fate of the soul at death, as he says at 29a-b, the truly adequate posture is to recognize that one knows nothing about "higher" matters. It is, in a word, precisely his absolute fidelity to the truth which causes him to describe the phenomenon as some sort of vague divine irruption into his conscious activity. Despite its "divine" character, it is nonetheless treated in a very matter-of-fact way by Socrates, indeed almost, as Burnet says, "quite lightly" and "ironically". It is concerned with the mundane and trivial, and not with the religious. Also, it is not part of his philosophy, though, as we shall see more fully below, it is complementary in a subordinate way. It is a special aid to Socrates, and unique to him, that guides him in *particular* matters to the goal of his philosophical way, whereas philosophical reasoning guides in general matters by determining the universally true ends of that way.

5. Xenophon's Account of the Trial of Socrates.

Having completed our examination of Plato's *Apology* it is now an appropriate time to examine and compare Xenophon's account of the trial in his *Defense*. Taylor once said, "Except on one or two points of detail, Xenophon does not formally contradict anything which Plato tells us about Socrates."[69] This is true enough, *with regard to specific points of fact*. But it is nonetheless true, as we have argued above (as well as below, in Appendix III), that their accounts are *fundamentally* and *systematically* incompatible. Nowhere is this more apparent than in their treatments of Socrates' defense. Xenophon confirms Plato at many points, yet his account lacks entirely the depth and power and self-consistency of Plato's. In Plato everything serves to delineate the dramatic pathos of the event: Socrates is being tried for ἀσέβεια when his philosophical way is the true religious way. Xenophon is oblivious to any religious dimension of Socrates' *philosophy*. To him as to Greeks generally the question of Socrates' religion has nothing to do with his philosophy. One proves one's religious orthodoxy simply by establishing one's orthopraxy:

> [Socrates] offered sacrifices constantly, and made no secret of it, now in his home, now at the altars of the state temples, and he made use of divination with as little secrecy. (*Memorabilia* I.1.2)

But Xenophon realizes that at least the latter aspect of his religious piety calls for further explanation: he conjectures that it was out of Socrates' claim to be guided by the δαιμόνιον that the charge of bringing in strange deities (καινὰ δαιμόνια) arose (*Memorabilia* I.1.2). Indeed, it quickly becomes clear that Socrates' personal divination was not as straightforwardly orthodox as Xenophon suggests. The form of Xenophon's attempt to buttress Socrates' case is: Socrates' δαιμόνιον was *really* as orthodox as the other, acceptable δαίμονες:

> He was no more bringing in anything strange than are other believers in divination, who rely on augury, oracles, coincidences and sacrifices. For these men's belief is not that the birds or the folk met by accident know what profits the inquirer, but that they are the instruments by which the gods make this known; and that was Socrates' belief too. Only, whereas most men say that the birds or the folk they meet dissuade or encourage them, Socrates said what he meant: for he said that the deity [τὸ δαιμόνιον] gave him a sign. (*Memorabilia* I.1.3-4)

Xenophon, attempting to come to Socrates' aid, makes it manifest that the equivalence of Socrates' divination to the standard forms needed proof. It was not possible for him to argue that Socrates did resort to the standard forms of divination, and so he had to attempt a higher, "theological" defense. He argues, in effect, that the well-known indeterminacy of Socrates' δαιμόνιον shows a better understanding than does the way that common folk talk.

Having said as much, however, Xenophon proceeds to turn around and claim that Socrates did recommend oracles to his circle of intimate friends. As Xenophon puts it, he had another policy with regard to his friends (*Memorabilia* I.1.6). We have seen Xenophon claim this sort of privileged information before. Being among those special intimates, Xenophon relates that Socrates distinguished between τὰ ἀναγκαῖα, things that are necessary, and τὰ ἄδηλα, things that are hidden and unclear. This distinction, as Xenophon explains it at *Memorabilia* I.1.6 ff., is hardly a perspicuous one, but it appears that by τὰ ἀναγκαῖα Xenophon means those things whose *outcome* is a matter of necessity (that is, certainty) and so can be predicted on the basis of acquired knowledge. In any event the gist of Socrates' view as Xenophon reports it is this: a man should use his reason to the fullest of his powers to determine his course of action; however, in some matters, namely, in particular future contingencies, it is not given to human powers to understand; in these matters man should seek out a supplement to his rational powers and consult an oracle.

Xenophon's account is suspicious. We know from the *Anabasis* that he once consulted Socrates for advice on a course of action he was contemplating (III, 1.5 ff.). The privileged information spoken of in the *Memorabilia* looks like a generalization of that event. Xenophon wanted to know if he should join the campaign of the young Persian, Cyrus, in his attempt to dethrone his brother, Artaxerxes. Socrates had nothing definitive to say, though he pointed out what must have been obvious to anybody—that Athenians would hardly look kindly on such a course of action since Cyrus had been the principal ally of Sparta in the Peloponnesian War which had just concluded. Since he had no opinion of his own to give Xenophon, Socrates enjoined him to consult the Oracle at Delphi. The manner in which Xenophon did this reveals the sort of head-strong individual Socrates was confronted with. Instead of asking *whether* he should undertake the journey, he begged the question: what gods should he invoke and sacrifice to in order for the journey to be a success? Xenophon had already made up his mind, oracle or no. We may suppose that Socrates perceived this. Instead of attempting to drive home to Xenophon the dire consequences of this for his career in his own πόλις, Athens, Socrates was hoping that the Oracle at Delphi would offer more wisdom than Xenophon himself was displaying, and have more influence over Xenophon than he himself had. But, alas, Xenophon seems to have sensed what the response would be, and thus obviated the undesired results. Socrates (that is, common sense) proved right, of course, in the long run, as Xenophon spent most of his later years in exile from Athens. This is perhaps what Xenophon chiefly had in mind when he said, "those who followed [Socrates'] advice prospered, and those who rejected it had cause for regret" (*Memorabilia* I.1.4).

If Plato was right to think that Socrates never gave out answers and always insisted on his disciples thinking things out for themselves—though perhaps with him guiding and testing the reasoning —then it is possible to see the episode in another light. Xenophon came to Socrates looking for an answer, but was put off. We might surmise Socrates' response as follows: "If it were a matter of reasoning to moral truths or testing the truth of some moral proposition I might perhaps be willing to join with you in discussing the matter. But what you ask is my opinion about a particular course of action, which is, so far as I can see, a matter indifferent to reason. In this matter you must use your own head and think the matter out for yourself. You must direct your own moral life. If you still must have the matter decided for you, go and consult the Oracle." This is of course arm-chair "probabilizing", but perhaps not so idle if we recall that both Plato and Xenophon agree that Socrates himself did not make use of the accepted forms of divination. Whether or not this reconstruction of the episode be correct, it is clear there are sufficient grounds for seriously suspecting the accuracy of Xenophon's representation.

Xenophon introduces the episode of the Delphic Oracle into his account of the defense, but its description and bearing on the defense is instructively different from Plato's account (see *Defense* 14-17). There is no suggestion that the Oracle constitutes a religious calling, or that its true meaning had to do with Socratic ignorance. On the contrary, the Oracle specifies straightforwardly that Socrates is the most virtuous in three respects: he is the most free (ἐλευθεριώτερον), the most just (δικαιότερον), and the most prudent (σωφρονέστερον). In Plato's *Apology* the Oracle's pronouncement had to do with the central virtue, σοφία: the assertion that Socrates was the wisest of all constituted a great riddle. There is no such problem, however, with the Oracle's pronouncement in Xenophon's account. Its sense is immediately apparent to all. Socrates is σώφρων, prudent, which he also takes to be equivalent to being σοφός, wise (see *Defense* 16). The grounds of the Oracle's assertion are as apparent to Socrates as to everyone else: "from the time when I began to understand spoken words [I] have never left off seeking after and learning [μανθάνων] every good thing I could" (16-17). This Socrates clearly knows a great deal; he is outstanding for his knowledge. Indeed, here lies the μεγαληγορία of Socrates' defense on Xenophon's account: it was because he did not shy away from parading "all the good, noble, beautiful things that had come his way from gods and men" (9). Socrates sets himself up as an expert in the education of youth (20-21); he teaches his disciples every good thing he knows (26).

In other respects as well Plato and Xenophon agree on basic

facts but diverge in what they represent as their significance. In Xenophon's *Defense* (26) Socrates likens himself to Palamades, who was put to death unjustly. This recalls Plato's simile: Socrates is like the great hero Achilles who accepted his duty unto death. The discrepancy over the particular hero is not what is striking. In Plato the simile serves to develop the basic theme: Socrates is faithful in the service of his God; he remains obedient unto death. But in Xenophon it is a brief, pointed allusion. Its significance is not in the least developed or connected with anything else in his defense.

Similarly, Xenophon relates that among Socrates' last words to the jury there was a prophecy. Plato too, we will recall, relates that Socrates felt moved to prophesy with regard to those who had passed judgment on him (39c ff.). Socrates urges that vengeance will be wrought on them—their attempt to stifle criticism will be to no avail. Young men will rise up and confront them with even harsher criticisms. But there is nothing "uncanny" or supernatural about this prophecy—it is simply a prediction based on insight into the present state of affairs. Xenophon, however, relates that Socrates made a prediction in the particular instance that Anytus' son would end in a dissolute state, disgraced and shunned by all (29 ff.). It was, Xenophon says, a special power to look into the future granted by Homer. There is, no doubt, more truth to the view that this is a "prophecy" derived *post factum* by Xenophon.

We have so far neglected Xenophon's most striking and fundamental divergence from Plato's account of the trial. Xenophon begins the *Defense* thus:

> It seems to me fitting to hand down to memory, furthermore, how Socrates, on being indicted, deliberated on his defence and on his end. It is true that others have written about this, and that all of them have reproduced the loftiness of his words,—a fact which proves that his utterance really was of the character intimated;—but they have not shown clearly that he had now come to the conclusion that for him death was more to be desired than life; and hence his lofty utterance appears rather ill-considered.

Xenophon wants to show how Socrates arrived at his decision that death was to be preferred over life. Socrates refused the path that led to acquittal, and, as both Plato and Xenophon agree, he spoke with μεγαληγορία, loftiness, with resounding words, with great courage and boldness. But Xenophon finds this ἀφρονεστέρα, "rather ill-advised." He does not understand this refusal to take the path of escape and finds it somewhat embarrassing to think of Socrates taking such an unreasonable stand. It is this scandal that his *Defense* is meant to explain. He suggests (5ff.) that Socrates came to the conclusion that since he was old and still in possession of all his faculties it was a good time to die. For if he were to die under sentence before his natural time came, the sense of loss and esteem among his friends and associates would be all the more acute. And if he were to die now Socrates could avoid "dying in the throes of illness or [being] vexed by old age, the sink into which all distresses flow, unrelieved by any good cheer" (8).[70] On Xenophon's account the key notions in Socrates' mind are: self-respect, the esteem of others, pleasantness (7), good-cheer, sense of personal satisfaction (5), the easiest way, the way least bothersome to one's friends (7). But this catalogue of thoroughly unexceptional values is constitutive of the εὐδαιμονία (well-being, good fortune) of the gentleman, the man of "decency" and "good taste." To suggest that these were the values which motivated Socrates' stand at the trial is to undermine the whole importance and significance of his life and final stand. Xenophon's Socrates differs in no important respect from the general run of fine, upstanding citizens in Athens.

Actually, close examination of Xenophon's account reveals what Vlastos calls its "self-refuting" character. The purpose of the *Defense*, Xenophon explains, is to show that Socrates did not try to gain acquittal (22). But Xenophon also says that Socrates tried twice to contrive a defense (4), to find some plea that would "*by fair means or foul*"[71] effect his acquittal (8). He was stopped by his divine sign. But this means that the rationale Xenophon has just given for his courageous stand is really his second effort. The dictate of his own nature, before the intervention of "the gods" (for such is the δαιμόνιον on Xenophon's account at *Defense* 8), was to seek to get out of the charge, even, by implication, by devious means if necessary. Where would Socrates' virtue be, one wonders, without the promptings of the divine sign? But let us recall that Xenophon records Socrates' words:

> [D]o I not seem to you to have spent my whole life in preparing to defend myself? . . . all my life I have been guiltless of wrong-doing; and that I consider the finest preparation for a defence. (3)

These are surely empty words if Socrates' natural response was to seek to gain his acquittal by any means at his disposal. For all its superficial plausibility there is a profound confusion and inconsistency in Xenophon's account.

6. Divine Inspiration and the Socratic Way.

Socrates discusses divine inspiration occasionally in the other Socratic dialogues, and almost invariably in those passages there is a certain ironic air. For instance, at the end of the *Crito* Socrates proclaims that his head is so filled with mystic strains that he can hardly hear opposing arguments such as Crito brings to bear on him. He is like one celebrating the Corybantic rites, who hears the flutes ringing in his ears. But what transports Socrates thus are the *arguments* (τούτων τῶν λόγων, 54d4) which he has put in the mouth of the personified laws of the city. The mystical element is only a fine metaphorical touch, a mere manner of speaking. This is even more evident in the *Charmides*. There Socrates has been confounding Critias by drawing a number of monstrous absurdities out of a proposition set forth as a definition of σωφροσύνη. Critias is speechless; he cannot pick his way through the contradictions. Then Socrates, concluding his argument, abruptly introduces a new consideration (169b): Even if there were a science such as you defined it, Socrates seems to say, I wouldn't be prepared to call it σωφροσύνη, self-control, until you showed me that it was something useful (ὠφέλιμον) and good (ἀγαθόν). "For," he continues, "I divine (μαντεύομαι) that σωφροσύνη is something useful and good" (169b). But that σωφροσύνη is useful, or advantageous, and good would be commonly assumed by the Greeks. It is hardly something that needed "divining." The reference is clearly ironic. But still, irony granted, why does Socrates use the term "divine"? The reason seems to be that the additional consideration (that is, whether or not the virtue σωφροσύνη is useful and good) does not naturally emerge from the logical argument. Neither is it offered to Critias' assent to become a premise for further argument. It is simply an intuitive, or more properly, an axiomatic truth which is brought into the argument out of thin air, so to speak: its having to be divined has nothing to do with its being religious or "divine".

The divine inspirations that Socrates received (according to the dialogues of Plato) seem to have been closely aligned with his philosophizing. The *Ion* carries on the discussion of the relationship between inspiration and knowledge, and at the same time provides us with a glimpse of Socrates' attitude towards other, more conventional forms of divine inspiration. Once again the dialogue is not positive doctrine, but logical dialectic, and we must attend to it.

Socrates meets Ion, who has won fame as a rhapsodist, one who recites the poets, and especially Homer, from memory. Socrates is not interested in the man's marvelous talents of memory as such. He is interested in a certain extraordinary claim of Ion, the claim that he *possesses knowledge* in the matters the poets talked about, or, alternatively, the claim that he possesses the τέχνη, the know-how, to interpret what the poet says on various matters.

The dialogue, then, is another example of the familiar Socratic scrutiny of those who pretend to wisdom and knowledge. Socrates' questioning quickly reveals that Ion has a rather inflated view of the scope of his talents: he thinks that by knowing all that Homer has said he thereby possesses a thorough knowledge of all the things Homer talked about. But Homer talked about virtually all the concerns of human life, including (by mention at least) each of the particular τέχναι. But this hardly means, as Socrates is anxious to point out, that Ion possesses, by possessing the τέχνη of the rhapsodist, all the other τέχναι. Actually Socrates does not ultimately concede that Ion's talents, real as they are, constitute a τέχνη. For a τέχνη must satisfy certain criteria: it must be knowledge which the individual himself possesses; it must be general knowledge of a certain domain of human affairs, and therefore a knowledge of what is good and bad in that domain. The dialectic here is negative: Ion cannot demonstrate what knowledge he has, or even what the subject matter of his alleged τέχνη might be.

The *Ion* is unusual in one respect: Socrates departs from the rigors of dialectic to offer his opinion of just what Ion's remarkable talents amount to. It is not a τέχνη or ἐπιστήμη at all;[72] it is a θεία δύναμις, a divine power (533d3). By virtue of the rhapsodist's participation in the poet's original divine inspiration, a deity (or "the Muse", 533e4) is said to inspire him (ἐνθέων, 533e4; ἐνθουσιαζόντων, 533e5) and to take possession of him (κατεχόμενοι, 533e7) like one partaking of the Corybantic rites (534a). He is out of his senses (ἔκφρων, 534b5); his reason is no longer in him (ὁ νοῦς μηκέτι ἐν αὐτῷ ἐνῇ, 534b6). He goes so far as to say, "So long as he has [νοῦς] in his possession, no man is able to make poetry or to chant in prophecy" (534b). Socrates resorts to the traditional view of inspiration to explain his attitude towards the practitioners of the poetic arts:

> Herein lies the reason why the deity [ὁ θεός] has bereft them of their senses, and uses them as ministers, along with soothsayers and godly seers; it is in order that we listeners may know that it is not they who utter these precious revelations while their mind is not within them, but that it is the god himself who speaks, and through them becomes articulate to us. . . . By this example above all, it seems to me, the god would show us, lest we doubt, that these lovely poems are not of man or human workmanship, but are divine and from the gods, and that the poets are nothing but interpreters of the gods, each one possessed by the divinity to whom he is in bondage.
> (534c-e)

Socrates' attitude thus appears to consist of, on the one hand, an orthodox view of divine inspirations of all sorts, and on the other, a strict refusal to grant the status of knowledge to any such "revelations". The cleavage between the two states of human consciousness is striking. Human reason and divine revelation are utterly distinct: evidently, they have nothing to do with each other. Socrates can accept the authenticity of a θεία μοῖρα such as Ion's alongside his own philosophy precisely because they are strictly and completely discontinuous with that philosophy.

If it is true that in the dialogue Socrates leaves standing the rhapsodist's claim to receive an authentic divine inspiration, there is nonetheless good reason to doubt whether Socrates himself really holds the traditional view. At the end of the discussion Socrates again allows that Ion, while possessed by Homer, utters many fine, really quite lovely things. Yet at the same time he maintains that Ion knows nothing (μηδὲν εἰδὼς, 542a) of what he is saying. This criticism is really more damaging than Socrates would here make it appear. He evidently has no intention of making all its implications clear to Ion. Socrates has granted only that Ion has a wonderful ability to *impress* his audience, to *inspire* them with *awe* at the fine, lofty words and deeds of men and gods, to *fire* them with sublime beauty. It was the rhapsodist's aim to *move* his audience with the appropriate emotion. The question arose, as it did again in the *Republic*, how does one decide the truth and rightness of poetry? Let us recall that in the *Euthyphro* Socrates was willing to question on moral grounds whether certain poetic myths about the gods were correct. The claim of the poet's myth to be divinely inspired was not sufficient in itself. There were other, independent criteria, criteria of moral reason. The rhapsodist was no doubt gifted in manipulating people's emotions, but did he really *know* what he was doing? Inspired rhapsodes such as Ion acted on certain conservative pedagogical assumptions of the day: knowledge of the poets, principally Homer of course, was taken to be sufficient for the intellectual training of good and noble young men. The poetic tradition was looked upon as a compendium of all the intellectual and moral cultivation a youth needed. Socrates, of course, resisted this view. He lived at a time when this older traditional means of defining a man of character and distinction was no longer adequate. The only solution, he urged, was to answer the question, what *is* ἀρετή? What is the proper excellence of a man? Not until one *knew* what one was looking for could one pretend to offer solutions to the cultural and pedagogical problems of the day—such was the crucial importance of knowledge in the Socratic way. Though Socrates did not make all this explicit in the *Ion*, he did make it clear that he viewed the whole system of the poetic arts, from the Muses to the poets, the rhapsodists, choristers, actors, down to their enraptured audiences, as a "chain of divine possession" (see 533d-536d). All who indulge in the poetic arts are men possessed; they are all equally "out of their minds." From the point of view of Socratic pedagogy the purveyors of the old poetic education subverted the true interests of the πόλις by working a kind of mindless mystification over the minds of citizens. Socrates believed that what was needed was clear-headed conscious dialectical inquiry into the question of human excellence. In a word, Socratic philosophy implied a deep and comprehensive criticism of the poetic tradition. *Prima facie* Socrates generously acquiesced in the traditional appreciation of inspiration. But the caustic irony of the dialogue cannot be ignored. Socrates granted that Ion had these "divine" powers to awe popular audiences. This much had to be granted. But what Socrates refused to grant, namely, that the "divinity" of these powers entailed a claim to truth, was an important, fundamental assumption of the traditional view. Much of what Socrates had given with the left hand he took back with the right. It may well be that Socrates did not intend a wholesale rejection of poetry or inspiration, just as the *Republic* does not; but neither can it be said that the *Ion* is simply and straightforwardly evidence of Socrates' traditional and orthodox attitude towards divine inspirations.

In the *Meno* there is a remarkable passage in which Socrates likens statesmen whose actions are not grounded in knowledge (ἐπιστήμη) to those under divine inspiration.

> Socrates: And ought we not to reckon those men divine who with no conscious thought [νοῦν μὴ ἔχοντες] are repeatedly and outstandingly successful in what they do or say?
> Meno: Certainly.
> Socrates: We are right therefore to give this title to the oracular priests and the prophets that I mentioned, and to poets of every description. Statesmen too, when by their speeches they get great things done yet know nothing of what they are saying [μηδὲν εἰδότες ὧν λέγουσιν], are to be considered as acting no less under divine influence, inspired and possessed by the divinity. (99c–d)

It is of course the statesmen's ignorance that qualifies them for the epithets "divine" (θεῖος), "inspired" (ἐνθουσιάζειν), "possessed by the god" (κατεχομένους ἐκ τοῦ θεοῦ). But that does not mean that "divine" is simply equivalent to "ignorant". The discussion has revealed that men outstanding for their virtue have not known how to teach it. Socrates did not want to question whether there have been good men in the past; there have indeed been many distinguished men of character and excellence (93a–b). But Socrates and Meno had already agreed that virtue was in whole or in part knowledge (88e–89a); the advantageous part of virtue was knowledge (89a). If virtue was knowledge, it should be teachable. But the facts of history seem to belie this conclusion. It is no wonder the perplexed Meno was willing to doubt whether there are in fact men of virtue (96d). But Socrates would not countenance such a conclusion—he suggested rather that they had overlooked a distinction: if a man acts from knowledge (ἐπιστήμη) he will act rightly. But so too will a man who acts from right opinion (ὀρθὴ δόξα or ἀληθὴς δόξα), that is, the opinion he believes is right and in fact happens to be right. From the *practical* point of view it makes no difference whether the act be out of knowledge or opinion (so long as it is right opinion). But that there is an important difference between the two Socrates is sure (98b). Knowledge is, speaking after the fashion of a likeness (εἰκάζων, 98b1), a "tether" which keeps the opinion from wandering about. Ἐπιστήμη is δόξα which is kept in its place by working out explanations by reasoning (αἰτίας λογισμῷ, 98a3-4), by careful logical argument that establishes once for all the truth of the proposition. The "tether" keeps the opinion from "running away from a man's mind" (98a)—that is, he is stable in his grasp of it. He is able to defend it, to give an account, to supply arguments in the face of objections. Socrates' attitude towards δόξα was respectful here—so long as it did not lay claim to be knowledge. Δόξα is valid and true enough, though its truth and validity derive from its being an implicit form of ἐπιστήμη. It is valid and true because it *can* be established by rational argument; but what *cannot* stand the test of rational argument is not valid and true at all. Δόξα is like a "shadow compared to the solid reality" (100a). To express the point somewhat paradoxically, (true) δόξα is ἐπιστήμη before it has been submitted to rational argument.

Now, all of this is philosophical justification of an evident fact: that there have been numerous men of outstanding virtue and excellence before the advent of Socratic philosophy with its curious dictum that virtue is knowledge. We are reminded too of the deep paradox in the Socratic way: Socrates was ignorant, yet he clearly believed he was virtuous (most evidently in his heroic stand at the trial). Though he did not possess "divine", absolute knowledge, he nonetheless possessed the "beginnings" of knowledge and virtue. In *this* context, then, it is clear why Socrates called such virtuous men "divine" and why he likened them to the various sorts of inspired men. It was not the lack of knowledge as such which thus distinguished them, but the fact that these "beginnings" of virtue, like the marvelous, awe-inspiring gifts of the poet, seer or oracle, made their appearance *in* human consciousness without having proceeded *from* any human, conscious mental processes, including knowledge. It was their inexplicable "marvelous", "beautiful", "awesome" quality beyond the control of human deliberation that Socrates acknowledged here. The very fact that Socrates was anxious to recognize the reality of the "beginnings" of virtue outside of knowledge is strong grounds for concluding that he was willing to recognize the reality of divine inspirations as well. It is true, of course, that divine inspirations are not precisely δόξα inasmuch as they do not always lend themselves to rational substantiation. However, this does not rule out Socrates' looking upon such inspirations as authentic if they were *consonant* with reason so far as they went. Socrates does seem to have supposed that reason was important in figuring out the real meaning of an inspired revelation (for part of the charge of ignorance levelled against the poets was that they did not even know the meaning of what they were saying). This was certainly so with regard to its truth, for no divine revelation could make its own truth-claim, it was not self-authenticating. Yet with these severe qualifications, the very form of Socrates' argument here in the *Meno* indicates that he was willing, at least in principle, to recognize the validity and authenticity of divine inspirations.

7. Socrates' Religion in Action.

As we have seen, Socrates claimed that his philosophy was service of the God. But all we see in the Socratic dialogues of Plato is impersonal dialectic. It is difficult to see how this intellectualistic duelling with words can have any religious significance. Certainly if we follow our *impressions* this view of the dialogues will be confirmed—they are devoid of any religious flavor. Nonetheless, in what follows we shall attempt to show by means of examples in just what respects Socratic dialectic is religious.

In the dialogue named after him, Crito urges Socrates to attempt to escape the death penalty. Socrates takes this as a questioning of his view (or λόγος, 46b5); he is willing to enter into a dialectical testing of this view to see if it is the best that reason can establish, to see if it still stands up under critical scrutiny as the rationally right thing to do. He submits his own view to philosophical ἔλεγχος. It appears to be just another example of disinterested dialectical inquiry after truth. But closer examination reveals that this typical conceptualization of the discussion is not a full and adequate one. First of all, Socrates rejects out of hand the considerations which Crito had adduced to persuade him to make an escape (4-c). They are, he says, "the reflections of the ordinary public" who do all sorts of contradictory things "with equal indifference to reason" (48c). So one could hardly say that the discussion is a consideration of dialectical objections to Socrates' position. In fact the steps in the argument are elementary, leading up to the familiar axiom of the Socratic way: one ought not to pay heed to the many, but to the one who knows (48a). And there is not the slightest difficulty on Crito's part in assenting to the intermediary premises Socrates adduces. Indeed, the crucial part of the "argument" might well be called question-begging:

> Socrates: Do we say that one must never willingly do wrong, or does it depend upon circumstances? Is it true, as we have often agreed before, that there is no sense in which wrongdoing is good or honorable? Or have we jettisoned all our former convictions in these last few days? Can you and I at our age, Crito, have spent all these years in serious discussions without realizing that we were no better than a pair of children? Surely the truth is just what we have always said. Whatever the popular view is, and whether the alternative is pleasanter than the present one or even harder to bear, the fact remains that to do wrong is in every sense bad and dishonorable for the person who does it. Is that our view, or not?
>
> Crito: Yes, it is. (49a-b)

As an example of rigorous philosophical dialectic the *Crito* fails miserably.

But a too superficial reading of the dialogue can obscure another facet of its dramatic dialectic. For essentially the discussion was a matter of quelling Crito's emotions (see 46b, 48e) and getting him to recall his own real opinions so that he might *emotionally* accept the course of action Socrates had decided upon. Socrates emphasized that the discussion was of no use unless they worked from Crito's *real opinions* (49d, 48b), for Socrates earnestly hoped to *persuade* Crito of the rightness of his line of action. The dialectic here is an exercise in emotional persuasion; it is an attempt to bring Crito back to his senses by taking him by the hand through arguments he was familiar with. The *Crito*, then, is good evidence that Socratic dialectic was not always impersonal, logical argumentation; occasionally, at least, it was very much personally orientated.

The *Laches* is an interesting example of what Socrates calls in the *Meno* (75c-d) his "friendly method." Socrates attends closely to where his partner is and works from there in a common, disinterested quest for truth. Unlike the discussions where the aim is to defeat the opponent's arguments, Socrates' basic attitude here is helpful. This is not to say, however, that truth is arrived at. But the manner in which Socrates denies his two partners in conversation the truth they are seeking is itself interesting and instructive. The first part of the discussion is a typical example of the attempt to answer the question, "What is *X*?", in this case, courage. From the start Socrates assumes a deferential attitude to his eminent elders, the two generals, Laches and Nicias. But before long he has discreetly set aside their first statements and steered the inquiry to the pursuit of a definition. Unsurprisingly the first attempt is in terms of a mental picture—courage is a soldier remaining at his post to fight off the enemy. Socrates gradually gets Laches thinking in the appropriate direction, but before long the elderly general is at the end of his rope:

> I am ready to go on, Socrates, and yet I am unused to investigations of this sort. But the spirit of controversy has been aroused in me by what has been said, and I am really grieved at being thus unable to express my meaning. For I fancy that I do know the nature of courage, but, somehow or other, she has slipped away from me, and I cannot get hold of her and tell her nature. (194a-b)

Along the way Socrates has managed to suggest to Laches that although most people think there is no necessary or essential relationship between courage and intelligence or wisdom there must indeed be such a relationship. But Laches is incapable of taking up the suggestion.

Socrates turns to Nicias who displays more philosophical acumen. In particular he takes up Socrates' hint that courage is closely related to wisdom. He cleverly submits a view which he has heard Socrates advocate on another occasion, "Every man is good in that in which he is wise, and bad in that in which he is unwise" (194d). At this point the argument becomes rather intricate, and we shall not attend to it here. But some of the dramatic features are interesting. First, Laches is clearly over his head and mocks what he takes to be Nicias' nonsense (though we should recall it is Socrates' opinion that Nicias is defending). Socrates strings Laches along, as it were, pretending that they are partners searching out Nicias' strange opinion. Keeping Laches' caustic jibes in check, Socrates submits Nicias' opinion to ἔλεγχος. It ends before long in the familiar confession of ignorance.

What is remarkable here is Socrates' pedagogy, his patient attention to the level of philosophical acumen of his partners. For Laches it sufficed to get his mind going on a relatively rudimentary level. He was introduced to some basics of Socratic philosophical inquiry and encouraged to go as far as he could. But for Nicias, a somewhat more advanced student of philosophy, a little more was demanded—but just enough to show that his vague, general grasp of the Socratic philosophical proposition did not amount to knowledge he could claim as his own. There are, it appears, levels of philosophical ignorance, and the Socratic method is designed to probe the limits of a man's philosophical understanding, to show him the infinitely complex set of problems just over the horizon which he must nonetheless be able to give an account of before he can claim to have real knowledge.

The Socratic dialogues always show us Socrates engaged with certain individuals on certain specific problems. Typically, Socrates is engaged in the scrutiny of a particular argument submitted by his companion. This implies that the Socratic philosophical method can never lay claim to exhaustiveness. It is always a particular avenue that is travelled, and, typically, found to be a dead-end. One will never be in a position to say that all the possible positions on the matter have been tried. By its very nature dialectic is always a fresh start promising unanticipated twists and turns depending on the intellectual acumen and idiosyncrasies of opinion of the person being tested. Repeatedly the results of this dialectic are negative. If Socratic philosophy were just what meets the eye then it would seem to be a meager thing indeed. It would seem by its very nature to be condemned to such repeated exercises in futility: its piecemeal approach would make it impossible to attain any larger, more comprehensive grasp of the truth; and its person-directed approach would guarantee that it will be limited by the subject's grasp of the truth. Yet Socrates never draws negative, skeptical conclusions about the possibility of arriving at the truth; nor does he ever falter in his faith in the method. There seems to be some hidden motivation, some understanding of what he is doing, that maintains him in his way. In this context a single, brief passage in the *Meno* is invaluable for the light it sheds on the unspoken positive backdrop to the Socratic way. It is, Socrates says, "a true and fine [or beautiful] λόγος of people *wise* in religious matters," for he adds, "they are the sort of priests and priestesses who are able to give an account (λόγον διδόναι) of the things they do."[73]

> What they say is this—see whether you think they are speaking the truth. They say that the soul of man is immortal. At one time it comes to an end—that which is called death—and at another is born again, but is never finally exterminated. On these grounds a man must live all his days as righteously as possible. . . . Thus the soul, since it is immortal and has been born many times, and has seen all things both here and in the other world, has learned everything that is. So we need not be surprised if it can recall the knowledge of virtue or anything else which, as we see, it once possessed. All nature is akin [τῆς φύσεως ἁπάσης συγγενοῦς οὔσης], and the soul has learned everything, so that when a man has recalled a single piece of knowledge—learned it, in ordinary language—there is no reason why he should not find out all the rest, if he keeps a stout heart and does not grow weary of the search, for seeking and learning are in fact nothing but recollection.
>
> (81b-d)

The passage offers a revealing insight into Socrates' conception of his philosophical way. There was a whole system or network of truth, and one could go from one piece of knowledge to the whole of knowledge.[74] This system of absolute truth was objectively there, and the mind could expand one's conscious grasp of it. Socratic philosophy was the attempt to isolate and clear away mistaken opinions, by working one's way in careful question and answer argument through the system. By reasoning out logical arguments, then, one was exploring this realistically conceived system of absolute truth, or testing the truth value or certain hypotheses (see 86d-e) to see if they stood in this system of true propositions.

To all appearances it would be hard to see anything of religious significance in dialogues like the *Lysis*, *Hippias Major* and *Hippias Minor*, for they show the negative, destructive side of the Socratic method. Indeed, the discussions seem *designed* to end in confusion and disarray: because of his partners' lack of philosophical acumen the discussions are almost completely in Socrates' hands. In the *Lysis* (211c) Socrates agrees on a scheme to "put his opponent down," to deliberately put him to confusion. After thus dispensing with Menexenus, Socrates embarks on another line of discussion with Lysis. The dialogue that follows so stretches our credulity that Socrates is here engaged in the disinterested quest of truth and virtue that we might be pardoned some attention to it to see how, if at all, this could be true.

Throughout the dialogue it is Socrates who proposes the theses to be considered. Each new consideration seems to take the discussion further afield, and it finally ends in a sorry state. But one thing is especially suspicious: elsewhere Socrates always insists on the priority of the "What is *X*?" question. When his partners take him off on the proverbial wild goose chase, he is persistent in trying to bring them back to more basic and essential matters. But here, with the reins in his own hands, he seems almost deliberately to steer away from that question. He introduces (at 214a ff.) the question of whether friendship is between likes or between unlikes (or, as he eventually will point out, possibly between like and unlike). They try what appear to be all the possibilities but end up with their hands empty—it has slipped through their fingers (see 216c-d, 222e-223a).

We shall not dwell on all the tortuous intricacies of the discussion (Socrates himself admits he is quite dizzied by the entanglements of the subject, 216c). But to appreciate the dialectic several things need to be noted. The discussion can be broken down into the following four parts:
(1) 214b-215c: the first possibility is rejected—friendship

cannot be between likes (between either good and good or evil and evil).
(2) 215c-216b: the second possibility is rejected—friendship cannot be between unlikes (contraries).
(3) 216d-218c: a third possibility, hitherto unnoticed, is introduced by Socrates and discussed. Socrates first adduces the class of things that are neither good nor evil. He then proceeds to entertain the hypothesis that, failing (1) and (2), friendship must be between things that are neither good nor evil, or between that which is neither good nor evil and that which is good. (That friendship is between that which is neither good nor evil and evil is rejected as unthinkable, 216e.) This part of the discussion ends in a positive conclusion which is received with enthusiastic self-congratulations—for they are now quite sure they have discovered the real solution (218b). It is an ingenious theory. Socrates adduces the distinction between that which is intrinsically or simply *X* and that which has *X* present in it (217c ff.). On this basis he can make sense of "that which is neither good nor evil" (218a-b). A man is not good or evil simply and intrinsically. He is a mixture of both. Only a god could be wise *simpliciter*, for men (and some gods) are, like Socrates, mere *lovers* of wisdom (φιλοσοφοῦσιν). They love, are attracted to, are friends of, that which they do not completely possess. They are a mixture of good and evil, knowledge and ignorance. The difficulty of giving an account of friendship seems to be resolved.

But it is *not* satisfactorily resolved. For while they are rejoicing at their good fortune at coming to know exactly what friendship is, something "occurs" to Socrates (218c). In fact this is the fourth instance in which Socrates has entered a new consideration into the discussion as a result of a strange intuition. One was said to be a "divination" (216d5; the others are at 214e2-3, 215c5). Here he says he does not know the why or the whence of the sudden intuition, but the gist of it is this (the fourth phase of the discussion):
(4) 218c-222e: Socrates in (3) had expressed the ingenious theory of friendship as that which is neither good nor evil being friendly with the good on account of the presence of evil (διὰ κακοῦ παρουσίαν, 218c1-2). Socrates now proceeds to show that according to the ingenious theory the good is the τέλος of friendship (that for the sake of which [ἕνεκα] one is friendly to something) not because it is good and useful in itself but because of evil. In other words, evil, along with the good, is the cause of one's being friendly with something. And the good is conditional upon and relative to evil as an explanatory principle of friendship. But this conflicts with the notion of the ultimate, single, independent end or first principle of friendship—that supreme value

for the sake of which all friendship occurs—which Socrates had independently established. Socrates points out (220c-e) that the ingenious theory represents an attempt to explain why we are drawn to and love a thing in terms of that which is intrinsically inimical and repulsive to us, namely, evil—which is patently absurd. Furthermore, it is evident that we can desire (be friendly to) a thing when there is no element of evil involved—so evil can hardly be the necessary explanatory principle of friendship (220e-221d). In short, even the ingenious theory falls to the ground.

There follows a brief sophistical argument (221d-222d), and an admission of their joint perplexity, the discussion having reduced them to a drunken stupor (222c), followed finally by the familiar negative ending of Socratic ἔλεγχος:

> What other way then is left us of treating the subject? Clearly none. I therefore, like our clever pleaders at the bar, request you to reckon up all that I have said. If neither those who love or are loved, neither the like nor the unlike, nor the good, nor those who belong to us, nor to any other of all the suppositions we passed in review—they are so numerous that I can remember no more—if, I say, not one of them is the object of friendship, I no longer know what I am to say. (222e1-7)

If, however, we step back somewhat from the bewildering intricacies of the discussion to obtain a modicum of perspective it is not difficult to discern what was no doubt Socrates' own real conviction: true friendship has as its aim the good, the good of both concerned in the friendship—indeed, that ideal norm of the Good which is good and useful in itself and not at all conditional upon or relative to evil as in the ingenious theory. This proposition stands as the central ground around which Socratic dialectic has led the bemused Lysis. Without Lysis by his own insight seeing his way clear of the dialectical hurdles which Socrates has thrown up, Socrates will not enter with Lysis upon that central ground. Socrates seems almost to want to steer Lysis close to the proper solution, but to dare him to see his way through to the real answer. But Lysis is too dazzled by this most subtle and convoluted of Socratic dialogues to perceive the implications of Socrates' notion of the ultimate τέλος or ἀρχή of friendship, or to see that Socrates' sudden intuition in step 4 obscures the import of the ingenious part of the theory in step 3, namely, the distinction between a person being evil (or ignorant) and having evil in him—a distinction fundamental to Socrates' conception of himself as an ignorant "lover (or friend) of wisdom" (see 217e-218b). Step 4 represents a hurdle which Lysis must jump before Socrates will proceed with his inquiry into the nature of friendship (and make *positive* use of the ingenious distinction in step 3). Lysis of course fails, and so the discussion is consigned to oblivion at a rudimentary level—they had barely gotten off the ground in what may ultimately be conceived as a dialectical exploration of the vision of the Good as the ultimate ἀρχή and τέλος of friendship in its full ramifications, implications, and consequences.

Lysis and company must have been thoroughly bewildered by the end of their discussion with Socrates. But for us the problem remains, what can all this negative procedure mean with respect to the search after truth? From what we have seen we can form some tentative conclusions. Socrates never left his partners with a sense that they possessed sound knowledge. And sometimes he was frankly destructive. But behind the apparently pointless procedure this much remained true: he guided their thinking in certain directions, sometimes (we recall the *Euthyphro*) dropping significant hints and clues, sometimes bringing his subject within arm's reach of a real insight. Certainly he showed his interlocutor many of the necessary ingredients in whatever truth or knowledge there was to be attained in a particular connection. But he would never do the work of assembling them, even where the discussion seemed to allow some further progress, where there were sufficient clues to be so assembled. Socrates always positioned the truth to be attained just out of reach of his subject's comprehension, urging him on, guiding his thought, but always leaving the actual progress in wisdom to the subject himself.

The *Hippias Major* is a more straightforward example of the negative method. It is essentially a demonstration that the renowned know-it-all, Hippias, is ignorant—and, indeed, ignorant of most elementary things. Socrates puts to Hippias the logically basic question, "what is beauty?" but the latter quickly shows his obtuseness. Socrates must propose definitions himself, though each time Hippias expresses his enthusiastic assurance that they have hit upon a good account (for example, 296b and 298b). But each time Socrates brings the attempted definition tumbling down, and in the end Socrates leaves Hippias in the lurch. No account of beauty is arrived at. *For the record* Socrates claims to have been seeking truth in Hippias' treasury of wisdom. But Socrates doubtless was thoroughly convinced of Hippias' profound ignorance —not least because he was caught in the delusion of wisdom. What purpose could discussion of this sort have? How is it the function of a serious, religious philosophical way? We do not have to look too closely between the lines to see the implicit, unspoken motivation at work in Socratic destructive ἔλεγχος. The necessary starting point for the true philosophical way is the realization of ignorance, of the radical limitedness of human intelligence. One must be fully conscious that one did not know and fully aware of the difficulty,[75] complexity, and tentativeness of what glimmers of truth one did obtain through philosophical inquiry. Where this consciousness was lacking, the negative method must be employed to bring the subject down, to fulfill the necessary pre-conditions for the philosophical search for wisdom and virtue.

We have seen that Socrates' religion was not some special extra-rational, extra-philosophical compartment of his thought. It was precisely and simply his philosophical way. The object of his religious outlook was not some divine being or beings, but divine excellences (ἀρεταί) united under wisdom. The philosophical way was concerned essentially with excellence, moral and intellectual. It aimed at knowing and living in full accord with the moral law, the nature of things so far as it pertained to human life and conduct. The Socratic way was an *intellectual* way—it did not concern itself with the "beginnings" of virtue. From the point of view of philosophy the beginnings were "divine" in the sense of "one knows not whence, but not ultimately of human source." Socrates recognized that people possessed virtues in different degrees, and always imperfectly. Philosophy was intent on bringing about a higher synthesis of, and more intense conversion to, the development of human character by the method of logical argument. This logical method had the effect of bringing individuals to recognize inconsistencies in their moral life, to order all the various, fragmentary virtues to the ultimate end of human life. Interest in logical dialectic became an instrument of moral advancement. The intellectual process brought with it as an essential ingredient intense realization. Above all, it led one to the realization of how unordered and inconsistent one's moral life was. Ἔλεγχος showed that one did not know the ultimate values and priorities in one's own life. But though officially Socrates insisted on the negative side of things, his philosophical way fostered the clear awareness of something very positive—the ideal which he did not possess. The Socratic way intensified one's awareness of the objective, absolute system of moral truth. It operated as a fundamental belief informing all that was done in the way. Objective ἀρετή transcended man not just as human individual but *as man*. Full, complete grasp of the nature of things was divine—it was not given to men to comprehend fully. Nonetheless, the Socratic method was a device to push ahead gradually the frontiers of human knowledge, or, to put it in terms of a simultaneous process, gradually to make one's knowledge more systematic and less tentative. Though man had no adequate *grasp* of the divine, he did nonetheless *apprehend* intellectually what eluded his grasp. Yet in that vision of the divine standards of moral and intellectual excellence one was not given to apprehend *all* that transcended man. There was nothing in that vision of the heavenly ideals to warrant the conclusion that these ideals constituted perfectly, simply and totally the divine realm. That would have been the height of intellectual and religious presumption. Man must resign himself to what was given to him to apprehend; he must follow his own lights and not presume to matters which were quite strictly beyond his ken. Knowledge of personal divine beings resident in the divine realm (including even *whether* there were any such beings) was one such item which exceeded his grasp. The appropriate attitude was one of openness, openness to either alternative. There may or may not be divine beings resident in the divine realm—one had no way of knowing. In the last analysis such lack of knowledge was not even an important matter. The only thing of real importance was to lead a life that was καλός τε κἀγαθός, good and noble and beautiful, for such values were beyond all question. It was the one thing man could commit himself to with full, even absolute, conviction and assurance.[76]

1 This Euthyphro is a μάντις (seer). There is a Euthyphro mentioned in the *Cratylus* who seems to be the same person. He is a man possessed by divine inspirations. He expounds the wisdom of his inspiring goddess in great, lengthy discourses. The topic of this wisdom is the etymology of the gods' names (396d-e). At 400a this Euthyphro is said to have a school of disciples. He seems, then, to have been a famous religious expert in the names of the Homeric gods. Cf. W.K.C. Guthrie, *A History of Greek Philosophy* (Cambridge, 1975), IV, 102 and note 2.

2 John Burnet may be right in supposing this is what attracted a μάντις like Euthyphro to Socrates, for they are unlike as can be intellectually, *Plato's Euthyphro, Apology of Socrates and Crito* (Oxford, 1924), 15, ad 3b5.

3 Though this is not to say that Attic law would not countenance, in certain special circumstances, one member of a family prosecuting another member of the family, including for murder—rather only that such a course of action was an abomination from the point of view of traditional religious sensibilities. Cf. Spiro Panagiotou, "Plato's *Euthyphro* and the Attic Code on Homicide," *Hermes* 102(1974), 422-23.

4 W.K.C. Guthrie's translation of fr. 4, *A History of Greek Philosophy*, III, 234.

5 W.K.C. Guthrie, *History*, III, 253; cf. also Laszlo Versényi, *Socratic Humanism* (New Haven, 1963), 16.

6 In the *Cratylus* (400d), however, Socrates makes a somewhat stronger statement:

> [T]here is one excellent principle which, as men of sense, we must acknowledge—that of the gods we know nothing, either of their natures [περὶ αὐτῶν] or of the names which they give themselves.

7 Such, for example, is the view of L. Versényi, *Socratic Humanism*, esp. 80-81, 105-10. There is no transcendent, religious dimension to Socrates' philosophical outlook: his horizon remained "immanent, worldly, humanistic," a straightforwardly naturalistic outlook.

8 Though we shall argue below that the premises Socrates elicits from Euthyphro in the course of the ἔλεγχος are quite standard and orthodox.

9 As R.E. Allen translates πόρρω που ἤδη σοφίας ἐλαύνοντος (4b1-2) in *Plato's 'Euthyphro' and the Earlier Theory of Forms* (London, 1970), 18.

10 W.K.C. Guthrie observes, *History*, IV, 104: "As with other Greek moral terms, no single word spans τὸ ὅσιον exactly. Holiness, piety, righteousness, religious duty, religion have all been suggested. As E[uthyphro] says at 12e, it was generally thought to cover all right conduct concerning one's obligations to the gods. For this, 'piety' seems as near as one can get."

11 See for instance A.W.H. Adkins, *Merit and Responsibility* (Oxford, 1960), 131-38.

12 We have departed from Lane Cooper's translation of the *Euthyphro* in E. Hamilton and H. Cairns, eds., *The Collected Dialogues of Plato* (New York, 1961) for the moment, and adopted R.E. Allen's translation of these technical phrases, *Plato's 'Euthyphro'*, 26.

13 "*A*ffection", not "*e*ffect", as for example Lane Cooper in his translation.

14 R.G. Hoerber misses the point of Socrates' distinction (misconstruing it as a relationship between "pairs of agents and patients implying causation") in his discussion, "Plato's *Euthyphro*," *Phronesis*, 3(1958), 103; consequently he views Socrates' argument as a "straw man" incorporating an illogical argument.

15 Though he adduces several considerations which are apropos of a correct understanding of the passage, still W.K.C. Guthrie, for example, fails to grasp that the distinction Socrates is making is not the grammatical distinction between active and passive voice—see his *History*, IV, 105, note 2, and 112.

16 R.E. Allen, *Plato's 'Euthyphro' and the Earlier Theory of Forms*, 40.

17 This is plainly true in Plato's dialogues. Xenophon represents matters quite otherwise. We shall discuss his testimony below.

18 W.G. Rabinowitz concludes his study, "Platonic Piety: An Essay Toward the Solution of an Enigma," *Phronesis* (1958), 108-20, with the statement:

> The monstrousness of the Athenians' treatment of Socrates, for Plato, lay in this: that they had condemned and put to death for impiety a man who, as Plato saw it, had practiced the true piety of dialectic all his life. And the hints of the *Euthyphro* record this judgment for posterity—for all, that is, capable of applying νοῦς thereto.

The conclusions of Rabinowitz' discussion thus converge with our own, though he finds much more positive (and much more Platonic) doctrinal content in the dialogue than we do, and arrives at his conclusions by a very different route: he sees in the phrase "to apply νοῦς to" at *Euthyphro* 14d4-6 a clue—an ingenious cryptogram as it were—placed there by Plato to suggest a substitution of νοῦς (understood in fully Platonic terms) for "the gods" in the proffered definition of piety as "service of the gods." The hidden teaching of the *Euthyphro*, then, is that the true service of the gods is to bring about apprehension of the Forms among men through philosophical dialectic.

19 See R.E. Allen, *Plato's 'Euthyphro'*, 6-7, 58. Such is also the view of George Grote, *Plato and the Other Companions of Sokrates* (London, 1867), 322-27.

20 A.E. Taylor's opinion that "there can be no doubt both that 'praying and sacrificing aright' are ὁσιότης and that ὁσιότης, since it is virtue or a part of virtue, is in the Socratic view an ἐπιστήμη or τέχνη, an application of knowledge to the regulation of practice" (*Plato: The Man and his Work* [1926; rpt. London, 1960], 148) can similarly be dismissed.

21 J. Burnet, *Plato's Euthyphro*, 57, ad 13d10.

22 R.E. Allen, *Plato's 'Euthyphro'*, 7.

23 *Ibid.*, 58.

24 R.E. Allen points out (*Ibid.*, 53-54) that while on the surface of things piety seems to be a virtue alongside the others (from the point of view of external behavior), on closer examination (of the οὐσία) it disappears as a separate virtue. It is assimilated as a subspecies of some one of the four cardinal virtues, likely justice.

25 Gregory Vlastos, "The Paradox of Socrates," *The Philosophy of Socrates*, ed. G. Vlastos (Garden City, 1971), 14. In marked contrast is the interpretation of R.G. Hoerber, "Plato's *Euthyphro*": the dialogue is a dramatic means of contrasting the views of Euthyphro and Socrates (105, 98-99); in contrast to Euthyphro's view that piety is a part of justice, a separate compartment of life, Plato intended to uphold—Hoerber infers from the *Epinomis*—the opposite view that piety is the highest virtue, of which justice is a part (105); and in contrast to Euthyphro's religious piety based on fear Plato intended to maintain that true religious feeling and worship should be based on reverence, not fear (105-6). W.K.C. Guthrie, on the other hand (*History*, IV, 123-24), identifies another, more modest set of positive, though "masked" conclu-

sions in the latter part of the dialogue: piety is a moral quality, with a single, constant essence; and piety is a form of knowledge.

26 James A. Coulter in his searching, detailed analysis, "The Relation of the *Apology of Socrates* to Gorgias' *Defense of Palamades* and Plato's Critique of Gorgianic Rhetoric," *Harvard Studies in Classical Philology*, 68(1964), 269-303, has demonstrated that Plato's *Apology* is "an illustration of the rhetorical counter-position" to Gorgias' *Defense of Palamades* which Plato has enunciated in the *Gorgias*. By pointing out the many striking verbal parallels (quite inexplicable in terms of chance) between Plato's *Apology* and Gorgias' *Defense*, and the inner agreement between the dramatic action of the *Apology* and the dialectic of the *Gorgias*, Coulter has shown how intricate and extensive is Plato's reworking of the trial "in an entire stratum of meaning." (For a critical discussion of Coulter's study see W.K.C. Guthrie, *History*, IV, 76-80.) While this suggests all the more that the *Apology* cannot be taken to be a court-report of Socrates' defense, still, within the bounds of Aristotle's understanding of poetic μίμησις, this does not affect our understanding of Plato's Σωκρατικὸς λόγος as an interpretation of the meaning of the historical facts that Socrates stood trial on the charge as recorded, that he was condemned by virtue of association with atheistic sophists, that he stood his ground on his practice of philosophy and suffered the consequences of their misunderstanding of it, that that conduct of philosophy was his devotion to the deity, and that he was ignorant of the kind of σοφία professed by the σοφισταί with whom they confused him.

27 Diogenes Laërtius, *Lives of Eminent Philosophers*, II, 40, ed. and trans. R.D. Hicks (London, 1925; rpt. 1938), 170. The Greek is:

> ἀδικεῖ Σωκράτης, οὓς μὲν ἡ πόλις νομίζει θεοὺς οὐ νομίζων, ἕτερα δὲ καινὰ δαιμόνια εἰσηγούμενος. ἀδικεῖ δὲ καὶ τοὺς νέους διαφθείρων. τίμημα θάνατος.

28 See J. Burnet's commentary on *Apology* 18c3, 24c1, and *Euthyphro* 3b3, *Plato's Euthyphro*; A.E. Taylor's discussion of the *Apology* in his *Varia Socratica* (Oxford, 1911); and R.E. Allen's translation of *Euthyphro* 3b3 and comments on page 62 of his study, *Plato's 'Euthyphro'*.

29 R. Hackforth, *The Composition of Plato's Apology* (Cambridge, 1933), chap. IV, "The Meaning of the Indictment," 58-79; J. Tate, "Greek for 'Atheism'," *Classical Review*, 50(1936), 3-5, and "More Greek for 'Atheism'," *Classical Review*, 51

(1937), 3-6; W.K.C. Guthrie, *History*, III, 237, note 2. See also Bruno Snell, *The Discovery of the Mind*, trans. T.G. Rosenmeyer (1953; rpt. New York, 1960), chap. 2, "The Olympian Gods."

30 Coleman Phillipson in his study, *The Trial of Socrates* (London, 1928), maintains:

> It was not, however, Socrates' alleged irreligion that was really the proximate cause of the formal accusation. The charge of impiety was introduced as a pretext, whatever ground there might be for it . . . . (203)

The ultimate grounds for Phillipson's view, however, are his acceptance of Xenophon's testimony regarding Socrates' religious beliefs (see 25-31, 118-31). As a result he says:

> [W]e have sufficient reliable evidence to show us the views [Socrates] held on several of the most important matters of religion, for example, the nature of God and his relation to man, the design of Nature and its bearing on divine purpose, benevolence, and providence, the object of worship and prayer, the office of oracles and divination, the meaning of piety, the immortality of the soul. (118-19)

Since Socrates gave so little grounds for offense to orthodox piety, Phillipson reasons, it must be "the political circumstances of the time" (204) that explain his condemnation.

31 R. Hackforth, *The Composition of Plato's Apology*, 63.

32 J. Burnet, *Plato's Euthyphro*, 105, ad 24c1.

33 R. Hackforth, *Composition*, 67-68.

34 See also R. Hackforth's article, "Socrates", *Philosophy*, 11 (1933), 271.

35 Burnet and Taylor's view that the δαιμόνια καινά of the accusation referred to Socrates' worship in a Pythagorean religious community (ἑταιρεία) will find few defenders today. (See Burnet's commentary on the *Apology*, 105, ad 24c1, and Taylor's essay, "The Impiety of Socrates," in his *Varia Socratica*.) For comprehensive and detailed refutations of Taylor's arguments see A.S. Ferguson, "The Impiety of Socrates," *Classical Quarterly*, 7(1913), 157-75, and G.C. Field, *Socrates and Plato* (Oxford, 1913).

36 See also F.M. Cornford, *Principium Sapientiae*, ed. W.K.C. Guthrie (1952; rpt. New York, 1965), 134-37.

37 See W.K.C. Guthrie, *History*, III, 227-28.

38 Coleman Phillipson, *Trial*, 215.

39 In this respect the state "defined" orthodoxy much as Euthyphro

defined ὁσιότης: it is what we do.

40 Martin Nilsson (*Greek Piety*, trans. H.J. Rose [New York, 1969], 5) observes:

> It is important to notice, as showing the significance of the domestic cult, that when evidence of citizenship was wanted, an Athenian citizen proved his civic rights by referring to his altar of Zeus Herkeios, to Apollo Patroos (i.e. inherited from his fathers), and his ancestral graves. Religion formed a part of everyday life in a way which is far from easy for us to understand.

41 See Coleman Phillipson, *Trial*, chap. X.

42 Callicles' statement at *Gorgias* 486a-b has been thought to imply (a knowledge on Plato's part) that Socrates was silent before his jurors, that he did not defend himsel[illegible] at all (implying in turn that Plato's *Apology* fills in [illegible]or Socrates what he *might* have said in self-defense). (See [illegible].A. Oldfather, "Socrates in Court," *Classical Weekly*, 31(1938) 203-11, for an argument of this view.) However, no such ra[illegible]cal interpretation is called for: in the context of the *Gor*[illegible]*as* Callicles is attacking Socrates' pursuit of philosophy, w[illegible]ch he finds shamefully useless and naive, a pursuit unbefit[illegible]ng a grown man. What life is all about, in Callicles' vie[illegible] is the pursuit of political power, fame, property—in a w[illegible]d, success in the eyes of the many. Thus it is easy to se[illegible] that in Callicles' eyes Socrates' defense, based on his [illegible]evotion to the deity, the care of his soul, and the convic[illegible]on that it is better to suffer than to do wrong, would be [illegible]tiably inept and ineffectual to the point of "having nothing [illegible] say at all." Socrates' tack was to take his stand, submit th[illegible]accusations to his customary ἔλεγχος, and state publicly th[illegible]nature of his life's pursuit of philosophy which had caused [illegible] offense —and this with utter disregard for the conseq[illegible]es to himself, and with utter contempt for the expectat[illegible] of the jury to be flattered and cajoled into [illegible]tting him o[illegible]he hook.

[illegible]ence [illegible] of [illegible] ty [illegible] were [illegible]erthro[illegible] of [illegible] honor[illegible] [illegible] even m[illegible]e immed[illegible] [illegible] is [illegible] for An[illegible]cides when he w[illegible] being [illegible]ed fo[illegible] that same year. (See J. Burnet, *Plato's Euthyphro*, 100-1, ad *Apology* 24a7, and Coleman Phillipson, *Trial*, 208-12.) The reason for his participation with the likes of Meletus and Lycon in the indictment, then, is perhaps to be found in some sort of personal grievance such as Xenophon alludes to at *Defense* 29. Next to nothing is known of the third accuser, Lycon.

44 R. Hackforth, *Composition*, 78.

45 The apparent contradiction between what Socrates says here in the *Apology*, namely that he would not obey the jury (and thus by implication the laws of the πόλις) if they demanded that he cease his conduct of philosophy among the citizens of Athens, and what he says in the *Crito* (50a-53a), that every citizen should obey every command of the πόλις, has been acutely discussed in a recent series of papers: A.D. Woozley, "Socrates on Disobeying the Law," *The Philosophy of Socrates*, ed. G. Vlastos (Garden City, 1971), 299-318; Gary Young, "Socrates and Obedience," *Phronesis*, 19(1974), 1-29; Robert J. McLaughlin, "Socrates on Political Disobedience," *Phronesis*, 21(1976), 185-97; Andrew Barker, "Why did Socrates refuse to escape?" *Phronesis*, 22(1977), 13-28. (And see McLaughlin's paper for references to other recent papers on the topic.) Young resolves the contradiction by the provocative view that in the two dialogues Socrates is speaking differently to different audiences, and to different ends. He argues that Socrates does not himself hold the arguments he makes in the *Crito* (in taking the part of the Laws of the πόλις against the arguments urged on him by Crito). Rather, Socrates' arguments are merely designed to persuade Crito, a close friend who nonetheless represents the views of the many.

To discuss the many complex issues involved in this problem is of course impossible in the present context, but for our part the resolution of the evident contradiction lies along the following lines. (Cf. McLaughlin's paper, which is a reply to Gary Young, for an argument to similar conclusions.) For Socrates that which is right or just (τὸ δίκαιον) is determined not by looking to the laws of the πόλις, but to that essential character or Form of τὸ δίκαιον perceived in and through philosophical dialectic. Socrates' divine command to conduct philosophical inquiry among his fellow citizens represents the absolute claim of τὸ δίκαιον, that which is right and just unqualifiedly, always and everywhere, regardless of circumstance or consequence. (Cf. *Apology* 29b where Socrates expresses his certainty on one point, that to do wrong and to disobey one who is his superior [τῷ βελτίονι], *whether God or man*, is evil and dishonorable—the avoidance of ἀδικία and the upholding of τὸ δίκαιον are primary, not the obedience of particular personages, divine or human. The superior is to be obeyed because it is δίκαιον to obey one who is βέλτιστος.) By conducting philosophical inquiry among the citizens of Athens Socrates is directing them to the one and only true standard of justice and right, and the criterion of the justice and rightness of the laws of the πόλις. Socrates' assertion in the *Crito* is true generally and so far as it goes (we should keep in mind that the arguments put forward by Socrates on behalf of the Laws are not submitted to ἔλεγχος): to obey the laws is normally part of τὸ δίκαιον. But for Socrates the claims of Athenian law on him derive from, are based on, and are justified by, the claims of that which is absolutely Right and Just. Thus, in any conflict of competing claims one must follow the dictactes of one's conscience, and philosophical insight, and act in accord with absolute Justice and Right. Should escape from jail have been perceived as a matter of the essence of τὸ δίκαιον, that is, as a matter of principle, and not of self-interest, then Socrates would no doubt, in our view, have felt obligated to "obey his God" and escape. But the arguments advanced by Crito for him to escape are considerations of personal self-interest (Socrates' own or that of his friends). Since Socrates will always and everywhere submit his personal interests and desires to the claims of absolute Justice and Right, he cannot exempt himself from the power of the πόλις to exact the death penalty and must suffer the personal consequences of his heroic, and tragic, stand.

46 Despite the shortcomings of his interpretation of Socrates in his *History of Philosophy* Hegel rightly perceived that it was this setting up of critical intelligence in judgment of the unreflective, traditional social order (summed up in the word νόμος, which corresponds roughly to Hegel's *Sittlichkeit*) that constituted the threat to the πόλις implicit in Socrates' conduct of philosophy. Hegel also saw that in this respect the jurors were right in lumping Socrates with the sophists.

47 J. Burnet observes (*Plato's Euthyphro*, 155, ad *Apology* 36d7):

> The πρυτανεῖον was the κοινὴ ἑστία of the πόλις, and the custom here referred to is a survival of the time when kings invited honoured guests to share their board. The privilege was granted to victors at Olympia (and possibly at the other great games), to distinguished generals, and to the representatives of certain families (e.g. the descendants of Harmodius and Aristogiton).

48 W.K.C. Guthrie, *History*, III, 402.

49 J. Burnet, *Plato's Euthyphro*, 16-17.

50 R. Hackforth, *Composition*, 96.

51 Little is said by Socrates about his dreams, and what is said has little religious significance. See *Crito* 44a-b, *Phaedo* 60e, *Charmides* 173a ff. See also F.M. Cornford, *Principium Sapientiae*, 67-68.

52 "Chaerephon's Inquiry about Socrates," *Classical Philology*, 56(1961), 249-50; *Greek Oracles* (London, 1967), 80-88.

53 The date of Chaerephon's consultation of the Oracle is a matter of some difficulty. H.W. Parke has pointed out that it would have been impossible to consult the Oracle during the war years, 431-22 and 413-404 (*A History of the Delphic Oracle* [Oxford, 1939], 412-13). "On the whole," Parke maintains, "it is much more likely that the oracle was given before 431, and so influenced Socrates from about the age of thirty-five" (413). There are two difficulties with this view: first, there is no reference or allusion to the Oracle's pronouncement in Aristophanes' *Clouds* (which appeared in 423); second, the identification of Socrates as the one preeminent in σοφία in the 430's (Socrates would have been about 35) seems somewhat anachronistic due to its evident prematurity. As John Ferguson (who supports a date in 421) observes: "it is hard to imagine, as PARKE and WORMELL saw (The Delphic Oracle I 402), what could have led the Pythia to make the assertion that there was no-one in Greece wiser than Socrates in the 430s" ("On the Date of Socrates's Conversion," *Eranos* [1964], 70). However, the first difficulty is removed by the fact that Socrates is represented as the σοφιστής par excellence in the *Clouds*: there is even the distinct possibility that the Oracle's pronouncement was the very reason why Aristophanes chose Socrates as the central, representative figure in the movement. The second difficulty is removed if we consider that the Pythia merely drew a black or white bean in response to Chaerephon's question, is there anyone wiser than Socrates? To explain why such a seemingly premature question would occur to Chaerephon in the 430's one need only have recourse to his well-known impulsiveness and over-zealous enthusiasm (*Apology* 21, *Charmides* 153). Thus we take Parke's early dating (before 431) as the most reasonable resolution of this complex question.

54 Cf. *Charmides* 153b, where it is said that Chaerephon "always behaves like a madman."

55 J. Burnet, *Plato's Euthyphro*, 92, ad *Apology* 21b8.

56 *Greek Oracles*, 111. See also M. Nilsson, *Greek Folk Religion*

(1940; rpt. Philadelphia, 1972), 129-32.

57 To paraphrase 21b4-5.

58 W.K.C. Guthrie, *History*, III, 407, and H.W. Parke, *Greek Oracles*, 85.

59 In a fragment from his Platonic writings Aristotle testifies that Socrates centered his inquiry into man on the Delphic saying, "Know thyself," cf. Th. Deman, *Le Témoignage d'Aristote sur Socrate*, 44 ff.

60 That is, arrogant self-assertiveness implying resort to one's own might to get what one wants in disregard of the claims of justice.

61 We are reminded of G.M.A. Grube's important remarks, *Plato's Thought* (1935; rpt. Boston, 1958), 150:

> The Greek word θεός and the English word God are by no means equivalent; their associations are obviously very different. The chief difference is perhaps best expressed by Wilamowitz where he says that to a Greek, god is primarily a predicative notion. Where the Christian says that God is love or that God is good he is first asserting, or taking for granted, the existence of a mysterious being, God, and making a qualitative judgment about him. He is telling us something about God. With the Greek the order is frequently reversed. He would say that Love is god or Beauty is god; he is not assuming the existence of any mysterious divinity but telling us something about love and beauty, the reality of which no one could deny. The subject of his judgment, the thing of which he speaks, is in the world we know, and in that world pagan thought was focused in classical times.

62 He thinks too that the failure of his δαιμόνιον to warn him of some impending ill-fortune is significant.

63 One might compare the puzzled musings of Bishop Theophilus of Antioch (second century A.D.) in this connection: "What was the point of [Socrates'] acceptance of death? What sort of reward did he expect to gain beyond death?"

64 He adds as well, "[the good man's] fortunes are not a matter of indifference to the gods." This certainly sounds like a belief in the providence of gods. However, there is reason for thinking this exceptional remark is a *façon de parler* for a more prosaic truth. Just as 30d, "I do not believe that the law of God [θέμις] permits a better man to be harmed by a worse," is merely an alternative way of expressing the conviction central to his religious conception of philosophy, that nothing can harm the good man, so this talk of the providence

of "the gods" is another way of expressing Socrates' conviction that doing the right is in *every* circumstance and without qualification, and therefore regardless of consequence, the good for man. Doing the right necessarily results in one's εὐδαιμονία.

65 Emile de Strycker, in his provocative article, "Socrate et l'au-dela d'après l'*Apologie* platonicienne," *Les Etudes Classiques*, 18(1950), 269-84, maintains that it was not Plato's intention in the *Apology* to present a Socrates who was ignorant and agnostic about the fate of the soul after death. De Strycker distinguishes between the agnostic reserve Socrates shows towards the description of the afterlife—a conflation of traditional (epic) and current (Orphic and Eleusinian) notions—and his firm conviction that there is an afterlife. The latter he finds, "si nous la replaçons dans les perspectives platoniciennes" (280), in *Apology* 41c-d:

> You too, gentlemen of the jury, must look forward to death with confidence, and fix your minds on this one belief, which is certain—that nothing can harm a good man either in life or after death, and his fortunes are not a matter of indifference to the gods.

For our part, we have argued that the evidence is on the side of the view that Plato's belief in the immortality of the soul evolved gradually from the *Apology* to the *Meno* and *Gorgias* to the *Phaedo*. Thus we find de Strycker's reference to the later dialogues to interpret the *Apology* unacceptable. As for the view that 41c-d is an assertion of a belief in Providence, we can only reiterate our view that the passage is a metaphorical statement of the Socratic truth that no matter what calamity befalls a man the only matter of importance is the state of his ψυχή, that is, whether he has attained his own proper ἀρετή, excellence, as a man. There is no question in the *Apology* of a Providence who will keep misfortunes from befalling the good man (see 30d where Socrates' belief in the "law of God" which will not permit a better man to be harmed by a worse is consistent with his suffering death, banishment, or deprivation of civic rights): the essential point, expressed metaphorically at 41c-d in terms of "the gods", is that the external misfortunes that do befall the good man work no harm on his ψυχή or character.

66 In his elenctic refutation of Meletus Socrates refers to his δαιμόνιον as δαιμόνια πράγματα, supernatural actions.

67 Eduard Zeller, *Socrates and the Socratic Schools*, trans. O.J. Reichel (from Zeller's *Philosophie der Griechen*)(London, 1885), 92-93.

68 At *Republic* 496c Socrates passes an interesting remark about his δαιμόνιον: "My own case, the divine sign, is hardly worth mentioning—for I suppose it has happened to few or none before me."

69 A.E. Taylor, *Socrates* (1933; rpt. Garden City, 1953), 22.

70 Plato's Socrates does mention his advanced years once in connection with his sentence to death, but only briefly in passing to try to put the distraught Crito at ease: "Well, really Crito, it would hardly be suitable for a man of my age to resent having to die" (*Crito* 43b).

71 O.J. Todd thus liberally, though justifiably, interprets the phrase ἐκ παντὸς τρόπου. The whole passage reads more literally, "it seemed to us that we should search out every possible means of escaping."

72 Socrates uses ἐπιστήμη as a near equivalent of τέχνη at 532c6.

73 My paraphrase of 81a-b.

74 Most scholars would agree that the use of the Orphic λόγος is an indication of the new religious and intellectual influences on Plato which were decisive in leading him to the theory of Forms as enunciated in the *Phaedo*. Many would thus be disinclined to take the passage as applicable to Socratic philosophy, particularly because of the metaphysical realism implied in the passage. We, however, have maintained that Socratic dialectic does imply a realistic theory of Forms, so that this objection does not hold as a reason for not applying the passage to Socrates' philosophy as well as to Plato's. Nor do we see any other good reason for not doing so.

75 Socrates' last words of the dialogue are: "I think now I appreciate the true meaning of the proverb, 'all that is beautiful is difficult'."

76 In his study, *Sokrates: sein Werk und seine geschichtliche Stellung* (Tübingen, 1913), Heinrich Maier rejects the traditional view of Socrates as a philosopher: Socrates had no philosophical doctrines or theories (103); he was concerned only with a purely moral dialectic (296, 303). In Maier's view Socrates' dialectical scrutiny of his compatriots constituted a Gospel (*Evangelium*, 304) of moral salvation (*die sittliche Erlösung*, 304). It was Socrates' achievement to identify traditional Greek eudaimonistic utilitarianism with the moral ideal (305 ff., 313-14): the ultimate ground, justification, and end of any moral precept, the Socratic Gospel proclaimed, was εὐδαιμονία, the perfection and well-being of the

individual (316). Socrates sought to convince each individual that he contained within himself the ethical ideal, which alone had an absolute claim on his conduct (316-17): thus the individual was liberated from a dependence on traditional, socially imposed moral precept to individual moral autonomy and freedom (320 ff.). It was precisely by pursuing the moral ideal contained within himself through a life of moral self-examination and knowledge that each individual achieved his own perfect self-realization and well-being (336, 339, 350, 369).

Maier's quasi-religious interpretation of the Socratic way is problematic in a number of respects: Maier represents the essential feature of the Socratic way to be the conscious realization by the individual of his moral autonomy: that perfect εὐδαιμονία is possible through the realization that the individual is an autonomous moral system, that the realization of his own nature constituted both the moral absolute and the end of all his life's activity. But the Socrates of Plato's early dialogues (on which Maier principally and ultimately depends) does not bring about any such *self-conscious* reflective grasp of one's total situation in life, nor particularly such an understanding of the moral ideal as opposes *in principle* the private and the individual on the one hand to the social on the other (389-90). Rather, Socrates' conduct of philosophy is wholly preoccupied with the nature of the moral ideals themselves as objective realities transcending the individual person. The important concern for Socrates was not to bring about a *subjective* self-consciousness in the individual of his moral mode of existence but to clarify the substantive questions, what (after all) *is* ἀρετή? what *is* εὐδαιμονία? what *is* the ethical ideal? Maier's distortion of the Socratic way here stems from the fact (consistent with his view that Socrates was no philosopher) that he totally ignores the philosophical *content* of Socratic dialectic, confining himself to a purely *formal* characterization of the Socratic way (382-83).

Further, Maier's quasi-religious characterization of the Socratic way is specious insofar as he maintains that the Socratic moral Gospel was a thorough-going secularization of morality (391). The only religious element in fact in Maier's Socrates is a religious belief which metaphysically grounds or supports his Gospel: there is a Providence which rules and orders all of nature and guides the life of the virtuous man to the good (430-32, 437). We have argued, however, that though it was certainly Socrates' personal inclination to believe that all was controlled by divine Mind for the good (as at *Phaedo* 96a ff.) it was still in the last analysis governed by his ignorance: to have maintained such a religious *conviction* would have been a form of knowing something about "higher matters" which were beyond the reach of human intelligence to comprehend.

The Religious Dimension of Socrates' Thought

1. Socratic Irony and Eros.

In the context of Greek civilization the Socratic philosophical way is an utterly remarkable phenomenon: one could hardly have been prepared, on the eve of Socrates' birth in the golden era of the Athenian πόλις, for the appearance of so singular, idiosyncratic, and paradoxical a figure as Socrates. He rose up out of the mainstream of Greek culture to take his solitary stand, and offering no teaching or wisdom of his own, with ignorance as his cornerstone, set his face against the wise, the experts and the pedagogues of the day, and called into question their wisdom about the most important concerns of life. He conceived it his duty, against the will and comprehension of his contemporaries, to be the gadfly: to goad, to jolt, to get under the skin, to sting, to paralyze with confusion and indignant rage. He is the one individual over against the many of his contemporaries—though here as always we are confronted by paradox: Socrates is driven by a dead-serious zeal, undaunted even in the face of death, for the individual well-being of his contemporaries, and thus ultimately for the glory and well-being of Athens. The idiosyncrasies of his philosophical mission are matched by his physical appearance: he went about shoeless and virtually impoverished, dependent on the hospitality of those with a taste for the kind of discussion he conducted. He was a decidedly unattractive figure with his snub-nose and protruding eyes, and his odd habit of looking from side to side (or perhaps, staring off to the side) as he walked about—he did not at all have the appearance or airs of the καλός τε κἀγαθός—to all appearances he was the exact opposite. His conduct of philosophy contributed to this impression as well: his questions were trivial, elementary, and seemingly innocuous, and his examples were homely and mundane. In every way the appearance of Socrates' own person as well as his practice of philosophy seemed designed to put off any comparison with the beautiful, the gifted, the successful, in a word, all those who commanded the admiration of their fellow citizens.

In Plato's *Symposium* (214e ff.) the handsome, brilliantly gifted youth, Alcibiades (who in his later precocious career in quest of power and glory was to fluctuate so wildly between the roles of awe-inspiring hero and ignominious rogue and traitor), complains bitterly of what he deems the perverse seductiveness of Socrates' personality. Alcibiades has been deceived by Socrates' feigned erotic admiration and desire of his physical beauty. In reality

Socrates does not care a whit for such beauty and laughs up his sleeve at it (*Symposium* 216d-e, 219c). Socrates pretended to be the ignorant, graceless, unattractive lover drawn by the beauty of Alcibiades. Alcibiades has grounds for complaint: Socrates has violated the pattern of Greek pederasty. For, in love between males, while reciprocal in the sense that both members experienced love and affection for the other, still one member normally was considered the lover and the other the beloved. That is, the elder was the lover: he was aroused with desire in the first place by the physical beauty of the youth; more secondarily he was attracted by the youth's promising abilities. What aroused the love and affection of the youth for his elder lover were his manly virtues and talents, the power he had achieved, and the name he had attained as a result of his accomplishments. The quality of their ἔρως was different, or perhaps more properly, it was the lover who experienced what most Greeks thought of by the term ἔρως; the beloved reciprocated with an affection and devotion based more on admiration and respect for strength of character and accomplishment.

Clearly Alcibiades' pride is grievously wounded by his discovery that his beauty counts for nothing in Socrates' eyes. Alcibiades has realized that Socrates' real mind is just the opposite of what he openly professes. He finds too that the respective roles they play in their relationship are just the reverse of what they ought to be according to public expectations: it is Socrates who is the beloved and not the beautiful Alcibiades. Alcibiades' beauty is only the semblance, while Socrates' is the reality, the thing itself (*Symposium* 218d-219a). Further, despite Socrates' characterization of himself at the beginning of the *Symposium* as possessing a very modest σοφία, a very meager, inconsequential sort of thing as tenuous and shadowy as a dream—in contrast, that is, to the awesome, brilliant σοφία of Agathon, whose play had recently met with such glorious success before all of Athens (*Symposium* 175d-e)—it is the philosophy of Socrates which enthralls Alcibiades and takes possession of his mind like a spell or a divine frenzy. Through his philosophy Socrates has insinuated himself into Alcibiades' mind and cast a spell over him; he suffers philosophy as a πάθος, like ἔρως, which takes possession of him. Indeed, Alcibiades uses stronger language than that of the human beloved to describe his new perception of Socrates: Socrates is like those little Silenus figures sold in the statuaries' stalls that open up down the middle to reveal little figures of the gods inside. Despite his unflattering satyr-like appearance, his cultivation of the common and the plain in his outward comportment and appearance, and his habitual profession of ignorance, there is something altogether sublime and divine about him. For those who can penetrate beyond the appearances, beyond seeming, to the reality within there is something god-like about him, or more properly about his wisdom.

This distinction between reality and seeming, between Socrates' real mind and the face he shows to the public, is crucial to the understanding of his personality and career. Or, to express the point in another way, one cannot arrive at a full and true understanding of Socrates unless one takes into account his irony.

> And [Thrasymachus], on hearing this, gave a great guffaw and laughed sardonically and said, Ye gods! Here we have the well-known irony [εἰρωνεία] of Socrates, and I knew it and predicted that when it came to replying you would refuse and dissemble and do anything rather than answer any question that anyone asked you. (*Republic* 337a)

Socrates' εἰρωνεία was well-known to his contemporaries. When Thrasymachus uses the word in the above passage in the *Republic* he has in mind Socrates' refusal to answer questions himself: he always puts the questions, but never answers them. But the word εἰρωνεία implies not only a refusal to say what one thinks, to give one's own opinion, but also a certain note of dissimulation, pretense, affectation, namely, in Socrates' case, that he is ignorant and has nothing to say of his own and so must ask questions of someone who does know.[1] Thus Socratic irony is not simply an incidental personal idiosyncrasy, but rather stands in the closest relationship to those two central categories in Socratic philosophy, ignorance and ἔλεγχος. Ἐιρωνεία informs the aporetic and maieutic aspects of his conduct of philosophy inasmuch as (1) it is inquiry out of "ignorant" puzzlement as to the truth of some claim, and (2) Socrates does not give of knowledge he possesses himself but acts only as midwife for the one he questions.[2] Further, this philosophical ἔλεγχος he carries out with various individuals is his religious duty, his "service of the God" (*Apology* 23b, 30a), and his service of his fellow Athenians by dedicating himself to the "care of their souls" by examining and testing their opinions and beliefs—which Socrates calls the greatest boon to befall his fellow citizens (*Apology* 29d, 31c). So εἰρωνεία is clearly not some isolated, incidental characteristic of the Socratic philosophical way, but stands at its very center in systematic relationship to its other essential features. The attribution of εἰρωνεία to Socrates amounts to the claim that his ignorance, and the elenctic method based on it, are a pose adopted by Socrates. It implies that Socrates' explicit words in professing to be ignorant, and his rationale or justification of the elenctic method, cannot be taken at face value and do not fully and adequately represent

Socrates' own real views. Furthermore, it implies that Socrates' assertion that his conduct of philosophical ἔλεγχος is his "service of the God" is only *ironically true*. Since the basis for this claim of a religious dimension to his practice of philosophy is the pronouncement of the Delphic Oracle that he was wise because he realized his ignorance, which on the present account is only an ironic truth, then this profession of philosophical service of the God would be merely a part of the face he shows the public. It is only the outward view of his philosophical career intended for public consumption. What is Socrates' real mind in this regard? Are we to think, with Alcibiades, that his religious vocation is part of Socrates' ironic play with the public and that in his real mind he "laughs up his sleeve" at us (and the jury)?

There are several reasons why we or Socrates' contemporaries might conclude that Socrates' official self-understanding as one devoid of σοφία was a pose: (1) Socratic dialectic proceeded by adducing premises wich were intuitively and axiomatically true. Without the ability to establish such propositions as truths (for example, that virtue is to be desired) Socratic dialectic would hardly have got off the ground. But this means such propositions were *known* to be true and thus were additional pieces of knowledge. (2) Socrates could be identified with a number of propositions which would not have been universally accepted as axiomatic or common-sense truths: that soul is the better and ruling part (that desires of the body ought to be submitted to rational control); that virtue is knowledge: that all the principal or cardinal virtues are united under wisdom; that the only essential consideration regarding human conduct was not what accrued to personal gain, but whether the act was right and good.
(3) Socratic dialectic implied that Socrates knew where he was going (despite his frequent protestations that to question implied no knowledge). Socrates certainly knew that the wisdom claimed by the one he was scrutinizing was no real wisdom, that no λόγος could be successfully given for it. Socrates could hardly direct the questioning (which he unquestionably does) so efficiently, succinctly, and inexorably to its conclusion without having a clear idea of its end, without, that is, knowing what was wrong with the claim and what were the right questions to bring the proposition so speedily to its downfall. The direction of the dialectic was not haphazard: all the thought input, as it were, was Socrates'; his subject just answered briefly, usually yes or no.

The objection may be raised, if this was perceived to be a pose on the part of Socrates, then why would his fellow citizens play along with it? The reason may partly be found in the vanity and complacency of his subjects. They after all had their reputations to uphold: they were generally held to possess a certain σοφία or ἀρετή, and indeed especially in the case of the sophists, they themselves cultivated, and profited by, this reputation. They could not afford to decline Socrates' ironic entreaty to learn at the feet of one so notable for his wisdom and virtue. Also, Socrates made the brief question and answer method his price for participation in the discussion, and Socrates' Athenian contemporaries seem to have had an extraordinary love for discussion and controversy. Indeed, the ability to speak forcefully and persuasively in the public forum, particularly of course in the discharge of one's duties as a πολίτης in the Athenian democracy, was quickly becoming the most important criterion for determining whether a man was καλός τε κἀγαθός, whether he was a success, a man of distinction. The brilliance of Socrates' interrogations was renowned: his participation in a discussion would have been highly valued. And finally, but not least importantly, we must remember that in fact Socrates was not always (or very) successful in getting his subject to submit to the question and answer method.[3]

There are many features of this ironic profession of ignorance that will inevitably appear problematic and paradoxical, or even morally objectionable, to the modern reader. In the latter category especially falls the implication that Socrates was deceitful, that he was guilty of willful duplicity, in assuming the pose of ignorance and insisting thereupon on putting the questions to those he engaged in discussion. Yet the temptation to interpret this ironic pose of ignorance as morally devious and culpable must be resisted. Socrates' profession of ignorance as the basis for the elenctic method was *transparent*: as the above remarks of Thrasymachus in the *Republic* indicate, Socrates' εἰρωνεία fooled no one—no one, that is, with any intellectual acumen or insight. Indeed, Thrasymachus' reference to Socrates' well-known or customary εἰρωνεία implies that Socrates was *commonly, generally* perceived to be assuming a pose, to feign ignorance in his characteristic conduct of philosophy. (This of course does not mean that there was no truth to Socrates' profession of ignorance—rather that its full meaning was non-apparent, hidden in paradox behind his public, ironic *persona*.) Socratic irony, then, is not aptly characterized as deceitful. Rather its most striking feature, we submit, is that *Socrates refuses to make known his own mind*. Herein lies the historical uniqueness of Socrates and the deepest stratum of the Socratic paradox. Why should Socrates assume such a resolutely negative posture?

It is important to note that the dialectical character of Socratic philosophy did not demand this inscrutable ironic negativity: Socrates might very well have made explicit the implicit workings of his philosophical way without sacrificing or compromising its character. He might have, after having shown by ἔλεγχος how imperfect, unstable and confused the human grasp of truth was, appealed to his subjects to look upon human knowledge as something necessarily *in-between* ignorance and true, divine knowledge, and as something essentially *on-the-way* to real knowledge. Human knowledge was only partial, tentative and tenuous, and so they ought to participate together in dialectical inquiry into truth realizing that whatever tentative advances they might make must necessarily fall short of real wisdom. Socrates might thus have made explicit what seems to have been the implicit actuality anyway, that he served as midwife to a community of lovers of wisdom, those who were fired by the love of wisdom and aided each other through philosophical discussion to attain as much as was given to human intelligence to attain.

Yet Socrates did not do this; he chose rather an attitude of silence and dissemblance. The question must be asked, what is the significance of this? What is the significance of Socratic negativity, given its non-essentiality to the Socratic dialectical conception of philosophy? Can any further light be shed on this ultimate facet of the Socratic paradox? The question may be asked in another form: what was Socrates' real mind behind the facade of irony and ignorance? Put in these positive terms our task is to open Socrates up and look inside in order to detect that something sublime and divine which Plato alluded to in the speech of Alcibiades. Only by penetrating thus behind the mask of irony and ignorance will we fully perceive the religious dimension of his thought.

Socrates was concerned with the *conduct* of philosophical inquiry, not with the self-reflective characterization of his conduct of philosophy. In the *Symposium* and the *Phaedrus*, however, Plato, Socrates' greatest disciple, elaborates a fundamental truth *about* the Socratic philosophical way which Socratic irony had concealed. If irony is the outer, negative face of the Socratic way, Plato there reveals, ἔρως is its heart and soul, its inner moving force or dynamic. Plato thus provides us with a speculative, reflective perspective on the Socratic philosophical way, with which Socrates, wholly taken up with the end and object of the life of philosophy, knowledge of divine reality, did not concern himself. When viewed from this second-order perspective as *process* and *way of life* philosophy was the highest form of ἔρως. In Plato's attempt to make manifest this implicit erotic dimension of philosophy we shall find the needed clues to an understanding of Socratic irony, and ultimately to an understanding of the religious dimension of Socratic philosophy.

In his second speech in the *Phaedrus* (242a ff.) Socrates attempts to make amends for what he calls the blasphemous argument of his first speech (242b-e). It was the import of his first speech that the irrational power of Eros should be kept firmly under the control of reason. To let Eros hold sway over reason was an evil, an evil directly opposite to the virtue of temperance, which was the subordination of the desire for pleasure to the rational choice of what was right and good. In his first speech Socrates argued that "when irrational desire, pursuing the enjoyment of beauty, has gained the mastery over judgment" it brings about the total ruin of the beloved, both physical and spiritual (241c).

But this account represents Eros in a negative light: it was an irrational force which tended to work contrary to the life of ἀρετή. It was this "terrible" injustice to Eros that Socrates' second speech set out to amend. Though in his second speech Socrates proceeds dialectically to destroy his first argument and to establish its opposite (namely, that to be possessed by love is a divine gift), Socrates' new argument does not in any way undermine his former conclusion that reason is the superior, ruling, guiding element in the personality (the pilot in the analogy of the chariot and unharmonious steeds). Rather, Socrates shows that his first account neglected and obscured the important, implicit, positive role of Eros in a life ruled by reason.

In Socrates' speeches of the *Phaedrus* and the *Symposium* Plato refers to Eros as a god (*Phaedrus* 242e), that is, something divine (242e), a great δαίμων (*Symposium* 202e), but not one of the high Olympian deities resident in the heavenly realm. Rather, Eros is a divine power which acts *in between* men and gods, between the world of mortals and the divine, eternal realm. Eros is divine in the sense that it is *from* the divine realm and acts on mortals to draw them to divine reality. The overall and ultimate thrust of the speeches of Socrates and Diotima is to direct attention away from Eros as a divine reality in itself, as a fitting object of religious emotion.[4] The divinity of Eros derives from its *relativity* to divine realities: it ought not itself be made the object of a religious enthusiasm or reverence. Its divinity resides in its function, its orientation, as well as its transcendent, non-human origin. Philosophically, the nature of Eros in itself can only be elucidated in terms of the realities to which it is oriented and on which it operates. Its being is *toward* the divine ἀγαθά and καλά, it is *for* them, it serves them, it points to them, its being is apprehended only relative to and in terms of them. And it operates on men to bring them to the good and lovely realities of the divine sphere. It is of the essence of Eros, then, to be a go-between, an envoy (*Symposium* 202e).

In the *Symposium* Plato subjects Eros to a metaphysical interpretation. Eros was commonly understood to be the emotional experience of love; it was the passionate desire aroused by the physical beauty of the beloved. At a crucial point in the *Symposium*, however, Plato, in the person of Diotima, expands the meaning of Eros to embrace the fundamental drive in mankind to attain the state of happiness. Eros is equivalent to nothing less than that innate, ineradicable longing in every human being to possess the good.

> Right, said she, for the happy are happy inasmuch as they possess the good, and since there's no need for us to ask why men should want to be happy, I think your answer is conclusive.
>
> Absolutely, I agreed.
>
> This longing, then, she went on, this love—is it common to all mankind? What do you think, do we all long to make the good our own?
>
> Yes, I said, as far as that goes we're all alike.
>
> Well then, Socrates, if we say that everybody always loves the same thing, does that mean that everybody is in love? Or do we mean that some of us are in love, while some of us are not?
>
> I was a little worried about that myself, I confessed.
>
> Oh, it's nothing to worry about, she assured me. You see, what we've been doing is to give the name of Love to what is only one single aspect of it; we make just the same mistake, you know, with a lot of other names. . . . For 'Love, that renowned and all-beguiling power,' includes every kind of longing for happiness and for the good. Yet those of us who are subject to this longing in the various fields of business, athletics, philosophy, and so on, are never said to be in love, and are never known as lovers, while the man who devotes himself to what is only one of Love's many activities is given the name that should apply to all the rest as well.
>
> (*Symposium* 205a-b, d)

In this light Eros is not merely an emotional state but a metaphysical drive, which, like the human instinct to reproduce the species, is more fundamental than particular emotional states and operates unconsciously in the human species independent of the experience of the emotion.

By its very nature this metaphysical drive to possess the good and the beautiful is unlimited: Eros in its most fundamental terms is the desire to be happy perfectly, fully, and without end. But this, of course, is a description of the divine condition of being. Thus, implicit in Plato's redefinition of Eros is the assertion that man by his very nature aspires to the divine condition of being. Yet at the same time in the *Symposium* and the *Phaedrus* Plato defines the idea of the immortal gods in terms of and relative to the idea of mortal human beings. In the *Symposium* (202) the gods are defined as those beings who *possess* the good and the beautiful, and thus happiness (εὐδαιμονία): that is, the gods are to be distinguished from men only in the *degree* of possession and enjoyment of goods (or the attainment of desired ends) common to both human and divine life. And in the *Phaedrus* Plato observes:

> '[I]mmortal' is a term applied on no basis of reasoned argument at all, but our fancy pictures the god whom we have never seen, nor fully conceived, as an immortal living being, possessed of a soul and a body united for all time. (246c-d)

Plato thus treats the concept of the immortal gods as a limit-concept: they are bodily, besouled (that is, created) beings just as men are, but they are *imagined* to endure indefinitely or eternally.

According to Plato's mythical speculation on the nature of the soul in the *Phaedrus* (246a ff.) it is the wings which account for the ability of the charioteer and the steeds of a living being to "raise that which is heavy and carry it aloft to the region where the gods dwell" (246d). Through the metaphor of the wings Plato refers to the ability of the soul to overcome the influence of the bodily, the material, and the earthly, and thus to be able to rise to the heavenly spectacles of bliss. This ability resides in the acquired capacity to attain the intellectual vision of the Forms. Furthermore, the wings are thought of as the seat of virtue (they are called fair, wise, good, and by the name of every other excellence), and they are nourished on virtue (that is, they increase their capacity to overcome the downward pull of the unruly steed) (246c-e).

In Plato's elaborate metaphor there are in mortal human beings a charioteer and two steeds, one good and noble, the other base and ignoble. The two steeds stand for two opposing *inclinations* or *dispositions*, not faculties or component parts, of the human personality. They stand for the two directions in which a human being is conditioned: by virtue of being a bodily being one is conditioned towards selfish, physical and worldly gratifications; but a human being is also drawn to higher, nobler realities. These two tendencies are in conflict with one another in the human person, though in the gods they are imagined to be in perfect accord. Thus, in terms of Plato's imagery, by nourishing the intellect on the vision of the Forms the charioteer is able to master the lower tendency and submit it to the higher aims of the personality.

At *Phaedrus* 253e ff. Plato extends his speculative metaphor to an analysis of love between males. The passionate erotic desire aroused by a handsome young male corresponds to the base, unruly steed. The steed drives blindly towards the gratification of its desire, but Plato describes the brutal, violent conquest of the steed. Through repeated, tempestuous struggles the steed is finally broken and submitted to the will of the driver: the sensuous erotic desires of the lover become suppressed in favor of a higher aim.

According to the mythical λόγος of the *Phaedrus* the gods ascend by chariot to a realm "beyond the heavens" (247c). (Alternatively it is said that access to the realm is gained by reason alone.) But the gods do not *dwell* there: they return to the heavens, to that compartment within the world which is designated their proper abode. This necessity for the gods to return into the world is due to the fact that they are bodily beings (they too have a chariot with steeds, albeit perfectly ordered ones). The region outside the heavens is not a realm of composite bodily beings at all: it is the realm of pure reality absolutely free of the bodily and everything particular. It is the realm of Justice and all the Forms, simply and absolutely, in and by themselves.

By virtue of their feasting and banqueting on the spectacles of bliss (Plato has so interpreted this traditional Homeric image of Olympian society in terms of contemplation) the gods are able to return to do their work, which for the train of Zeus is the loftiest, most royal function, to order and care for all things (246e). The gods are informed (in metaphorical terms, nourished) by their vision of the Forms in the performance of their work.[5] But in this regard the divine condition is essentially no different from the state of mortal human beings, in particular, philosophers: they too must draw on their vision of the Forms in ruling their bodies and in the performance of their obligations in the social and political domain. The only difference between gods and men in this connection is that the gods have a perfect, permanent hold on the divine realm: no struggle with an unruly steed is required to gain access to the vision of divine reality. The gods have attained by birthright and possess without jeopardy what mortals must toil ceaselessly to attain. Or, to put it differently, the gods are merely the imaginative idealizations of the end-state of the philosophical life. All human existence expresses Eros, the longing for good, beauty, wisdom, in a word, the fullness of all excellence or ἀρετή, as well as the possession of it without limitation. The gods, of course, are imagined not to die. But more than that, the gods represent a humanity free of all the downward pull of one's lower, appetitive nature: they represent a humanity permanently informed by rationally perceived truth. This is their blessed εὐδαιμονία. The gods have bodies, but by virtue of their ready access to the sublime spectacles, by their habitual, trained vision on true, eternal ἀρετή, they are free of the conditioning of their bodies. The external and internal conditioning of their bodies has no power to obstruct their soul's vision of real and true Being, nor interfere with the conduct of their work guiding and controlling the cosmos. Their divinity, and by implication that of men who approach the divine condition, rests not in their escape from the bodily condition of being—for that is as much a contradiction of the notion of immortal gods as it is of mortal men—but rather in their liberation from every influence of the body contrary to the higher life of ἀρετή, from every influence that is contrary to the vision of the Forms and the life (bodily activity in the world, whether heavenly or earthly) informed by that vision.

There is implicit in the metaphorical λόγος of the *Phaedrus* an interpretation of the Socratic philosophical way. It represents the full elucidation of Alcibiades' assertion that if one opened up Socrates one would find something divine inside: the implication of Plato's account of Eros in the *Symposium* and the *Phaedrus* is that Socrates is the mortal who has transcended his mortal condition of being; through the philosophical life he has ascended to a divine condition of being. Through the practice of philosophy Socrates' vision has been trained on divine ἀρετή in "that place beyond the heavens [which] none of our earthly poets has yet sung, and none shall sing worthily" (*Phaedrus* 247c). He is free of the influence of the body; his lower nature is completely in check and submitted to the life of ἀρετή. Through years of struggle his wings have been nourished; they are able to lift him clear of the downward pull of his lower nature. He is free to soar to the divine realm in company with the gods. Steadfast continuance in the philosophical way has given him a habitual hold on those spectacles of bliss that nourish the soul. Socrates' only concern is divine ἀρετή: he has become indifferent to his own selfish ends, to his own death, to every demand of his nature not in accord with the highest ἀρετή. In the metaphor of the *Phaedo*, philosophy has been for Socrates a process of dying, dying to the blind dictates of his lower, bodily nature. As with the gods, Socrates' conquest of his mortality and rise to a divine condition rest not in his escape from the bodily condition of being (in the metaphor of the *Phaedo*, the separation of soul from body), but rather his liberation from those influences of the body contrary to the divine life of ἀρετή. To put it in terms of another metaphor, Socrates has gained his salvation from the body while still in it.

If Plato's account in the *Phaedrus* prescribed only the suppression of physical erotic love for the sake of the life of reason and virtue it would amount to little more than his first, "blasphemous" account. Thus far the philosophical life as an approach to the divine condition of being would appear to be the suppression and control, rather than the sublimation and fulfillment, of erotic passion. According to Plato's apology, perhaps here based on Socrates' own statements during his lifetime, visible beauty, such as that of the handsome young males for whom Socrates professed such passionate admiration, "reminded" the lover of wisdom of the Good under the aspect of the Beautiful.

Yet there is a difficulty here: we are to remember Alcibiades' bitter words that Socrates only feigns this passionate erotic admiration of young men. In reality he cares not a whit for their charms. Thus, irony pervades and complicates the picture even here. There would appear to be the same ironic discrepancy between Socrates' profession of passionate erotic desire and his own real mind as there is between his own unattractive outward appearance and the something divine within to which Alcibiades alluded. What Plato represents as the positive continuity between physical ἔρως and the sublimated intellectual ἔρως of the philosopher is found once again to be pervaded with irony.

The resolution of this difficulty lies in the recognition of a certain complexity of Plato's account of Eros: Plato recognizes an important difference between those who are predominantly lovers of beauty and those who are lovers of wisdom. This distinction is based on an ambiguity in the Greek notion of the Good: the sum total of good or excellence was represented by the words καλός τε κἀγαθός. The Good had both aesthetic and moral elements: it included all that was lovely and beautiful, as well as all that was right and just. The former was paradigmatically aligned with the visual, aesthetic mode of experience; the latter with the judgments of moral reason. Let us examine this important distinction between the Good as moral right and the Good as beauty, and its implications for an understanding of Socratic philosophy as Eros.

> Now in the earthly likenesses of justice and temperance and all other prized possessions of the soul there dwells no luster; nay, so dull are the organs wherewith men approach their images that hardly can a few behold that which is imaged, but with beauty it is otherwise. Beauty it was ours to see in all its

> brightness in those days when, amidst that happy company, we beheld with out eyes that blessed vision, ourselves in the train of Zeus, others following some other god; then were we all initiated into that mystery which is rightly accounted blessed beyond all others; whole and unblemished were we that did celebrate it, untouched by the evils that awaited us in days to come; whole and unblemished likewise, free from all alloy, steadfast and blissful were the spectacles on which we gazed in the moment of final revelation; pure was the light that shone around us, and pure were we, without taint of that prison house which now we are encompassed withal, and call a body, fast bound therein as an oyster in its shell.
>
> (*Phaedrus* 250b-c)

Plato here acknowledges that particular examples of eccellence of moral character do not have the ability, by virtue of their very perception, to fire the perceiver with passionate desire and attraction. Unlike beauty, wisdom as the culmination of all moral ἀρετή is not apparent, even in an imaged form, to physical sight. Thus Plato recognizes a difference between the aesthetic mode of ἔρως on the one hand and the rational, moral mode on the other.

Plato's distinction between "the train of Zeus" and "the train of other gods" is significant in this regard:

> Now if he whom Love has caught be among the followers of Zeus, he is able to bear the burden of the winged one with some constancy, but they that attend upon Ares, and did range the heavens in his train, when they are caught by Love and fancy that their beloved is doing them some injury, will shed blood and not scruple to offer both themselves and their loved ones in sacrifice. And so does each lover live, after the manner of the god in whose company he once was, honoring him and copying him so far as may be, so long as he remains uncorrupt and is still living in his first earthly period, and in like manner does he comport himself toward his beloved and all his other associates. And so each selects a fair one for his love after his disposition, and even as if the beloved himself were a god he fashions for himself as it were an image, and adorns it to be the object of his veneration and worship.
>
> (*Phaedrus* 252c-d)

Those who are possessed by the divine madness of Love and who travel in the entourage of Ares, the blood-thirsty, impulsive and unpredictable god of war, will commit serious offenses against the virtues of σωφροσύνη and δικαιοσύνη. In a word, they will be like that disorderly chariot in which the unruly steed runs wild. Clearly Plato envisions that many forms of divine possession by Eros will seriously contravene the life of reason and moral virtue.

Indeed, it would appear that only in the train of Zeus, in whom σοφία reigns supreme, and who rules and orders all according to his great wisdom, might a mortal human being be a lover of wisdom. No doubt Plato would recognize other, more blessed, divine companies that that of Ares, such as, most notably, those of Athene and Apollo. For it was their function to inspire the poet, the sculptor, the painter or the architect with aesthetically perceived forms—the realization of a form discerned in the imagination in a plastic medium. This aesthetic mode of discerning lovely, divine form did not entail giving a λόγος, which was of course a prerequisite of the philosophical mode. Those, however, who followed the Socratic philosophical way belonged in the train of Zeus.

> Thus the followers of Zeus seek a beloved who is Zeuslike in in soul; wherefore they look for one who is by nature disposed to the love of wisdom and the leading of men, and when they have found him and come to love him they do all in their power to foster that disposition. And if they have not aforetime trodden this path, they now set out upon it, learning the way from any source that may offer or finding it for themselves, and as they follow up the trace within themselves of the nature of their own god their task is made easier, inasmuch as they are constrained to fix their gaze upon him, and reaching out after him in memory they are possessed by him, and from him they take their ways and manners of life, in so far as a man can partake of a god. But all this, mark you, they attribute to the beloved, and the draughts which they draw from Zeus they pour out, like bacchants, into the soul of the beloved, thus creating in him the closest possible likeness to the god they worship. (*Phaedrus* 252e-253a)

There are two striking features of this passage: the first is that it stands as a thinly veiled reference to Socrates: love for Socrates is a divine Eros, and Socrates is an image of Zeus, who represents the highest embodiment of divine σοφία.[6] The second remarkable feature is its complete contrast to Alcibiades' speech in the *Symposium*. Let us consider these points at some length.

Physical beauty was a visible image of true, divine Beauty, but of divine Wisdom itself, the object of the philosopher's love, there was no *visible* image. A quantum leap from the outward and physical to the inner realm of intellectually discerned reality was required. The discontinuity was emphasized in Socrates' case by his thoroughly unlovely physical appearance. One had to open Socrates up and peer inside in order to perceive the god in him. Alcibiades, unable to keep his lower nature in check and raise his soul to the life of reason and the vision of heavenly reality, was confused and irritated. He was caught in the interplay of the two steeds, unable to make the steep ascent. He could not penetrate beyond appearance to the inner mystery of the Socratic way as a condition of life. Alcibiades complains in the *Symposium*:

> What [Socrates] reminds me of more than anything is one of those little sileni that you see on the statuaries' stalls; you know the ones I mean—they're modeled with pipes or flutes in their hands, and when you open them down the middle there are little figures of the gods inside. And then again, he reminds me of Marsyas the satyr. . . . Now the only difference, Socrates, between you and Marsyas is that you can get just the same effect without any instrument at all—with nothing but a few simple words, not even poetry. Besides, when we listen to anyone else talking, however eloquent he is, we don't really care a damn what he says. But when we listen to you, or to someone else repeating what you've said, even if he puts it ever so badly, and never mind whether the person who's listening is man, woman, or child, we're absolutely staggered and bewitched. And speaking for myself, gentlemen, if I wasn't afraid you'd tell me I was completely bottled, I'd swear on oath what an extraordinary effect his words have had on me—and still do, if it comes to that. For the moment I hear him speak I am smitten with a kind of sacred rage, worse than any Corybant, and my heart jumps into my mouth and the tears start into my eyes—oh, and not only me, but lots of other men.
>
> Yes, I've heard Pericles and all the other great orators, and very eloquent I thought they were, but they never affected me like that; they never turned my whole soul upside down and left me feeling as if I were the lowest of the low. But this latter-day Marsyas, here, has often left me in such a state of mind that I've felt I simply couldn't go on living the way I did. (215a-216a)

Plato, unlike Alcibiades, was able to discern the "god" in Socrates. In Socrates divine wisdom had become physically manifest, not to physical eyes, but for one whose intellectual vision could penetrate to the divine mysteries. For those with eyes to see, the life of Socrates became an "image", leading to the vision of divine reality. For those who had gained admittance to the path, those who had glimpsed the sublime mysteries through ceaseless, negative dialectic and attained to the philosophical way as a new condition of being, Socrates became a paradigm, an incarnate pattern or image of divine σοφία. The human emotional ties of disciple to mentor served to lead one to divine Wisdom just as surely as physical beauty led one to divine Beauty.

Nonetheless, despite Plato's implicit view that the disciple's love for the master was an *emotional image* of that transcendental intellectual vision of divine Good-Beauty, the same cannot be true for Socrates himself. We are left with an evidently ironic profession of erotic attraction to the beauties of youth. Socrates' real mind has been revealed behind the mask of dissemblance: the direct and immediate object of Socrates' love is absolute Good-Beauty itself; and it is only because he is "reminded" of the divine Good-Beauty that the physical beauties of youth have any erotic impact on him at all. Properly speaking it is only by virtue of the attractive, possessing power of this transcendent ideal that Socrates can be said to be under the influence of ἔρως.

By taking into account the ironic factor in Socrates' public self-understanding, and the metaphorical element in Plato's account of ἔρως, we have discerned something of Socrates' own real mind. Yet the fact of irony itself still remains to be explained: what is the significance of negativity and paradox in the Socratic way? why did Socrates insist on hiding his real mind behind the public *persona* of ignorance and irony? To ask such questions is to seek to gain access to the hidden recesses of Socrates' personality, and to go beyond the bounds of Plato's explicit testimony. In order, then, to penetrate to this deepest stratum of the Socratic paradox, in order to gain a vantage point for critical reflection, we are forced to take an indirect route: to that end we now turn to consider the interpretation of Socratic irony of one of the greatest thinkers of the last century.

2. Kierkegaard and Hegel on Socrates.

Soren Kierkegaard, in his study, *The Concept of Irony*,[7] viewed irony as the essence of Socrates. Socratic irony was infinite, absolute negativity. Socrates' negative, destructive questioning left nothing but an emptiness. This was as true for Socrates as for those he questioned: for Kierkegaard there was no positive content constituting the mind of Socrates behind the negative, ironic method. Nonetheless this infinite, absolute negativity of Socrates was for Kierkegaard a fact pregnant with significance. It meant that through his infinite negativity Socrates had risen above all actualities and determinations of life (whether concrete or notional) and self-consciously confronted the fact of his existence in its totality before the empty, infinite mystery of the cosmos. Socrates thus constituted a world historical turning-point: he had taken the first step toward the Idea, that state of self-conscious reflection independent of tradition-bound, socially determined existence, which was in turn necessary before a return of reflective self-consciousness to concrete actuality, which would thus complete the circular dialectic of an authentic human existence. To Kierkegaard, then, Socrates was wholly negative and empty; he was wholly negatively related to the historical actuality in which he lived. His stance in life was to remain poised (to "hover") at the edge of the abyss without being able to make the leap across to the infinite positivity of the Idea (a privilege reserved for Plato).

For Kierkegaard irony was a category of authentic *human* existence: it was not a religious category, though it did prepare the way for faith, which was the authentic human response to revelation (for which Socrates, of course, lacked the opportunity). Through his irony Socrates was wholly negatively related to his age, including the religious life of his age. Socratic irony represented a necessary first, negative phase in an authentic human existence, and was only a preparation for the leap of faith (which Kierkegaard would distinguish sharply from religion), the ultimate, consummate phase in an authentic human existence.

In thus conceiving Socrates' historical relationship to his age in wholly negative terms Kierkegaard followed in the footsteps of Hegel. Indeed, Kierkegaard's whole interpretation of Socrates may be seen as a transposition of Hegel's interpretation of Socrates from the speculative level to the level of personal, individual existence. Thus, at many points, Kierkegaard follows Hegel in the latter's (implicit) view that there was no authentic, intrinsic religious dimension to Socrates' thought. Though Kierkegaard transposed Hegel's speculative interpretation of Socrates on to the level of personal, individual life, for him too there was no authentic religious dimension to Socrates' thought.

In Hegel's view Socrates attained intellectual insight into the abstract, universal principles of moral conduct through individual reflection in his own consciousness.[8] Socrates represents the dawn of moral consciousness insofar as there emerges with him the consciousness of self as an independent critical subject over against the social organism. In the project of critical reflection on custom (νόμος, or *Sittlichkeit* in Hegel's thought), the way things are, and always have been, done in the πόλις, Socrates became conscious of himself as a moral individual over against, and sitting in judgment of, the social order. Hegel differentiated Socrates from the sophists not with respect to the subjectivity of the rational, critical form of consciousness (for in this they concurred), but insofar as Socrates reflected the universality and objectivity of what was revealed within the individual's moral reflection (which was lacking in the sophists). Thus, to Hegel Socrates represents the emergence of critical moral *reason*, which challenged the old unreflective and non-rational synthesis. Hegel discerned no intrinsically religious dimension of Socrates' conduct of philosophy: in Hegelian terms Socratic philosophy represented the dialectical negation of Greek religiousness.

Hegel viewed Greek religion as the product of a free, self-conscious act of artistic creation on the part of Spirit: through the poets in the verbal mode and the sculptors in the plastic mode, Spirit became conscious of itself through acts of the artistic imagination or fantasy. Spirit brought itself, that is, the spiritual, to consciousness through the imaginative *idealization* of nature (seeing the *ideal* in nature). In the Homeric depiction of the gods and the sublime sculptures of the Periclean age the Spirit became conscious of the spiritual under the aspect of beauty. In the hands of the Greek poets and sculptors Spirit became transparently manifest in the material, the concrete, and the specific (in the case of poetry, not physically, but imaginatively). Thus Greek religion was for Hegel a religion of beauty. Through the concrete, aesthetic mode of experience the Greeks had attained a state of perfect harmony and equilibrium between Spirit and Nature, between Thought and objective Reality. They were perfectly, spiritually at home in the world as no civilization before or since. They experienced no alienation between themselves and the world about them; thus they experienced no need for reconciliation or salvation. (It was for this reason that Greek aesthetic-religious culture stood as an ideal for Hegel, for it was a principal aim of Hegelian philosophy to overcome antinomies by a higher resolution, or synthesis, of the opposed principles.) Nor did their religion alienate the Greeks from themselves, for the gods were nothing more than an idealized humanity.

In terms of Hegelian philosophy it was the function of art and religion to bring to consciousness the common, universal *truths* of the Spirit. Thus religion and art were ultimately to give way to philosophy, in which Spirit became conscious of itself in its own proper, that is, universal and abstract, terms. Thus, for Hegel religion did not have any authentic, specifically religious content: it was merely a non-reflective, non-rational expression of Spirit. It was an expression of Spirit before it became self-conscious, critical *reason*. Though Kierkegaard replaced Hegel's abstract, objective reason with subjective individuality he nonetheless concurred with Hegel in this non-religious reading of Socrates and his relation to the Greek religious tradition.

The lasting value of Kierkegaard's study of Socrates lies precisely in its attendance to deep structures, and in its serious attempt to formulate a holistic view of the phenomenon of the Socratic way. Of prior significance to particular discussions and arguments, or even to their sum-total, was the implicit fact that in his philosophical activity Socrates the individual had confronted his own existence in the wide universe, or in Kierkegaard's phrase, before the absolute infinity of the universe. All, including the individual subject himself, was submitted to the rational tribunal within consciousness. Socrates had reflectively, consciously confronted the fact of his existence, not as Greek, as Athenian, as a member of such and such phatry, deme, etc., but as a mortal human being. Not that the meaning of life (either of the world as a whole or of his own individual existence) was ever the subject of philosophical discussion. Rather, it was the ignorance and irony which informed the conduct of philosophy that represented Socrates' understanding of his existence, as well as his personal response to that understanding. Socrates' life-stance was *expressed by* his conduct of philosophy; it was not a matter for direct enunciation *in* his conduct of philosophy.

In viewing Socrates against the stark, empty infinity of the absolute, Kierkegaard found no positivity in Socrates. Both Hegel and Kierkegaard spoke of the world historical importance of Socrates: Hegel thought of Socrates as a critical moment in the world historical dialectic of *Geist*; Kierkegaard thought of Socrates as the individual who transcended history, the individual who self-consciously came to grips with his own existence before the absolute. Yet, as important and illuminating as his "correction" of Hegel's interpretation was, in the last analysis Kierkegaard neglected and obscured the positive historical relationship of the Socratic philosophical way to the Greek tradition, and particularly to the Greek religious experience of life. That positive historical continuity lay in the central category of the Socratic way, ἀρετή. Socrates was wholly preoccupied with the care of the soul, which was the pursuit of ἀρετή, personal excellence, virtue, character. Socrates was wholly, even absolutely, committed to ἀρετή: to speak in terms of Plato's religious metaphor, Socrates was possessed by divine ἀρετή. But ἀρετή was the central category of Greek civilization: the whole of the Greek experience of life was shaped around it. In the rapidly changing circumstances of late fourth-century Athens traditional thinking about ἀρετή was undergoing a severe test. The basic value system of Greek culture was in the process of redefinition. Socrates' *via philosophiae* was a response to that cultural confusion: indeed, it was, in a sense which we shall elucidate below, *a specifically religious response* to the cultural upheaval in Athens at the close of the Periclean era. The Socratic way was a reformulation and revitalization of some of the essential features of the Greek religious experience of life. But in order to see how this is the case an understanding of the religious attitudes and convictions informing the traditional ἀρετή ethic is necessary. To this end we undertake at this point an analysis, both phenomenological and structural, of the Greek religious world-view, particularly as it was authoritatively enunciated, in an imaginative literary-pictorial mode, in the epics of Homer.

3. The Religious Experience of Homeric Man.

The *Iliad* is Homer's epic account of the deeds and words of the gods and heroes of old as they contributed to the siege of the great Trojan city, Ilion. The *Iliad* is a dramatic restaging in epic poetry of that epoch-making event, a scene by scene reconstruction in our imagination. Everything is vividly pictured for us, everything is three-dimensional and concrete. The *dramatis personae*, both gods and men, move and act before our mind's eye. Poetic artistry serves the representation of what happened, of what was said. Of course, Homer is not interested in recording "the bare historical facts." He is interested in the full meaningfulness of the events. The gods are the principal means Homer uses to draw out this greater significance. His purpose is to eulogize the deeds of the heroes and thus to set them up as ideal patterns of what a Greek of excellence and nobility is like. Though the primary focus is thus on the deeds of men, the gods are essential to the process of idealization. Indeed, to reveal the divine personage whose hand is at work *is* Homer's way of showing the greatness of the heroes' deeds, for the mark of the greatness of a mortal deed is the intervention of a god.

When we consider these Olympian immortals in themselves, however, as Homer so vividly portrays them moving behind the scenes intervening here and there at critical points in the action, there is little that is noble or dignified about them, much less evocative of deep religious emotions of awe or reverent submission before the sublime. They are depicted as a privileged society of immortals who dwell up above the heavens in a region of bright, etherial light (or alternatively, atop Mount Olympos) and spend their days without end in self-centered leisure and indulgence of their appetites. They are motivated in their dealings with men essentially by vanity and self-interest: that is, by the gifts and flattery of mortals. And when denied such gratifications, or when they have their honor flouted in any way by god or man, they react with a sulky petulance befitting a child. Throughout the *Iliad* the sons and daughters of Zeus direct their bitter invective at one another. And their foibles and antics are notoriously all too human. Zeus, for instance, the ultimate authority in heaven and on earth, is depicted as easily swayed and fickle in his decision-making, though stubborn and willful once his mind is made up. And he is easily seduced and duped by his wife Hera, and at times found to be quite ignorant of what is going on about him, or behind his back. Hera, the first lady of Olympos, is depicted as a shrewd, scheming, nagging wife who is filled with venomous spite when she does not get her way. The lovely divine maiden Athene, Zeus' beloved daughter and favorite (though throughout the period of the

Iliad there is a temporary falling out), can be as ruthless and bloodthirsty as the mad god of war, Ares. In the Homeric gods, then, we would not seem to have the stuff of a profound religious experience of life.

It is hardly surprising, then, that many modern commentators have failed to see anything particularly religious in Homer's world-view:

> To some classical scholars the Homeric poems will seem a bad place to look for any sort of religious experience. "The truth is," says Professor Mazon in a recent book, "that there was never a poem less religious than the *Iliad*." This may be thought a little sweeping; but it reflects an opinion which seems to be widely accepted. Professor Murray thinks that the so-called Homeric religion "was not really religion at all"; for in his view "the real worship of Greece before the fourth century almost never attached itself to those luminous Olympian forms." Similarly Dr. Bowra observes that "this complete anthropomorphic system has *of course* no relation to real religion or to morality. These gods are a delightful, gay invention of the poets."[9]

On the surface of things there is much to be said for this non-religious reading of Homer. In general Homer seems to take the gods for granted. As Wilamowitz put it, "*Die Götter sind da*,"[10] that is, the gods are simply objective facts of life, part of the basic furniture, so to speak, of Homer's universe, who need to be duly acknowledged in appropriate circumstances. But such an attitude is not conspicuously religious or profound. For the most part, Homer's preoccupation with the gods seems to be governed by artistic rather than religious considerations. However, Walter Otto, in his study, *The Homeric Gods*, takes an entirely different view of the matter:

> [The impression of the strangeness and remoteness of ancient Greek religion to modern man] is most striking for the observer who looks not at the centuries of waning creativity but rather at the early age of genius whose first and greatest monument is the body of Homeric poems. This is the period where belief in the gods was maintained with the liveliest conviction; and it is precisely here that conceptions of the divine have so little capacity to touch the heart of modern man directly that many critics have denied them any religious content whatever.
>
> This is understandable, and yet most extraordinary. Consider Homer, who is the prime object of the charge. We admire not only the art of his poems but also the richness and depth and grandeur of his thought. Who could think of attributing superficial views on cosmic issues to a work which can still thrill us after nearly three thousand years? And yet upon his belief

in gods we bestow an indulgent smile at best, or we explain him as a primitive—as if in a world so spiritually mature a primitive belief would not be the greatest paradox of all. Is not the fault to be found in the prejudices of the critics themselves? One may truly wonder at the assurance with which judgment is passed upon a nation's most inspired ideas on matters of supreme import without testing whether the position assumed produces valid insights into an alien realm of thought.[11]

For the purposes of the present inquiry we shall proceed on the assumption, following Otto, that the non-religious reading of Homer is *prima facie* the most extraordinary and improbable one, and that rather what is most likely is that we have simply lost the key to the interpretation of the religious dimension of Homer's world-view. Thus we address ourselves to the following question: what *experience of life* does the Homeric pantheon represent? Instead of treating Homer's religion as consisting simply of belief in and cultic obeisance to putative beings in some Olympian heaven where we today discern none—thus forcing us to treat it as something supernatural, something quite inscrutable and opaque to our understanding—can we translate it into terms we can recognize from our own experience? Our aim, then, is to penetrate beyond the explicit terms of Homer's artistically elaborated depiction of the gods to the religious experience of life implicit therein.

The key to the interpretation of the religious experience of Homeric man is the *Götterapparat*. The Homeric *Götterapparat* refers to the use the poet makes of the Olympian pantheon to effect the course of events at particular points: that is, by their intervention in the human sphere the gods determine the development of the plot (despite its various twists and turns, the realization of Zeus' will to give Achilles his day of great glory) at critical junctures. Through this device the gods, an independent, parallel society, emerge in the world of human experience. The identity of the god acting in the various scenes of the epic drama is of course known to Homer's audience, but only infrequently is the god's identity discovered by the human characters of the *Iliad* and the *Odyssey*. This is because the poet's vantage-point is a privileged one. He is able to peer deep into the dimly remembered past and relate to his audience with utter concrete clarity and detail just what happened so many generations before on the far shores of the Aegean sea. In this act of poetic recollection and representation the poet is well assisted: he is inspired by the Muses. Through these daughters of Zeus who know everything that is happening or has happened (though not evidently everything that will happen) the poet lays claim to knowledge which is not given to men to know —not only precise knowledge of events in a foregone era, but also who the divine actors were who moved behind the scenes and accounted for the numerous shifts in the action.

Even in those relatively infrequent episodes where a god is revealed to a privileged human character there is a distinction to be made between the dramatic pictorialization of the episode and its real, operative, functional lines of force. For instance, in Book One of the *Iliad* Athene intervenes to stop Achilles' fury (193 ff.). Achilles has become furious with Agamemnon and ponders, divided in mind, whether to draw his sword and seek revenge or to check his wrath. Into this breach steps Athene, at Hera's behest. Appearing in bodily form behind Achilles, she catches him by the hair: Achilles turns and, alone of all those present, recognizes her awesome gaze. The theophany is curiously—and magically—personal and individual. However, it is by her words and not her gaze that Athene accomplishes her purpose (which is ultimately Hera's). She directs Achilles to a certain course of action and Achilles obediently assents. He is to hold in his anger, except to chastise Agamemnon verbally. For this forbearance he will receive at some time in the future three times over the gifts and honor momentarily denied him. Now, one can easily distinguish here between the pictorial dramatization and the real, operative lines of force in the episode. It is by her gaze that the goddess is identified as Athene, but it is through her words that she accomplishes her purpose: through her intervention a thought is placed in Achilles' mind which happens to be Hera's will in the situation. It is not the point of the theophany to reveal anything *about* Athene or Hera, but rather to make occur to Achilles a possible course of action which is Hera's wish. The poet's inspired insight enables him to identify whose divine will was behind the decision Achilles took. The mysterious quasi-bodily theophany is merely the artistic technique the poet used to convey this to his audience.[12]

The most characteristic activity of the gods in their dealings with men in the *Iliad* is putting μένος in the breasts of favored warriors. Μένος is the surge of valor, the sense of courage and bravado welling up inside the breast; it is the divinely given surcharge of feeling that impels one to valiant, fierce conduct in battle. Let us take as an illustration the numerous descriptions of inspirations of μένος in the Diomedeia, the poet's depiction of the great day of glory of the Achaian warrior, Diomedes, commencing with the opening of Book Five. The opening verses stand as a summary of the detailed account to follow:

> There to Tydeus' son Diomedes Pallas Athene
> granted strength and daring, that he might be conspicuous
> among all the Argives and win the glory of valour.
> She made weariless fire blaze from his shield and helmet
> like that star of the waning summer who beyond all stars

> rises bathed in the ocean stream to glitter in brilliance
> Such was the fire she made blaze from his head and his shoulders
> and urged him into the middle fighting, where most were struggling.[13]

Here it is said that Athene simply "gave" (δῶκε) courage and might (μένος καὶ θάρσος) to Diomedes. Later Diomedes prays to Athene for her intercession in a specific encounter. The goddess responds by "putting" (ἧκα) μένος in his chest, then speaking to him to tell him *that* she did. At 5.782 ff. Hera takes on the likeness of Stentor and through his great voice "stirred up" (ὄτρυνε) the μένος and θυμός in each man. At 513 Apollo is said to "thrust" or "cast" (βάλε) μένος into the chest. At 10.482 μένος is "breathed" (ἔμπνευσε) into the breast. Much later (17.210-12) there occurs the most unusual description of all: Ares is said to enter Hektor "so that the inward body was packed full of force and fighting strength."

What is striking is the variety and ambiguity of the relationship of the μένος to the deity. Sometimes the god puts the μένος in the breast directly and without any visible manifestation of self. At other times the inspiration takes place through a magical transformation of the god into some human whose words stir up the μένος in the breast of the hero. Or at still other times it may be just men who by their words stir up the μένος in their comrades. Thus at *Iliad* 11.284 ff. Hektor calls out to his troops admonishing them to "remember [their] furious valour" (that is, to call forth the sense of courage they had formerly). The poet continues with the formula used of the gods' inspirations, "So he spoke, and stirred the spirit and strength in each man."[14] It is interesting to compare *Iliad* 10.475 ff. where Odysseus' words to Diomedes spur him on to great valor. There we find an intermediary form of the formula: "He spoke, and grey-eyed Athene breathed strength into Diomedes and he began to kill them one after another." It is a human who speaks but a god who causes the μένος. It is likely that some such formula is to be understood in the above examples of humans inspiring humans: it is their fuller, appropriate characterization. We would in that case be expected to suppose that there are two levels in operation. Through the words of the human warrior and leader the god acts to bestow the gift of valor. If we suppose such a two-level theory implicit in these Homeric formulae we can see how superfluous and over-determined are those other forms of μένος-inspirations, the gods assuming human form. Such transfigurations seem to add nothing to the religious dialectic of the situation, and appear to be merely a *façon de parler*. The words spoken are perceived by the human actors in the situation to be the instrument or occasion of that which is not in human hands to give. The transfigurations of the gods in the form of men are over-elaborate representations of the fact that deities are co-agents, with the human speakers, of the divine result. Or to put the point more theologically, they are the real agents of the valor; men are mere occasions. The account of Poseidon's μένος-inspiration in Book Thirteen (59-80) is especially noteworthy, for it allows us to translate Homer's dramatic representation into human experience. The poet tells us that the agent of the inspiration is Poseidon, but the two Aias's relate to us the human experiential element. Their words are an exact account of what part of the inspiration-theophany is manifest to human experience. Kalchas the seer has been talking to them; his words have evidently become the occasion of a "divine" inspiration. But although the poet tells us that the agent is Poseidon, shaker of the earth, the two Aias's know only that "some one of the gods" (τις θεῶν), one of the Olympians (οἳ Ὄλυμπον ἔχουσι), they believe, has acted through Kalchas. The poet marks the divine happening by two rather disparate signs: the appearance of a hawk (a divine omen to the early Greeks) and the curious mention of the divine form of Kalchas' legs—it is not Kalchas but a god in disguise. But the human truth remains clearly distinguishable from the magical transformations, and the magical transmission (by magic wand or staff) as well: the inspiration they have received is not simply the result of Kalchas' words to them. Though their own experience does not permit them to penetrate to it, another dimension, the sphere of unknown divine agents, must be taken into account.

As the above examples suggest, there is a systematic discrepancy between the poet's vivid *pictorial, magical dramatization* of events and the *experience* of Homeric man. In this connection let us consider the role of magic in Homer's epics.

The relative escalation of the magical element in the *Odyssey* has often been noted. Indeed, Athene has become a mistress of magical powers and transformations—a kind of fairy god-mother. She transforms Odysseus into a ragged, wizened old man and back again with a wave of her wand (*Odyssey* 13.396 ff.; 16.172 ff.; 16.207 ff.). She causes a magical mist to drift about him to make him invisible (*Odyssey* 7.14, 41, 139). At 13.189 she pours a mist over Odysseus' own countryside to make it unrecognizable to him. And she even transforms herself into a bird and flies away from the scene on a number of occasions.[15]

This sort of marvellous event is not unusual in Homer: magic is one of the ingredients in the Homeric synthesis. This is true even of the *Iliad*, where, however, it is a more occasional element. On one occasion Athene is said to transform herself into a vulture (*Iliad* 7.59), and at one crucial moment in the drama Athene snatches up Achilles' first spear cast and returns it to him while remaining invisible to Hektor (22.276). A snake-omen is struck to stone at *Iliad* 2.318-19. Athene sends a golden cloud (halo?) to encircle Achilles' head and a bright flame to shine above it—magical manifestations of his great honor and valor and might as a warrior (*Iliad* 18.203 ff.). More frequent are the mentions of a magical mist, often as a means the gods use to rescue humans from the battle (*Iliad* 3.380; 5.344; 20.321; 21.597) and sometimes to prevent themselves from being seen (14.346; 15.307; 16.788; 20.443).

The magic we are speaking of here, of course, is not ritual magic, sometimes called sympathetic magic, which is the attempt to copy the workings of certain powers, natural or supernatural, to establish a kind of ritual or formulary power of suggestion, as it were, over them in order to bring them to bear on the immediate situation. The magic of Homer's epics is of a different sort. It belongs under the heading of folklore, that is, the exercise of the literary imagination to *entertain*. There is no ritual or in any sense religious dimension to the magic in Homer. Magic is simply one species of the fantastic and extraordinary in the epics. It represents the sheer imaginative appeal of instantaneous, miraculous control over nature.

Now, there is nothing different in principle between the gods' magical transformations of men and things and their transformations of themselves. In both cases it is a matter of the power to change a bodily being instantaneously, at will. In a word, the theophanies (disguises in the first place, but also occasionally apparitions), and indeed the entire anthropomorphic Olympian *Götterapparat*, is a function of purely literary, non-religious, secular interests. They are a species of magic, which in turn is a species of folklore. But as we have already had occasion to see in particular respects, the *Götterapparat* is also the full literary elaboration of the religious experience of Homeric man. This is especially clear in the *Odyssey*. In Book One, for example, the poet tells us that it is Athene who appears to Telemachos in the guise of a stranger (the poet has given us a bird's-eye view of the gods in consultation formulating the plan Athene here sets in motion). The goddess departs from Telemachos by flying off like a bird leaving courage and might in his spirit (320). But all Telemachos discerns is that it must have been a θεός, a divinity. If we eliminate the magical element we are left with this: what the Homeric man *experiences* is a sense of inspiration and awe at the words of the stranger. He does not perceive the identity of the deity; that is the work of the poet's inspired divination. But he does *experience* the effect the stranger has on him *as* the work of some deity. A human speaks and some divine agency inspires; a man falls in battle and some transcendent power is credited with bringing about the occurrence; an idea, a plan occurs to a man and some deity is perceived to have communicated it to him; a man (or woman) steps forward with a handsome or beautiful or fearsome look about him and the action of some divinity is recognized—these are the principal forms of Homeric man's religious experience to be discerned behind the poet's artistic elaboration.

So far our treatment of the religious experience of Homeric man amounts to a structural analysis within the framework of its own categories of self-understanding. In what follows we shall attempt a more psychological interpretation: we shall attempt to recast three principal types of Homeric religious experience in terms of human experience as such: we shall concern ourselves with the μένος-inspiration, the divine "grace", and the divine "monition".

The μένος-inspiration, of which we have seen a number of examples above, expresses the truth that it is virtually impossible to prevail against a strong, gifted warrior once he is aroused. When he feels that surge of strength and might welling up, when he is moved to a wild fury, there is little for one without it to do except to give way. The *Götterapparat* represents the poet's magical over-determination of the basic experience of a natural "grace". Homeric man feels this valor come into him; it does not proceed from his conscious willing and thinking. Perhaps an illuminating analogy to us, a people with less familiarity with warfare, at least of the hand-to-hand combat type, is athletics. The most gifted, brilliant performer can be "hot" or "cold" and there is nothing he can do to change it. He may of course, if he is "cold", perform at a quite respectable level, falling back on habitual ability. But as long as the cold spell lasts he will miss some shots (pitches, passes, plays, or whatever) that would be easy to the relative beginner. He is lacking in his customary easy grace and rhythm—every move will be tight and a bit forced. Yet when the tide turns there is little a mere uninspired opponent can do. Everything works, he can do nothing wrong, and he can feel that this is so. A fluidity and complete confidence infuses him. He can execute moves which he never before executed. Yet the joy and frustration of these "inspired" and "cold" periods is that there is ever so little one can do to bring them on (or prevent them). An accomplished athlete of any modesty at all will continually speak of "luck" or "the breaks", and with no false modesty either. He perhaps better than anyone else knows how much this is so, not only in external circumstances, but in the mysterious mental factors as well. A dedicated athlete always tries, but a brilliant performance always comes as something of a surprise.

In the *Iliad*, a tale of war, the gods' principal activity is inspiration with courage and might, as well as interventions to prod the heroes to a certain course of action. But the *Odyssey* is a tale of adventures; accordingly Athene, whose presence there far overshadows that of any other god, is engaged in new activities. To be sure she still intervenes to direct the course of action—for example, her appearance in Book One as the stranger Mentes to encourage Telemachos to seek out news of his long-lost father; the goddess even outfits him with a precise plan and sets Telemachos in motion on the course of action we are to observe throughout the epic. But generally Athene appears in the *Odyssey* in a role we have not seen accentuated in the *Iliad*: she is the bestower of special *graces*. At *Odyssey* 2.1 ff. Telemachos is described emerging from his chamber in the morning; he is "like a god in presence" (θεῷ ἐναλίγκιος ἄντην). Athene has bestowed an enchantment of grace (χάρις) upon him. At *Odyssey* 6.224 ff. there is a fuller description of one of Athene's graces. Odysseus washes the brine that had encrusted him from his long hours in the sea. He anoints himself with olive oil and dresses,

> then Athene, daughter of Zeus, made him seem taller
> for the eye to behold, and thicker, and on his head she arranged
> the curling locks that hung down like hyacinthine petals.
> And as when a master craftsman overlays gold on silver,
> and he is one who was taught by Hephaistos and Pallas Athene
> in art complete, and grace is on every work he finishes,
> so Athene gilded with grace his head and his shoulders,
> and he went a little aside and sat by himself on the seashore,
> radiant in grace and good looks [κάλλεϊ καὶ χάρισι στίλβων]:
> and the girl admired him. (6.229-37)

At *Odyssey* 18.66 ff. Odysseus, disguised by Athene as a ragged old man, is challenged to a fist-fight. Athene stands close to him and magnifies his limbs so that his challenger and the onlookers are struck with awe.

There is another frequent grace bestowed by Athene in the *Odyssey*—the divinely restful, beautifying sleep bestowed on Penelope—that helps to shed light on this mechanism of the "revival of spirits" mentioned above:

> Then the goddess gray-eyed Athene thought what to do next.
> She drifted a sweet sleep over Ikarios' daughter,
> and all her joints were relaxed so that she slumbered reclining
> there on the couch. Meanwhile she, shining among goddesses,
> endowed with her gifts immortal, to make the Achaians admire her.
> First, for her beauty's sake, she freshened all her fine features
> with ambrosia, such as fair-garlanded Kytheria uses
> for salve, whenever she joins the lovely dance of the Graces.
> She made her taller for the eye to behold, and thicker

and she made her whiter than sawn ivory.
(*Odyssey* 18.187-96)[16]

Homer relates the effect of Penelope's entrance on the suitors:

Their knees gave way, and the hearts in them were bemused with passion,
and each one prayed for the privilege of lying beside her.
(212-13)

We must again attempt to project ourselves into the situation to discern what *experience* the poet wishes to mark. There are times when we merely sleep. We have been tired by our activities and we lie down for a rest. But there are a number of grades or qualities of sleep. In particular there is a certain kind of deep sleep from which we wake in a transformed state. In our normal conscious hours we are usually caught in particular roles; our conduct is governed by the expectations of both ourselves and others. Often this socialized self represents a narrowing and shallowing of the personality. We are perhaps more petty in our attitudes and conduct, and display less character and virtue than we might expect from our true potential selves.[17] It seems probable that neurosis is largely a conflict between the larger, deeper self, the self we would like to be, and the self which we have actually been able to realize in the concrete historical world. Yet sometimes, rarely, a sleep can accomplish a passing, partial breakthrough. On occasion a sleep can be so deep and profoundly restful that we awake with a wholeness which transcends the habitual level of existence whence we entered sleep. We possess a sense of being at one with ourselves and the world. Such a sublime state of inner peace and harmony cannot fail to show itself outwardly.

To return to the example of Penelope—a woman is not really beautiful if she merely possesses perfect features. For without that inner radiance and charm, that special brightness or play of light in the eyes, and that special spiritual grace manifesting itself in bodily movement, a woman is a mere pretty but essentially static object to look at, a lifeless mannikin. True beauty necessarily implies inner spiritual presence. Thus it is that a woman is not always uniformly beautiful. Indeed, as the Greeks deeply perceived, beauty is as much an *event* as it is a habitual possession. There is, of course, the permanent characteristic of physical beauty, but that is a relative thing. "True" or "divine" beauty is essentially a *manifestation in event*. It is such a sublime manifestation that the poet wishes to mark when Penelope comes forth from her chamber. Lacking a psychological mode of expression the poet resorts to the *Götterapparat*—but the reality he thereby describes is the sense of quiet, noble, radiant beauty Penelope exudes as she reenters the company from her sleep. The muscles have all relaxed; the tensions of normal, waking, socialized existence have eased. She is fully composed and at ease. Grace and tranquillity pervade the look of her face, her bearing, her every movement.

There is another domain of experience which must not go unexamined—what E.R. Dodds calls the divine "monition":

> Whenever someone has a particularly brilliant or a particularly foolish idea; when he suddenly recognizes another person's identity or sees in a flash the meaning of an omen; when he remembers what he might well have forgotten or forgets what he should have remembered, he or someone else will see in it, if we are to take the words literally, a psychic intervention by one of these anonymous supernatural beings.[18]

On the negative side there are the many visitations by the gods of ἄτη, fateful folly, on the minds of men.[19] Here again Homeric man experiences these as irruptions from without. And again from a pure phenomenological perspective it is not too hard to see the point of their description thus. When we ponder a matter for a long time we often "get into a bind"; no clear way through the impasse presents itself. We may stubbornly apply ourselves in the attempt to come up with the answer. But quite possibly, despite our most serious efforts, the impasse remains. Then, when and if the solution comes, it comes all of a sudden, in a flash of insight. It "occurs" to us—the common phrase in our language representing an accurate, appropriate description of the facts. We may, if we like, take a naturalistic (that is, reductionistic) view of the matter—in which case it will be seen only as our own mental powers coming through in the end. But this does not obviate the fact that what we here call "our own mental powers" is not co-extensive with our conscious experience. Label the source of the idea as we may, it does not proceed *from* our own conscious willing and thinking; it *comes into it*. And even if we take "our own mental powers" as a larger, unconscious, objective dimension to our own natural being, still a greater mystery remains. We are born with certain powers and learn to use them; we are appointed, as it were, their stewards. In our conscious activity we act as if they were subordinate aspects of our ego. But ontologically they are prior to our ego, and indeed form the very *grounds* (or materials) for it. Relative to the ego, these mental powers are "givens", given from where or whom we do not know. Yet the fact remains, we are "placed" in existence, and we "find" ourselves in the situation of managers of the particular set of characteristics and abilities we *happen* to possess. To reiterate, the *Götterapparat* (for example, Hera sending Athene to advise Achilles of her will), as well as the lower level δαίμων-interventions, are external representations of a basic inner experience of transcendence.

It would be the modern tendency to see these experiences in a subtle, and perhaps unconsciously, reductionistic fashion. To the modern, secular, scientifically-informed point of view the religious, transcendent dimension of these experiences is not itself a matter of *experience*—it is a superfluous, irrational extra. The feeling of courage, the occurence of an idea, the perception of radiant beauty (or a terrifying "look") are all purely "natural" processes. Everything is within our purview, everything belongs to the purely natural history of a physical organism.

But it is precisely at this point that the Homeric account would claim to be a precise description of what is *given* in human experience. It constitutes a direct, frontal challenge to the secular outlook: Homeric man would say that the transcendence is *given*, and that we moderns have become culturally blinded to it. The simple yet religiously profound truth is that we do not perceive any more than Homeric man did where a sense of courage, and insight, a beautiful or terrifying "look", moral determination, a brilliant musical performance "comes from", that is, what is involved in them in their totality. We cannot comprehend all the ingredients, all the dimensions that enter into these happenings. Our conscious life proceeds along a fairly narrow route. We think and we exert our wills, but in such instances as the above the happenings are radically incommensurable in their physical, intelligible and ontological reality with the amount of conscious thought and will we contribute to their outcome. Let us attempt to elucidate the point generally with an example not drawn from the Homeric poems.

Let us consider for a moment a person who has given a virtuoso performance on some musical instrument. Certainly an incalculable amount of conscious effort, practice and discipline has gone into such a performance. But the most basic factors are not those which are the direct outcome of conscious willing and thinking. For the performer simply *finds* himself born a human being, a human being who can think and learn, and in particular learn skills such as to play the violin. And he finds that his particular physical-motor-nervous constitution such that he can execute the most complicated, demanding piece with great power and sensitivity. When he succeeds in a virtuoso performance he realizes that his execution of the piece is not the simple and direct outcome of his *trying* to do so. It is rather that he manages forces and powers which are at once his and yet transcend him. This we suggest, at its most fundamental level, is the profound spiritual insight at work in Homer's use of the *Götterapparat* alongside the human factor to describe the special occurrences referred to above.

Certainly this outlook is strange to the modern mind which systematically ignores those dimensions of reality which do not fit within its ability to "explain" things. The spiritual outlook of modern technocratic man is geared only to that which he can manipulate and control. The world is a system of forces to be pressed until it yields up its secrets and then subjugated to man's own arbitrary needs and desires. There is no sense of a permanent, ultimate mystery of creation, the sense of wonder at the very fact of life and existence itself, that there *is* a world of infinite variety, beauty and complexity, both immediately experienced as well as more subtly approachable through theoretical and experimental science, and that the human situation as such is to be placed as a comprehending being in the midst of what is ultimately incomprehensible mystery. To a Greek there would be something profoundly irreligious, an expression of monstrous ὕβρις, in the spiritual horizon of technocratic man that the world is something which man holds *in toto*—if not already in fact, at least in principle—and which he can "grasp", comprehend, and submit to his will and domination. When, on the other hand, the Homeric world is understood from within it becomes clear that it is far from crude and primitive. It does not need to be explained away. On the contrary, it confronts modern man with a spiritually more profound and powerful way of experiencing the world than the technocratic outlook. And in contrast to the *tendency* in the western Christian religious tradition to place transcendence outside the bounds of all human experience and knowledge as human, human experience *as such* opens out on the mysterious. Man finds his natural experience caught up with processes that are much larger than human experience itself. And these dimensions are transcendental "givens" clearly perceived within human consciousness.

4. The Depth-Logic of Homeric Religion.

The Homeric gods are idealizations of human beings. We are dealing here with a commonly appreciated fact: the anthropomorphism of the Homeric gods. The very fabric of divine life and being is through and through of human form: the gods engage in the same activities as men, experience the same needs, act for the same values, and possess basically the same physical constitution, differing only in degree (of power, excellence, size, etc.). However, this truth is to be taken one step further. Homer conceptualizes the gods by taking the human condition as his basic model and imagining it in an ideal state. He does so by adding negative operators: he denies certain limitations of the human condition.

First of all, the gods are a class of bodily beings that do not die. The concept of the gods as the ἀθάνατοι is arrived at by a simple act of the imagination: the poet pictures in his mind (and asks us to picture in ours) a form of human existence that does not end. We are to imagine beings whose bodies remain forever at the apex of their development. They are born and grow to maturity, but there their development is perpetually arrested. Their flesh is not given to decrepitude and corruption. This in turn depends on another, analogous act of the imagination: imagining a kind of (magic) food and drink (nectar and ambrosia) which does not entail corruption of the flesh. Both ideas constitute a kind of negative theology, in an imaginative mode. We do not have to know what kind of food or drink it is, or what the mechanism of uncorrupting flesh is. All we need do is imagine a bodily existence which goes on and on just as it is pictured at the height of its development. Thus we conceptually prescind from a truth otherwise absolute and undeniable: that all flesh, having reached its acme, devolves; that death is the terminus for all bodily beings.

Similarly, with regard to the gods' magical powers of transformation. They all reduce to this: the gods are a class of bodily beings not (always, or absolutely) subject to the laws of nature, the ordinary laws of physical reality. The mental process implied in this conceptualization of the gods is no more difficult, abstruse or esoteric than that implied in a typical Grimms' fairy tale or a Walt Disney cartoon. Again, the concept of the gods is arrived at by imaginatively negating certain limitations of the human condition.

Implicit in these two Homeric characterizations of divine nature are two "theological principles": one is the principle that whatever is divine is pre-eminently more perfect, greater, nobler, more excellent than the human. The second principle, or rather fundamental assumption, is the adequacy of human nature as a conceptual model for the divine. The divine pre-eminence, as we have indicated previously, is not absolute or infinite, but rather subject to the limitations of the imagination. That is, the theological principle is governed and limited by the logically prior assumption of human nature as a conceptual model. It is only by transformations of the basic human model that the principle is realized. The limitations enforced on the realization of the principle by this prior assumption can be observed in the social sphere.

Commensurate with their status, and in observance of the theological principle, the gods are characterized as living in an ideal condition. They are believed to enjoy a completely happy, trouble-free existence in heaven. They do not have to toil, do not get sick, and of course do not grow old and decrepit. Even the weather is ideal on Olympos (*Odyssey* 6.41 ff.). They forever spend their time in leisure, enjoying themselves in the company of their peers. We can see here a kind of wish-fulfillment projected heavenward.

The supreme value for men, the apex of life for a Homeric hero, was the reception of honor from his peers. This was bestowed at the great courtly banquets where the warrior nobles sang the praises of each other's great valor, their great deeds in war. Nilsson once claimed that the honor of Homeric man depended more on what another man did to him than on what the man himself did.[20] This is true enough, but it appreciates only imperfectly the integral relationship between the deed and the honor. First comes the great deed; without great deeds there could be no honor. But the honor does not reside in the deeds themselves. Honor is rather the expression of the worth great deeds have in the eyes of society. The attainment of honor, the esteem of one's peers for deeds accomplished, is what motivated Homeric man. But the actual moment of glory was the reception of the praises of his peers in the public forum of the ἄριστοι, the communal banquet, and in particular the victory celebration. This was the climax of human happiness for the Homeric noble. All ἀρεταί, all a man's ability and might, were for this end: they served to attain this esteem. However, great though the glory might be, the labors and sufferings (and we might add, the risks) were great. And the glory too, when finally in hand, was a mere fleeting moment of exultation. For men, that is. It is precisely in this respect that the Homeric conception of divine society is an idealization (by way of a negative imaginative projection) of human society. The gods did not have to sweat and labor and struggle to attain such glory. They reaped without sowing, and they reaped without interruption or end. To bask eternally in glory and honor, as well as to enjoy the good life attendant upon such status, were the great blessings of those belonging to the race of the gods.

But precisely how does the assumption of human nature as the basic conceptual model limit the realization of the theological principle in this regard? Homer, we have seen, greatly developed and exploited the basic anthropomorphism of the gods for his own dramatic purposes. The *plurality* of the divine beings is a basic fact for Homer and the Greek society he immortalized. Deity, or the divine γένος, comprises a number of distinct individual beings. This is the basis for the divine drama which Homer relates. Because each god is a freely willing individual acting for his own ends, it is inevitable that the family of the gods comes into conflict. Eventually this means hatred, suffering, misery. In the epics they wound each other both physically and emotionally; they make each other frustrated and miserable, and even (what is the worst calamity for god or man) humiliated. On the one hand, there is in Homer the supposition that the lot of the gods is all happiness and blessings; man in contrast is doomed to unhappiness and suffering with only a meager portion of blessings. Yet what is given with the one hand is taken away with the other: because of the needs of drama the same fabric of existence as the human is projected upon the gods.

Similarly with respect to the belief that, commensurate with their status, the gods are eternally at leisure. Men must work,[21] but the gods are continually taken up with their own good pleasure. But since the gods' social life too is human in form, there are necessarily certain tasks to be performed. Thus Hephaistos must build the palaces and make the furnishings and the utensils. This exception to the rule of the gods' leisured existence is forced upon the poet (though of course the idea is not his creation) because of the necessities of the human form of the life of the gods, as well as the recognition of their dignity. For it would not be seemly for the accoutrements of divine life to be fashioned by mere human hands. We have, then, in effect, two principles, anthropomorphism and divine transcendent pre-eminence, working at cross-purposes. Rather than being perfectly consistent principles, the observance of the former hinders and restricts the observance of the latter.

So far we have concerned ourselves with the Homeric conceptualization of divine being, the very nature of the gods. Let us move for the moment from mythical ontology, as it were, to religion. What is the religious significance of divine beings so conceived?

The truth of the matter is that there is very little of *religious* significance in the gods *as* immortal, *as* supernatural beings with magical powers of transformation, *as* residents in a utopian leisured society. These features of divine existence do not become objects of religious yearning on the part of men. Rather they are the qualifications that constitute the gods as objects of reverence and obedience. The gods do not give of their immortality or their magical powers to men. Nor do they hold out the prospect of any kind of union or any sharing of the happinesses of Olympian life. Divine life is completely closed off to men, in death as well as in life. Even if we are to take the allusion to the Isles of the Blessed as an authentic Homeric belief, such blessed existence is nevertheless in a world apart from the divine realm. In fact, it is repeatedly emphasized in the tradition that it is distinctly *impious*, a sin of ὕβρις, to aspire to divine status in any of these three respects. So much is this the case, and so distinctive of Olympian piety through the centuries, that it needs to be recognized as a religious principle in itself. It constitutes a formal rule governing religious attitudes which is of the greatest importance in the mainstream of Greek religiosity. In a sense the criterion of piety was the degree to which a man *abjured* a claim or hope to the divine condition.

Though these defining characteristics of divine being did not enter into the divine-human relationship as *objects* of religious piety, they did enter in in another way. As we suggested above, they constituted the gods as a social class preeminently higher, nobler and more privileged than any human ἄριστοι. The gods were the ἄριστοι *par excellence*. This is far from a mere interesting analogy, for it explains the very nature of the relationship between gods and men. The relationship was in fact precisely the same as the secular relationship between lord and subject. Gods no less than men were motivated first and foremost by the maintenance of τιμή, honor or worth in the eyes of the society at large.[22] The gods, of course, were an exception in that they were not impelled by the desire to extend their material wealth and holdings—they already, by definition, possessed all they could desire.[23] But even for men there was an important distinction between actual wealth used and enjoyed (measured in land and flocks and herds, principally cattle) and wealth that was hoarded. The institution of gift-giving was a function of the latter. For Homeric man these gifts constituted valuations of worth; they were testimony of the individual's honor in the eyes of the giver. As such they were to be hoarded in the treasury and did not enter into use in the lives of the Homeric nobility (even though typically the items were designed for some use or other).

Gods were given gifts for the same reason human lords were given gifts: as honor-tributes. The gifts sacrificed to the gods were no more practically needed by them than were the gifts awarded to humans. Virtually all of popular, cultic religion, with its prayers and offerings, exemplifies this logic of honor-tributes. Indeed, religion comes down to a basic reciprocal relationship: men by their prayers and offerings render the gods τιμή; in return the gods grant men particular material favors. In short, Socrates' characterization of piety in the *Euthyphro* as "commerce with the gods" is quite apt.[24] Religion, from the human point of view, was not concerned with the gods in themselves, but rather in what the gods could give men: the *do ut des* concept of religion. The devotion and gratitude men displayed toward the gods was no genuine love, that is, love of the gods for what they were in themselves. Religious piety was thus the projection of a purely secular relationship. The *content* and *quality* of the conduct of religion did not express a genuine relationship to transcendence. This, however, is not to say that Homeric religion was not in *any* way the expression of a religious experience of transcendence—it is to say only that the formulation of that primal experience as a subject-lord exchange of τιμή for material favors was not genuinely religious.

In the Homeric scheme of things the gods, and particularly Zeus, perform an important function with respect to human morality: they uphold the authority of earthly laws and rulers.[25] Human morality, justice, right was a matter of "what is done." For Homeric man, just as for man in any other society, there was a code of behavior which ruled that some actions were acceptable and others unacceptable to society at large. Law was not a matter of conventional written statutes, but of tradition. Judgments and arbitrations always had their basis in customary practice. And the king, together with the warrior-nobility, was the depository of this knowledge of tradition. New legislation was of course always necessary, but this was judged for its "straightness" or "crookedness" on the basis of traditional practice. The θέμιστες were a set of laws only in the sense that they codified what the king together with his nobles in council took to be the traditional practice, based on the memory of "what was done" and on past judgments (δίκαι).[26] It is important to note that the θέμιστες constitute a system of customary law designating what practices were right and what wrong independent of and over against the authority of the king. They are the right practices independent of the king's will, and they judge his actions. This is clear from *Iliad* 16. 386-88 where Zeus is said to send storms to punish men for crooked θέμιστες passed in assembly, for driving out δική (that is, for departing from customary, "right" practices) and impiously thinking they could get away with it. Conversely at *Odyssey* 19.106 ff. we find the notion that Zeus rewards those kings who are righteous and fair in their dealings with the people they rule:

> as of some king who, as a blameless [ἀμύμονος] man and
> god-fearing [θεουδὴς],
> and ruling as lord over many powerful people,
> upholds the way of good government [εὐδικίας], and the black
> earth yields him
> barley and wheat, his trees are heavy with fruit, his
> sheep-flocks
> continue to bear young, the sea gives him fish, because of
> his good leadership, and his people prosper under him.

The θέμιστες are continually mentioned in Homer in conjunction with the institution of assembly (ἀγορά). At *Odyssey* 9.105 ff. the arrogant, coarse and uncivilized Cyclopes are contrasted with god-fearing men, who live under the reign of the Olympians, by their lack of assembly and laws. We can see here the seed of the later Greek pride in the democratic polity and their differentiation of themselves from the βάρβαροι on just this count. The Olympians are held to be the guardians of this civilized order.

No doubt this role of the gods, and more particularly of Zeus, as the sanctioning powers of the θέμιστες remained for the most part an empty pious theory. After all, the problem of the unjust man who prospered could emerge for later generations only because those in power had disregarded this sanction with impunity. The extraordinary statement at *Odyssey* 17.485-88 appears to be something of an exception, in that it credits the gods with very direct and active intervention in the affairs of men to enforce justice:

> For the gods do take on all sorts of transformations, appearing as strangers from elsewhere, and thus they range at large through the cities,
> watching to see which men keep the laws, and which are violent.

However, the connection with strangers and guests is significant. The θέμιστες surrounding hospitality were one of a set of institutions in which the gods played an exceptional role. For the most part the logic of right and wrong was based on personal honor and status. To commit a wrong was to transgress a person's honor; the wronged person subsequently had the right to seek vengeance or retribution. Thus the immediate sanctions of most θέμιστες were human and social, through αἰδώς (internalized sense of shame in the offender) and νέμεσις (the combination of righteous indignation, disapproval, disdain, and disgust on the part of the offended—the external counterpart of αἰδώς). Basically, justice was a matter of the offended individual (or his family) evening the score directly with the offender. It was the individual's responsibility to right his offended honor; the assembly and king essentially played the role of mere arbiter. However, in some respects the honor of Zeus was much more closely associated with the θέμιστες: respect for the stranger-guest (and all the protocol that went with hospitality), observance of funeral rites, respect for the suppliant (one who throws himself in an attitude of complete defenseless submission on the mercies of a strong man). In these areas the offense bore on Zeus himself and one could expect his vengeance for thus flouting his honor.[27] G.M. Calhoun makes a valuable observation regarding these institutions:

> It is worth noting that the offences which invite divine reprobation are precisely those for which human justice in a simple society will be least likely to offer adequate remedies—neglect of the dead, injuries to suppliants or guests, the perversion of justice. Religion enters the field of morals where secular custom does not suffice.[28]

That is, the general, vague rule of the justice of Zeus became more of a reality in those areas where the offended was not in a position to defend his honor and thus to uphold the θέμιστες.[29]

We have seen that the gods, particularly Zeus, function as *sanctions* of the authority of earthly laws, as well as of the authority of the earthly ruler. It now becomes important to consider in what sense or to what degree the gods are paradigms or models of action. We have already seen that the gods are not themselves the ends of human action, and that they do not hold out to men the prospect of any union or shared life and status. Is it the case that they serve as paradigms, moral or otherwise? In this connection we shall have to consider the logical relationship between the gods and the divine ἀρεταί with which they inspire men; and also what the relationship is between this system of ἀρεταί and morality as such (and even, as we shall see, in what sense there *is* a morality for Homeric man). Let us begin with an analysis of the value-system of Homeric man.

According to A.W.H. Adkins, ἀγαθός and ἀρετή represent the supreme value-words in Homeric society.[30] 'Αγαθός, the adjective, is used as a substantive to refer to the "good" or "noble" man. A man is (an) ἀγαθός by virtue of his possession of ἀρετή, in which is summed up all manly virtues and excellences, which Adkins calls the "competitive virtues."

> *Agathos* commends the most admired type of man; and he is the man who possesses the skills and qualities of the warrior-chieftain in war and . . . in peace, together with the social advantages which such a chieftain possessed. To be *agathos*, one must be brave, skilful, and successful in war and in peace; and one must possess the wealth and (in peace) the leisure which are at once the necessary conditions for the development of these skills and the natural reward of their successful employment.[31]

'Αγαθός and ἀρετή are not *moral* terms; though they are evaluative terms, they do not represent moral evaluations. Adkins, in his *Merit and Responsibility: A Study in Greek Values*, adduces a number of considerations in this regard: the following is offered as a summary of his account. The competitive virtues represent the supreme value which Homeric society put on the natural endowments and developed skills directly connected with warfare. The main concern of Homeric society was, of course, its own survival. It had to be strong enough to defends its order of life and its wealth against marauding forces. Thus, power was put into the hands of the individual (or more precisely, the class of individuals) who could best guarantee their survival. But the competitive virtues were not the only virtues held in esteem. There was another set of virtues which Adkins calls the "cooperative virtues." These represented the social or "quiet" virtues, values not crucial to the survival of society but rather to its good order. These virtues were represented by a set of adjectives: δίκαιος (just, fair, observant of "what is done," observant of another person's rightful claims), πινυτός (wise, understanding), πεπνυμένος (wise, prudent), σαόφρων (sensible, moderate), and we ought to add, even though Adkins, confining himself to the *Iliad*, neglects it, θεουδής (godly, pious, god-fearing).[32]

Through a close examination of Homeric usages of these terms Adkins has shown that the competitive virtues overrode the cooperative virtues. The claims of the latter always gave way, in the last analysis, to the former. The ἀγαθός could, out of his sheer power, disregard society's expectation that he be δικαιός, πινυτός, etc. That is, the exercise of his ἀρετή for his own ends, whether to increase his wealth or simply to accomplish his will, always outweighed the obligation to the cooperative virtue. Society was unable, or unwilling, to coerce him or to punish him. So far as the competitive virtues went, society did exert an efficacious sanction on the noble. If an ἀγαθός (a status-term as well as a conduct-term) did not exemplify the competitive virtues he incurred shame (αἶσχος). To be thus scorned by one's society was the ultimate disaster for a Homeric noble. But with regard to the cooperative virtues there was no such sanction of shame. This is evident in the *Odyssey* where the suitors dishonor the house of the king by a number of serious offenses against the code of conduct which the cooperative virtues represent: they devour the king's possessions, plot to kill his son, maltreat guests of his house, molest and violate the servant-women, and (in the person of Antinoös, one of the foremost among them) violate the debt of the suppliant. To do all this does not alter the fact that the suitors are ἀγαθοί; they do not thereby become κακοί (bad, low, inferior). Now, it is true that Antinoös himself terms the deeds of the suitors "bad" (κακὰ ἔργα, *Odyssey* 16.380), but that the word is not being used to denote moral evil should be clear from the fact that without hesitation Antinoös immediately terms the punishment they might receive from the assembly κακόν (381). Rather κακός, and its correlative ἀγαθός, are terms indicating whatever is "bad" or "good" for the honor of the noble, measured in public esteem, wealth and power.[33]

Adkins makes a further observation on the logic of κακόν:

> [T]o do *kaka*, to do harm, is not to be *kakos*; to be *kakos* is to be the sort of person to whom *kaka* may be done with impunity, since he cannot defend himself; and it is the condition which is *aischron*.[34]

Κακά are woes, misfortunes. They are things *suffered* (as opposed to moral evils, which are things *committed*). We find in evaluations of ἀγαθόν and κακόν a wholly amoral perspective. Subjective intention is consistently disregarded;[35] though Adkins notes a few exceptions, only tangible results are relevant.[36] One can look in vain in Homer for any word expressive of the *moral* badness of the one who commits a κακὸν ἔργον. Similarly with regard to expressions of guilt—Homeric nobles nowhere evidence a personal sense of guilt (conscience). It was shame, the feeling of being held in disrepute—a negative esteem, as it were—by one's society that sanctioned the code of conduct.

There are, however, difficulties with Adkins' interpretation. According to M.I. Finley:

> Even in the distribution of booty . . . the head of the *oikos* (household) or . . . king or commander-in-chief . . . was obviously bound by what was generally deemed to be equitable. The circumstance that no one could punish him for flouting custom, as in the conflict between Agamemnon and Achilles, is irrelevant to the issue. For the very fact that just such a situation gave the theme for the *Iliad* illustrates how dangerous the violation could be. In this world custom was as binding upon the individual as the most rigid statutory law of later days.[37]

Commenting on these remarks Adkins observes:

> This reflects the general situation: *agathoi* must be *pinutoi* most of the time, if only from lack of opportunity to be anything else.[38]

Apparently Adkins sees the force of the "must" in the obligation to the cooperative virtues to derive only from the force of circumstances. Evidently he feels that as soon as it was not in the interests of the ἀγαθός to observe the virtues he could and would ignore them—which is really a way of saying there was no moral obligation at all involved in their observance. It might be asked, however, just how true it is that most of the time the ἀγαθός, a man of power, lacked the opportunity to depart from "what was done" in order to pursue his own advantage. At any rate, Adkins' remark appears to agree with Finley's statement, but in fact fundamentally disagrees with it. Adkins makes this disagreement plain in the next, the *key* statement:

> It must be emphasized, however, that to say that Agamemnon 'was (normally) bound by what was agreed to be equitable' is not to say that Agamemnon was either legally or morally bound to act equitably. Since 'no one could punish him for flouting custom' (and since there are no laws to enjoin this), he cannot be legally bound; and since Homeric society cannot even censure Agamemnon effectively provided that his flouting of custom does not entail, as it does in the *Iliad*, failure to perform those functions which society demands of him, he cannot be morally bound either.[39]

The thrust of Adkins' assertion is that to say someone was normally bound by what was agreed to be equitable is not equivalent to saying that someone was legally or morally bound to act equitably. But "what was agreed to be equitable" in Homeric society was precisely customary right, or δίκη. As such it was *law*, all law in Homeric society being traditional, customary law, "what is done." All such law constituted a system of public morality that bound everybody. That is, the νόμοι, or θέμιστες, were by definition the set of legal-moral prescriptions designating what behavior was acceptable or not to the society. This does not mean in the least that they could not be violated with impunity; nor, for that matter, that they could be enforced. It only means that there was a (relatively) clear *sense* of what was right and wrong. Adkins' point that there was no formal legal machinery that could effectively be brought to bear on an ἀγαθός—*ante factum*, to force him to the right course of conduct, or *post factum*, to punish him—is to be granted. But that is a matter of the strength and effectiveness of the *sanctions*. And in this case the νόμοι of Homeric society had rather weak sanctions. Basically justice (essentially exacting revenge and retribution) was a matter to be settled directly between the offender (and his house) and the offended (and his house). Thus the sanctioning of the νόμοι in general depended on the power of the offended family. The assembly under the leadership of the king only entered the picture to adjudicate disputes and to deal with those matters that pertained to the commonwealth as a whole. Otherwise the sanctioning of the laws was left up to the gods, which of course depended on how god-fearing the ἀγαθός was. A powerful ἀγαθός might well know that he could get away with an offense against what was "right", against one of his peers or much more easily against one of his inferiors, and be willing to risk divine punishment, but this does not alter the fact that there *was* a code of right and wrong, even for him.

This public morality was the perfectly natural consequence of the hierarchical social structure—wrong was essentially a violation of a person's τιμή, honor. Within and between each social class there was a network of crisscrossing, reciprocal rights and claims bound up together with a protocol-system. As soon as this unstated code was violated the offended party had the sense of being "wronged". The *reality* of a moral code is clearly at work herein, even though it remains implicit in the workings of Homeric society; that is, even though Homeric man does not give expression in explicit terms to a moral consciousness, or conscience.

It might be pointed out that Adkins is certainly right in arguing that this legal-moral code was not sanctioned by shame. No ἀγαθός would incur shame or disgrace by committing such an offense. Yet it is interesting to consider that despite the general view today that Homeric society is not yet a guilt society,[40] there is guilt and moral conscience, albeit in under-developed form, implicit in this moral code. Because of the weakness of the sanctions the observance of the code of quiet virtues must have rested in part on Homeric man's knowledge that it was *right* to respect so-and-so's τιμή as an ἀγαθός, or the claim of a suppliant or guest, or to honor one's parents, or to give protection to a member of one's household. So there is warrant for attributing moral conscience (sense of fair play, respect for the code of social protocol, whatever one wishes to call it) as a subordinate "moment" in the Homeric ethic of ἀρετή.

The conflict between Achilles and Agamemnon in the *Iliad* is an interesting test case in the interpretation of the Homeric code of conduct. As we might expect, Adkins sees no "moral" dimension to the conflict: Agamemnon, according to Adkins, does not see the recompense he offers to Achilles (in the famous episode of Book Nineteen called Agamemnon's Apology) in the light of retribution for a moral wrong.[41] The only *wrong* the king acknowledges is a *mistake* in judgment. And only the conspicuous lack of success his course of action yielded brings him to recant, to admit he was wrong. But, Adkins stresses, he does not confess his mistake out of moral considerations. It was Agamemnon's due as supreme ἀγαθός to take what he could regardless of the claims of any quieter virtues. Indeed, it would have detracted from Agamemnon's ἀρετή and τιμή to give way to Achilles; the ethic of ἀρετή impelled him to override Achilles' claim to the maiden Briseis as his spoil.

We may suggest, however, an alternative reading. At *Iliad* 9. 109-13 the venerable old warrior, Nestor, intervenes in the discussion to beseech Agamemnon to consider making amends to Achilles on the grounds that the king refused honor to a great warrior on whom the very gods heap great honor. In effect, he is saying it is *wrong* to do such a thing. But Nestor goes further; he accuses Agamemnon of giving way to his "great-hearted spirit" (μεγαλήτορι θυμῷ, 109). "Yes," Agamemnon admits (119), "I lost my wits having been swayed in my wretched heart." We should note too that in the original scene of the conflict Nestor urged Agamemnon to "curb his spirit and check his rage" (*Iliad* 1.282). Agamemnon gives as the reason for this blind foolhardiness the ἄτη from the gods. It is to explain why he gave way to his emotions that he spins his tale of the gods who blinded him. We may agree with Adkins that Agamemnon's account is not meant to excuse himself from responsibility.[42] Nonetheless, Agamemnon does fail to point an accusing finger at himself in the speech. It is to be noted, however, that the gist of Nestor's speeches is much different. He charges Agamemnon directly with two specific offenses, the one the cause of the other, with no mention of the gods: Agamemnon is conducting himself improperly in letting his emotions run away with him and denying Achilles his rightful honor. Agamemnon has violated the code of τιμή because he failed to be πινυτός, πεπνυμένος or σαόφρων. It is to the aged mediator we must look for an unbiased reading of the situation; Agamemnon's speech is very likely to be an attempt at face-saving, an attempt to protect his kingly τιμή. Accordingly, we must disagree with Adkins' view that Agamemnon bore responsibility only for a mistake and not a moral error.

In every conflict, of course, there are two sides, and the same is true in this case—Achilles too offends against the quiet virtues. Agamemnon extends a most generous recompense to Achilles, more than enough to make up for the dishonor he has suffered at the king's hand, and it becomes the great warrior's lot to accept and submit to the commander-in-chief:

> All this I will bring to pass for him, if he changes from his anger.
> Let him give way. For Hades gives not way, and is pitiless,
> and therefore he among all the gods is most hateful to mortals.
> And let him yield place to me, inasmuch as I am the kinglier
> and inasmuch as I can call myself born the elder.
> (*Iliad* 9.157-61)

But Achilles' hatred still rages (strongly emphasized at 9.312, 378); he is not about to forget the wrong done to him. Indeed, this is an instance of a basic character-flaw in Achilles: he is the mightiest, awesomest warrior of all, but he is lacking in counsel and restraint of temper. Odysseus reminds Achilles of his father's words of advice:

> My child, for the matter of strength, Athene and Hera will give it
> if it be their will, but be it yours to hold fast in your bosom
> the anger of the proud heart, for consideration [φιλοφροσύνη] is better.
> Keep from the bad complication of quarrel, and all the more for this
> the Argives will honour you, both their younger men and their elder. (*Iliad* 9.254-58)

So Achilles too is wrong: refusing to recognize the rightful authority of the king, he too fails to exemplify the quiet virtues.

We see here that the quiet virtues are intimately related to the ἀρετή-ethic. The cooperative virtues do not form an independent system of morality. Rather, morality is a subordinate system complementing and supporting the ἀρετή-ethic, specifically by curbing it to meet the needs of social existence. The quiet virtues represented by the adjectives δίκαιος, πινυτός, etc. reflect society's need to restrain the purely egoistic, competitive pursuit of honor and glory. It was necessary for each ἀγαθός to recognize and in certain circumstances to defer to each other's honor. In a word, the very workings of the ἀρετή-ethic demanded the observance of some protocol and mutual self-restraint and respect. While it remains true that possessing ἀρετή *implied* being moral, it did not necessarily entail it.[43]

Having examined the relationship between the ethic of ἀρετή and morality as such, we are now in a position to make some general observations on the role the gods played in the two related systems. While the gods sanction morality, they do not simultaneously sanction the ethic of ἀρετή. They bring no recriminations to bear on those who fail to display ἀρετή; the shame before men is the sole sanction. Conversely, strength and might and the honor that accrues from them were values in themselves. Men were motivated toward their acquisition independently of the gods.

On the other hand, the gods are idealized realizations of the ἀρετή-ethic, though not of the moral code (as was often noted by later tradition). This can be most clearly seen in the case of Zeus. As Aeschylus has Prometheus say in *Prometheus Bound*:

> There is nothing without discomfort except the overlordship of the Gods. For only Zeus is free. (49-50, trans. David Grene)

Aeschylus characterizes Zeus as the original tyrant whose severity and willfulness is unmitigated by the quiet virtues of a benevolent king. This characterization of Aeschylus' is true of the Zeus of the *Iliad*—there, as we have seen, Zeus is repeatedly criticized for his stubborn willfulness and disregard for the rights and prerogatives of the other members of the divine family. While the other gods must, depending on their position in the social hierarchy, respect the rights of their peers and superiors, Zeus is a law unto himself, precisely because he has no peer with respect to the power that he wields. In Zeus we have a projection of an ideal only implicit in human thinking: that if a man were strong enough he would not have to bother with the moral code. Indeed, this puts morality in its proper focus: from this point of view we can see that morality represents the hold, however tenuous, the general populace had on the power of the ἀγαθός. It is to be noted that Zeus in this regard represents a mere *idealization* rather than a *paradigm for human conduct*. It would have been impious for any mortal to model himself on Zeus in this respect. In his freedom Zeus represents only the explicitation of something in the logic of ἀρετή, rather than a paradigm of real practical application in human affairs, and so in this respect represents only a form of idle religious speculation.

From all that we have seen there is nothing in the nature or being of the gods which, from a philosophical point of view, specifies them as authentic, religiously transcendent objects. In every respect the being of the gods is nothing more than an idealized projection of human being. Similarly with regard to the character of man's relationship to the gods: it fails to differentiate itself from the ordinary human, mundane relationship of vassal to lord. Further, the values and motives of the gods are identical with those of men. In short, there is nothing specifically "religious" in Homeric man's religion understood as the relationship between himself and a class of divine beings.

We have seen in the previous section, however, that an examination of the content of Homeric man's experience does reveal various forms of religious transcendence. But these divine powers, or forms of being, do not necessarily in themselves imply a relationship to a class of divine beings. They display a certain "open" or "indeterminate" character: the experienced "divine" irruptions do not carry in themselves any clues as to whence or from whom they come. They simply irrupt into the here and now as if from outside the normal flow of events, from a completely open, undefined "beyond". It is of course true that Homeric man (and not only Homer) conceptualized these transcendent irruptions as proceeding from a class of divine beings. He took the irruptions to be the *acts* of conscious, willing beings. The concept of the δαίμων is very instructive in this regard. Its frequent occurrence in the speech of Homeric men (as opposed to the poet's more definite, privileged knowledge) indicates that wherever an extraordinary power was experienced it was always supposed that *some divine being* had acted. Δαίμων is in fact perfectly equivalent in Homer to θεός τις, "some god." Knowledge of the identity of the god depended on that fund of traditional knowledge of the defining functions and special domains of each god. Indeed, the personality of the god was, before Homer's imaginative depictions, defined in terms of these functions, or epithets. God *X* was known as the god who did *a*, *b*, *c*, etc. For the most part pre-Homeric popular cult ignored the characterization of the gods in themselves.[44]

All this points to one conclusion: to construe the divine powers and forms of being as bestowals of personal beings was a gratuitous inference. There was no such this as empirical experience (knowledge by acquaintance) of divine *beings*. The concept of the "gods" did not answer to a set of experienced objective realities; rather it reflected a need of the human imagination to represent what it experienced in a concrete manner. In this sense, then, the Homeric pantheon and the entire system of religion which was formulated in terms of it, are not part of the logically fundamental stratum of Homeric man's religious experience of the world.[45]

Yet the gods served another purpose than simply to be the purveyors of various ἀρεταί to men. The gods as idealizations of the human condition functioned dialectically to express a truth about the limits of the human condition. That is, though the concept of the gods was arrived at by negating certain features of human being, and thus failed logically to designate a class of beings radically distinct and separate from the human race, and intelligible in their own right, the gods could nonetheless enter dialectically into the expression of a truth about the limits of human existence. Superficially Homer's narrative was a story about the acts of supernatural beings in a celestial realm: the ultimate meaning and purpose of such celestial narrative, however, was to express a basic insight into the nature of the *human* condition. By imagining beings who enjoyed the full, unending measure of τὰ ἀγαθά, the things supremely valued by Homeric man—power, honor, success, glory, wealth—and then demarcating the divine mode of life sharply from the human, the Homeric myths implicitly taught that there were severe and strict limits on man's striving for power and success. The ἀρετή-ethic was essentially a competitive ethic: to attain power and success was always to win out over others and at their expense. The ἀγαθός was taught to strive egoistically for as much honor and glory as he could attain. In this context the axiom of traditional Greek wisdom, that with respect to the race of gods and the race of men there could be no real comparison and no real intercourse, was a means of inculcating in the hero a healthy resignation to the limits in the very nature of things according to the ἀρετή-ethic.

The fullest and most explicit expression of this insight was the fifth-century encomiast of aristocratic ἀρετή, the poet Pindar. There is, for instance, his famous utterance in the sixth Nemean ode:

> There is one
> race of men, one race of gods; both have breath
> of life from a single mother. But sundered power
> holds us divided, so that the one is nothing, while for
> the other the brazen sky is established
> their sure citadel forever. Yet we have some likeness
> in great
> intelligence, or strength, to the immortals,
> though we know not what the day will bring, what course
> after nightfall
> destiny has written that we must run to the end.[46]

The view being enunciated here is wholly Homeric in its logic. On the one hand there is the basic isomorphism of gods and men arising from their single origin, and extending to a likeness in mind (νόον) and even to a likeness in nature (φύσις).[47] But at the same time the point is made (by sheer emphasis or *fiat*, rather than from logic or considerations of fact) that there is a *radical* difference, a basic cleavage, between the two races. The conviction is a matter of theological axiom; Pindar no more than Homer can pick out a radically differentiating feature.

The important aspect for Pindar of this very orthodox view is not the paradoxical ontological cleavage, but rather the *relative contrast* between the condition of divine existence and that of the human: the race of men who amount to nothing and the race of gods who abide in their illustrious heaven forever. Pindar's maxim, "Seek not the life of the immortals, but enjoy to the full the resources that are within their reach,"[48] is in the first place a monition to accept the extreme infrequency and unpredictability of success and glory. The egoistic will to power which the ἀρετή-code represents is in itself blind, voracious and unlimited. Its very essence was to desire complete victory over one's opponent, to crush him down and so win great glory at his cost. The ἀρετή-code was necessarily competitive and relative: one only attained glory by surpassing the achievements of one's fellow competitors (one's comrades in arms). But the human condition did not allow unlimited realization of ἀρετή. There was the shortness of life; even more there was the limitation imposed by the strict necessity of a fitting situation: it required a great battle. And even then, given the social relativity of glory and the contingencies (luck) of human events, there could be very few genuine, recognized heroes. In Pindar's time, when the aristocratic ἀρετή-ethic had to a great extent become transferred from singlehanded combat in war to athletic contest in the panhellenic games, there could obviously be only one winner to an event. Thus Pindar emphasized that honor and glory were the fruit of many long years, and even perhaps generations, of toil whose final season of bearing fruit was granted by the gods' gratuitous will. Another respect in which the man of distinction was admonished to resign himself was the transience and insecurity of human success. It was one of the most constant themes of traditional παιδεία that the human lot was to enjoy great bliss one day and suffering and despair the next.

In each of these respects the gods were privileged idealizations. The divine condition became the projection of a fully realized ἀρετή-ethic; it was the imaginative wish-fulfillment of how the life of glory and honor might be lived if the limitations of earthly existence could be cast off. But there were other than ontological limitations: the limitations imposed by the necessities of social life. Glory and fame were, of course, nothing if they were not glory and fame in men's eyes. Thus, despite the egoism of the basic drive, it could not disengage itself from the social situation. The retributive necessities of life in society forced on the drive to ἀρετή limitations from without. If a man was to receive his rightful acclaim, there must be procedures to *give* it, and thus obligations, duties and protocol impinging on others to do so. The ἀγαθός was thus necessarily drawn into relationship with the community. This meant in turn that society was in a position, albeit relatively weak, to curb the egoistic drive to power in accord with its needs. There could be no basking in the glory and esteem of men if there was not an orderly society to render that esteem. The very code of individual self-assertiveness contained within itself the necessity of a certain degree of submissiveness.

From the Mycenean age down to the archaic age society was organized around its source of livelihood, the land. Due to a variety of factors, ethnographic, geographic and economic, social units tended to remain relatively small and autonomous. In this context societies needed strong leaders with bands of strong, proficient warriors as their retainers to protect their source of livelihood and holdings from invaders. Warfare between clashing groups consisted principally of one-to-one combat between these warriors, and above all, between their leaders. In this perspective the ἀρετή-ethic was a function of the social form of life: society needed the powerful individual who excelled.

The pressure of frequent and serious fights for survival spurred men on to make innovations in the techniques of warfare which in turn had momentous, far-reaching implications for their very form of life. Instead of individual combat between competing heroes, battle was waged with tight formations of heavily-armed soldiers. The necessities of the situation are obvious: no Homeric hero could hope to stand up to these phalanxes of hoplites. Thus the individual hero began to lose his privileged place: the crucial need was for a great number of foot-soldiers who could be regimented into a single fighting-unit. There was still glory and honor to be won, but the warrior was denied some of the sublimity of victory in the Homeric era. In the wake of these developments the feeling that present generations could cast only the weakest shadow in comparison with the great deeds of heroes of old was quite natural. In the new era, as Tyrtaeus, poet laureate of the Spartan martial ideal, relates, heroic valor consisted of planting one's feet and standing firm against the onslaught of the enemy's forces and encouraging the comrades at one's side.[49]

The expanded military operations inevitably created pressures for the expansion of political sanctions. This realignment of political power, together with the social and economic discontent brought about by inequitable land distribution and debt, as well as the emergence of a non-noble *nouveaux-riches* class, made the archaic age of Greece a time of great turmoil. The old order was under attack. Gradually the rule of the ἀγαθοί under a Βασιλεύς (king) gave way to that supreme achievement of Greek civilization, the πόλις.

In the old social arrangement the administration of δίκη was in the hands of the Βασιλεύς. This of course meant that δίκη depended on the virtuousness of the ruler, and in particular how pious he was, since a powerful ruler could, as we have seen, if he did not fear divine reprisal, override traditional practice. But the standards for what was just and holy were largely independent of his will: relative to his will they were objectively determined. It was society at large, and in particular the established practice of countless generations of families or households living in community, that determined them. For the most part an injustice was an offense against the τιμή of a family, and punishment was therefore the direct responsibility of the offended family. The role of the βασιλεύς was essentially merely that of assessor and adjudicator of conflicting claims.

The code of ἀρετή and the code of δίκη then represented two different perspectives of valuation: the former that of the individual, the latter that of society. The former was essentially non-religious in the sense that it had no logically necessary relationship to the gods. The latter, however, in the old scheme of things, depended on religious piety. Reverence for the gods was the mortar of the old social order. Ἀρετή remained the supreme value and the pinnacle of achievement for Greeks of the classical period, as is amply evidenced in the persisting emphasis on success and distinction in military service. Yet the individual hero was no longer exalted to the same degree as he had been during the Homeric age; his achievement was assimilated not so much to his γένος as to his πόλις. In Sparta the emphasis was wholly on obedience. Valor was won only by accomplishing with distinction one's function in the extremely regimented and disciplined Spartan fighting-units. As was pointed out, the very style of warfare denied the warrior the sublimity of Homeric victory. Actually the panhellenic games continued the Homeric warrior heritage, though in a tamed form: mortal combat had become competition in sport.

The significant development at this point, however, was the emergence of law. The Greek πόλις was founded upon the positive, rational formulation of constitutions and legal codes. Under the pressure of social and economic change men were taking into their hands, often in the name of the great, legendary lawgiver (νομοθέτης), the devising of their own social form of life, as well as the codification and promulgation of the laws they were to live by. From the perspective of the old sensibilities man was assuming a divine function. While the formality of recognizing the gods of the πόλις as the hallowed sanctioners of the laws persisted, in actuality man's attitude became (especially in Athens) secular and rationalistic.[50] The fund of traditional unwritten laws was wholly inadequate for the needs of the πόλις, and so receded more and more into the background, and indeed was in some cases reformed or annulled by human legislation.

It is, of course, in Athens that we can observe the developments in their most interesting and acute form. It was this city's special genius to accomplish the introduction of the whole body of citizens, the three στάσεις or factions (small farmer; merchant and artisan; and large land-holding aristocracy) into political responsibility on an equal basis. This had important implications for the ἀρετή-ethic: it greatly expanded the context and social base for the quest of ἀρετή. Instead of the traditional aristocratic definition of the ἀγαθός, and even instead of the Spartan definition of the obedient hoplite, Athens defined the ἀγαθός as the outstanding citizen. This still entailed in the first instance, of course, distinction in military service; but in place of the aristocratic ideal of the leisured existence of sport and banquet, it emphasized participation in the political processes of legislation and adjudication. It was excellence in the public forum, in the wisdom and judgment displayed in the formulation of policies which would lead to success, as well as the power to influence the course of events, that measured a man's worth.

The code of ἀρετή became redefined in democratic terms: participation in the political processes, to which every citizen had access, became the framework for the quest of ἀρετή. It was in this new context that the sophists made their great contribution. They rendered to noble and non-noble citizen alike the service of teaching the requisite skills for success in public debate.[51] The traditional παιδεία taught gymnastics and music, that is, physical education and "culture", or the social graces expected of the leisured aristocrat. The young noble was tutored in the poets, voice, dance, and self-accompaniment on the cythera—the skills he would be expected to display on occasion at the symposium. The poets were, of course, Homer and Hesiod: through the recitation of their works the youth was inspired with the love of glory and the patterns of great and noble deeds.[52] The educative process took place in this respect more by immersion in the climate of the epics than in actual words or maxims expressed. But for the moral education of the youth the great authority was Solon.[53] His was the traditional message of εὐνομία, everyone in his "proper place" (in the traditional social hierarchy). This entailed the ἄριστοι accepting the limits of the quiet virtues in their quest for ἀρετή; they must beware of ὕβρις, arrogantly stepping on someone's rights or prerogatives, even an inferior's. And the non-nobles must respect the rights of the noble class and defer to their status in grasping for their (non-nobles') own measure of wealth and success.

The crucial vulnerability of the old moral code was of course its dependence on the old social order. Never clearly formulated, it consisted more of a system of sensibilities of what was acceptable, rather than a system of specific, much less codified, laws. Generally speaking in the old scheme of things the moral uprightness of an individual was characterized as fidelity to one's oaths and not committing wrongs (ἀδικίας). The definition of the moral code remains frustratingly vague and obscure to the modern observer. It only becomes explicit in specific offenses: it is always this or that action that is wrong, not permitted, unholy. Another perspective on the traditional morality is obtained from the familiar summary of παιδεία as reverence for gods, parents, and strangers (-guests).[54] But this summary too points back to the basic institutional realities of Homeric society: family, religious cult reinforcing the family and the socially vulnerable, and the exchange and mutual recognition of τιμή.

It was most natural, then, that when the social and economic form of life, and the distribution of power and wealth, changed, this moral order was, short of radical reform, doomed. Of course we may see Hesiod, Solon, and Theognis as valiant attempts to expand and adapt the moral code. Hesiod in particular reformulated the ethic of ἀρετή for the aspiring class of non-nobles by basing it not on bloody combat but healthy competition in the economic sector. However, transgressions against justice remained essentially breaking oaths and committing "wrongs". The story of the golden age of Athens is the story of the failure of this old morality. The old sensibilities with regard to right and wrong became increasingly irrelevant to Athenian life. They receded into the background as "the unwritten laws"; they represented the groundwork of tacit assumptions on which positive legislation was founded. Plato well appreciated the importance of this function of the unwritten laws:

> All that we are now discussing [says the Athenian] is what people in general call 'unwritten laws', and all such injunctions amount to what they call the 'laws of our ancestors'. And what we said recently, that one should neither call them laws nor yet pass them over, was well said. They are the bonds that hold a political society together, links between laws already on the statute book and those still to be enacted, in truth a body of ancestral and age-old precepts which if rightly conceived and put into practice protect and safeguard the written laws of the time, but if they swerve from the right path they cause everything to collapse like a building when

> the builder's supports give way. With this in mind we must bind your new city together with everything possible that goes by the name of law, custom or usage. (*Laws* 793a)

The truth is that while few would be so impious as to deny them, the unwritten laws were increasingly ignored in the conduct of political affairs in Athens. The old formula for balancing the pursuit of ἀρετή with δίκη had broken down. We can see this best in large scale in Pericles' philosophy of empire.

Under Pericles Athens was engaged in the clear-sighted, conscious pursuit of power politics. After the Persian wars Athens found herself in the forefront of the Greek community. Her response to this new-found but precarious hegemony evidenced the extent to which the democratic life of the Athenians was saturated with the new secular, rationalistic spirit.[55] Men faced their new situation with a bold confidence in the ability of human insight and judgment, as well as energy and courage, to steer them on their course. What impelled them to embark on such a danger-fraught course was the promise of glory: the Athenians were fully prepared to take the tremendous risks involved (that Athens would be completely destroyed and enslaved). The attitude of the Athenian city-state is most cogently expressed in Thucydides' great work, in the speech of the Athenian envoy to the Lacedaimonians (who were deliberating on whether they should declare war with Corinth on Athens):

> We have done nothing extraordinary, nothing contrary to human nature in accepting an empire when it was offered to us and then in refusing to give it up. Three very powerful motives prevent us from doing so—security, honour, and self-interest. And we were not the first to act in this way. Far from it. It has always been a rule that the weak should be subject to the strong; and besides, we consider that we are worthy of our power. Up till the present moment you, too, used to think that we were; but now, after calculating your own interest, you are beginning to talk in terms of right and wrong. Considerations of this kind have never yet turned people aside from the opportunities of aggrandizement offered by superior strength. Those who really deserve praise are the people who, while human enough to enjoy power, nevertheless pay more attention to justice than they are compelled to do by their situation. Certainly we think that if anyone else was in our position it would soon be evident whether we act with moderation or not.[56]

Another revealing episode recorded by Thucydides is the Melian debate. The Athenians had sent a large force to the pro-Spartan island of Melos and, threatening to lay waste the land and to lay siege to the city, attempted to persuade the Melians to capitulate to their superior force. They urged the Melians to agree that conventional appeals would be pointless; only frank talk and a hard-headed facing the facts would do them any good:

> we recommend that you should try to get what it is possible for you to get, taking into consideration what we both really do think; since you know as well as we do that, when these matters are discussed by practical people, the standard of justice depends on the equality of power to compel and that in fact the strong do what they have the power to do and the weak accept what they have to accept. (V. 88 ff.)

The Athenians refused to hear any appeal to traditional rights and practices; nor did they accept the Melians' argument that there would be anything shameful or impious in destroying their city and killing their men. They chided the Melians for relying on "vague, blind things" like prophecies and oracles, or the pious hope that the gods would defend them out of the righteousness of their cause. The only fitting response for the Melians in the Athenians' eyes was to accept the facts of the situation and act realistically to one's best advantage as reason indicated it. But the Melians stubbornly held to their old-fashioned views and their fate was sealed. The Athenians clearly had nothing but scorn for the Melians' faith in the gods and honor and blood relationships.

What is remarkable about these episodes is that they show the extent of the breakdown of the old religious piety. Athenian thinking had become untethered from traditional standards of justice and piety. Athens confronted her situation with the cold, clear-sighted calculation of what accrued to her power and advantage. Considerations of justice and piety were quite incidental and peripheral; indeed, it is recognized that "the mighty have no need to appeal to right." It was those in the position of weakness that clothed their policies in the guise of concern for justice, piety, and the hallowed, time-worn practices of the Greeks. If they were in the position of power they too would act for their glory and honor. Athens claimed to have discerned in this regard the universal law of human nature which undercut considerations of justice.

Aeschylean tragedy, too, illustrates the new thinking. In the *Eumenides* (848 ff.) Athene gives expression to Athens' concept of herself in the golden age: Athens is the favored of Zeus; it is his will to raise her up as he did Achilles and grant her her day of great glory. And Aeschylean tragedy teaches that what was the lawful, rightful order of things under the rule of the Olympians was a law and right founded on superior brute strength, violence and bloodshed:

> Hephaestus: "Might and Violence, in you the command of Zeus has

its perfect fulfillment." (*Prometheus Bound*, 12, trans. David Grene)

Chorus: "For new are the steersmen that rule Olympus: and new
are the customs by which Zeus rules,
customs that have no law to them,
but what was great before he brings to nothingness." (148-51)

Chorus: "A disposition none can win, a heart
that no persuasion soften—these are his,
the Son of Kronos."
Prometheus: "I know that he is savage: and his justice
a thing he keeps by his own standard . . ." (186-89)

Chorus: "Such are the actions of the younger gods. These
by unconditional force, beyond all right, a throne hold
that runs reeking blood,
blood at the feet, blood at the head." (*Eumenides*, 162-65, trans. Richmond Lattimore)

By his youthful power Zeus has set himself up as a law unto himself and like a tyrant ignores the laws and customs of the previous reign. In the *Eumenides* (213 ff.) Apollo argues against the age-old law of blood-vengeance by appealing to the sanctity of marriage which he says is guaranteed by "a right of nature" stronger than oaths. At 619-21 Apollo affirms that right is what Zeus wills and that this right is stronger than the age-old right founded on oaths. This view assumes tremendous importance in connection with the belief of fifth-century Athens in her manifest destiny: in bringing other Greek cities under their rule Athenians committed numerous sacrileges and offenses against traditional standards of right. No doubt the subtle conviction informed their action that in thus exercising power they were acting like Zeus (who was after all behind their rule): thus to override traditional laws and sanctions was merely the necessary consequence of assuming "divine" power.

In the *Gorgias* Socrates expresses a dissident view of Periclean Athens. He evidences a sense of the moral decadence of the unchecked exercise of power:

You praise those who have banqueted our citizens with all the dainties they desire. And men say it is these who have made our city great, never realizing that it is swollen and festering through these statesmen of old. For they have filled our city with harbours and dockyards and walls and revenues and similar rubbish, and so, when the crisis of her infirmity comes, they will hold their present advisers responsible and will sing the praises of Themistocles and Cimon and Pericles, who caused their misfortunes. (518e-519a)

Socrates evidences the conservative sensibilities of the traditional outlook. The Athenian πόλις is lacking in σωφροσύνη and δικαιοσύνη: they commit the sin of ὕβρις against the old Delphic faith of order, moderation, self-control, respect for due limits. But however conservative his sensibilities, his tack in meeting the challenge of the new amorality is, as we shall see, a *radical* one in the true sense of the word.

In Callicles of the *Gorgias* and Thrasymachus of the *Republic* (I) Socrates meets his two most radical opponents. They are men who boldly, self-confidently proclaim themselves to have broken the hold of society over their conduct. "What men think" no longer has any hold on them. They declare that they have seen through public standards of right and wrong, proper and improper, and have seen in them the design of the weak and inferior to curb the naturally strong and so prevent the strong from dominating and exploiting them.

> But if a man rises endowed with a nature sufficiently strong, he will, I believe, shake off all these controls, burst his fetters, and break loose. And trampling upon our scraps of paper, our spells and incantations, and all our unnatural conventions, he rises up and reveals himself our master who was once our slave, and there shines forth nature's true justice. (484a)

They proclaim the true, or the real, justice: not the artificial, conventional sort, but natural justice. It is the law of nature that the stronger impose his will and enforce whatever is in his interest. The rule of law in a society too obeys this universal law of nature, for right and justice are nothing else than the advantage of the weak and inferior. When the many weak and inferior are stronger than the few strong and superior individuals, the many weak impose the rule of equality before the law in their own best self-interest. But there is no such thing as a natural right or justice binding on the truly strong; to give way to the interests of others is only to concede one's weakness and inferiority.

Callicles and Thrasymachus are of course profoundly antidemocratic in their views. Their thinking expresses the old aristocratic code in its crudest, most blatant form. Nonetheless, they illustrate just as surely as any democrat the prevailing philosophy that right is might; for, like their democratic opponents, they are not restrained by δίκη.[57] The spirit of secular rationalism pervades the thinking of these new elitists just as thoroughly as that of the Athenian democrats. In setting himself against them, then, Socrates shows his response to the new irreligious spirit.

Gorgias' assertion that rhetoric is the purely technical skill to speak effectively (that is, persuasively) in public debate, and so is morally neutral, is damning enough for Socrates. In the context of an egoistic ἀρετή-ethic relatively free of the restraints of justice, this would only mean the manipulation of traditional norms and values for the sake of personal power and advantage (or that of the πόλις). Thus Socrates sets himself against the sophistry of a Protagoras, a man who in himself stood for the traditional values of δικαιοσύνη, σωφροσύνη, and ὁσιότης. The problem was that he was no more able than the ordinary man in the street to give a λόγος, a conscious, positive, rational account of what right, self-control, and piety were. The sophists were on the same footing as the ordinary man: the moral values were what social conventions said they were. Thus they were vulnerable to the new secular cynicism. As Glaucon and Adeimantus observe in the *Republic*, the conventional recommendation of justice was not based on the intrinsic value of right as such: they were to be "practiced for the sake of rewards and repute due to opinion" (whether of gods or of men). To illustrate this Glaucon asks us to conceive a situation where the just man and the unjust man had unlimited power to do as they pleased: would the just man persevere in just actions if he could get away with the opposite with impunity?—"no one could be found it would seem of such adamantine temper as to persevere in justice" (360b). As he sees it, this means that it is really the *implicit teaching of traditioral* παιδεία that justice is no value in itself, but is observed only because society demands it. What was needed, Adeimantus insists,[58] is a λόγος, a *grounded* account of what justice was in and by itself independent of all opinion and independent of all consideration of constraint, rewards or reputation. Adeimantus makes it clear that he includes the gods in this "seeming". He asks for an account of justice that prescinds from the gods and disregards them.

At *Gorgias* 466d ff. Socrates denies that a man who does what seems best to him does what he wills. The implicit premises for this paradoxical-sounding statement are: it is a truism of Greek life that everyone wills the good, that is, what is advantageous to him. But some things only seem good and do not really produce a good result. However, the truism should thus be changed to read: everyone wills for himself what is *really* good (advantageous). Now, for Socrates this implies knowledge, a sure knowledge of ends. Here the influence of the Eleatic quest for reality beyond seeming becomes apparent: philosophical dialectic is the attempt to gain a firm intellectual grasp of the ends of human conduct by defining the virtues. This implies cutting through the maze of conflicting common-sense *opinions* to the *real* nature of justice, wisdom, courage, temperance, piety, etc., and ultimately of the good itself. Only by anchoring one's conduct on real, absolute values can one escape the aimless flux and circularity of the prevailing morality. Sophistry, far from overcoming the moral cynicism of the times, actually contributed to it.[59] As Socrates characterizes it, sophistry is no τέχνη (know-how) but a routine or knack (ἐμπειρία) lacking any conscious understanding of the grounds (αἰτία) for what it recommends. Thus it ends, like cooking, a flattery of the body, serving up to man's lower nature what it desires. In effect, sophistry becomes an instrument of the amoral drive to power.

It is crucial to realize that Socrates' response to the breakdown of traditional moral values was not to evoke moral conscience. He did not appeal to any internalized sense of moral shame in the individual, that is, to transform the basis of morality from public shame to personal guilt. Rather, Socrates accepted the basic character of the Greek ethic: that the supreme value was individual excellence, the perfection of one's nature and powers. Yet there was the problem to be faced: how was the basic disharmony between the competitive and cooperative virtues to be overcome? how was it possible to give the quiet virtues a firm basis without simply making a moralistic appeal to traditional practice?

Socrates was a "radical" thinker in the true sense of the word: that is, he shunned both conservative reaction and liberal accommodation in favor of an attempt to get at the "roots" of the problem.[60] Though he had the conservative's sense of the moral decadence of the age, he saw too clearly the weaknesses and inadequacies of the old synthesis to take a conservative stance. And though he could share the liberal's conviction that the old situation was irretrievably lost, he could not accept mere accommodation to the new situation as an adequate response to the crisis. Indeed, it was because he was too steeped in the traditional form of religiously experiencing life that these responses were unacceptable. Because of his radicalism, no doubt partly a function of the rational spirit of Greek philosophy itself, he was willing to cast the religion as traditionally understood into the crucible and allow that essential experience of life to take on a new shape. The fundamental apprehension of ἀρετή as divine, lovely, awesome and good became transposed onto the level of philosophy. What was formerly merely the human *experience* of the disparate, individual forms or modes of divine ἀρετή—principally in the inspiration with μένος, the fury of the inspired warrior; the divine monition; the divine inspiration of the artist or seer; the grace of a divine loveliness—became sublimated in the Socratic philosophical way to the *intellectual apprehension* of the

Forms of Justice, Wisdom, Courage, Beauty, and above all, the Good. Through his gospel of care of the soul Socrates preached that the soul, as the better, higher part, should be the primary focus of ἀρετή. It was the individual's prime concern to develop a superior spirit or character, one in which wisdom reigned supreme. Accordingly, Socrates repeatedly called into question the prevailing assumption that the competitive virtues were logically independent of the virtues of mind and moral character, the cooperative or quiet virtues. It was a mistake, for instance, to view courage as having no necessary relationship to knowledge and wisdom. Indeed, all the virtues were distinguished by knowledge, and were even in some important sense a species of it. Ultimately virtue depended upon the soul maintaining a vision of the Forms of personal excellence, as well as their interrelations, and above all, an intellectual grasp of the Form of the Good, according to which all acts were to be ordered. The moral life thus became one with the life of personal excellence and power. The fundamental disharmony between the two value-systems was overcome by collapsing them into one system under wisdom.

5. The Religious Dimension of Socrates' Thought.

The immediate context for Socrates' personal project of reconstructing the essential features of the Greek tradition was the tradition of Greek philosophy. Greek philosophy was from its very outset a kind of arm-chair, *a priori* speculation about the physical world. It was by its very nature an attempt to select, from a genuinely rational, theoretical point of view, a material category which was at once as logically primary and simple (and general and abstract) as possible, yet which had the maximum explanatory power to account for the being and the coming-to-be of all other more particular, derivative forms of being. Thus natural philosophy was materialist and rationalist in its chosen perspective on things. But this does not mean that it was immediately or in its basic conception antithetical to traditional belief in the gods. After all, even pre-critical Homeric man had his conviction that all material beings were basically earth and water.[61] From this point of view Thales represents an attempt to develop a more aesthetically appealing theory by reducing reality to a single explanatory category instead of the traditional two or four.[62] And indeed, some myths of the pre-philosophical period have for their purpose *speculation* about the nature and origin of the world. Instead of a fully rationalized perspective, those early mythopoeic speculators employed the technique of personification of material essences or powers (Ouranos, Eros, Nyx, Gaia, Chaos, Okeanos). The fact that the philosophers subordinated the gods of popular religion to the ultimate impersonal but divine material ἀρχαί did not itself have radical implications for popular religious belief. For the gods, even in the myths, had only lately come on the scene; they were begotten from earlier, more primordial generations of gods whose role they had usurped. Further, Thales, Anaximenes, and Xenophanes, at least, showed that the divine material ἀρχαί were compatible with belief in the gods of myth and religion.

The crucial thing about natural philosophy was the *form* of thought. The emergence of a second-order, genuinely theoretical point of view implied a self-consciousness about the basic terms of one's account of things. For instance, the process of reducing one's account to simplest and fewest terms possible implied a reflective grasp of the relative logical appropriateness of different possible explanatory terms. The systematic, internal self-consistency of the theory also had to be a prime concern. To be sure, in satisfying these theoretical criteria alone the natural philosophers did not guarantee the truth of their theories. What is of special interest, however, is that the very commitment to these criteria had certain epistemological implications. It meant that theoretically proper statements had a privileged status compared to statements of the uncritical mind. We can see this sort of distinction emerging very clearly in the growing sense that the world of seeming, the ordinary common-sense world, did not manifest the real nature of things. In effect, a wedge was gradually driven between appearance and the really real (to anticipate Plato's phrase, τὸ ὄντως ὄν). For the philosophers, of course, this really real was divine and transcendent, though not in any popular religious sense (no philosopher, for instance, ever recommended praying to his philosophical ultimate). But the gods of religion were traditionally conceived to be beings in the same three-dimensional world as men, though, as it were, in a separate, more privileged compartment. The popular mind confusedly represented the transcendent dimension as a realm within the world—a logical consequence of projecting the categories pertaining to a class of existent personal *beings* on to experienced *powers* or ultimates for thought. Only a genuinely reflexive, critical perspective could clear up the confusion. It accomplished this by drawing the limits to thought. This can be seen most clearly in Parmenides, whose formal criteria of what really is, set the bounds of human thought such that man had an *a priori* grasp of real being, but could find no *bona fide* candidates in the world in which he lived that would satisfy the criteria. The central part of Parmenides' philosophical achievement was a set of *a priori* deductions from the abstract idea of thing being what it was. From this followed a whole set of formal and necessary criteria of being. Given the idea of a thing being what it was, it followed that the thing was not what it was not. On purely formal grounds this very thought, as well as all other thoughts which displayed this basic logical form, was ruled out. From this a whole set of logical entailments regarding ἐόν (or ἔστι) followed: it must not have come into being; it must not be destructible, nor in any way terminable; it must be one, whole, without parts; it must not move or in any way be altered. By working out these entailments Parmenides formulated for the first time in a clear, succinct form the metaphysical concepts of "absolute being," "ultimate reality," "reality in and by itself," reality beyond the relativism of the common-sense world.

In elaborating these new metaphysical insights Parmenides used a set of traditional religious metaphors to convey the *sense* of a realm of being that transcended human grasp. A. Mourelatos, in his study, *The Route of Parmenides: A Study of Word, Image, and Argument in the Fragments*,[63] has demonstrated the integral connection between literary, artistic expression and philosophical thought in the Parmenidean fragments. Parmenides has selected certain images and motifs from traditional epic sources (the preponderance being identifiable as Homeric) and pressed them into the service of speculative inquiry. The overarching, organizing motif is that of a journey or quest under the guidance of a polymorph goddess (principally characterized as Fate-Constraint) who reveals the "measures" or "signposts" of the route. Parmenides brilliantly uses these epic images and motifs as vehicles for enunciating metaphysical notions never before expressed. After careful scrutiny Mourelatos concludes that the blurred lines of the mythical motifs and images, making particular identifications of persons and places impossible, is intentional. Parmenides has deliberately fashioned a vague amalgamation to preclude old meanings and to provoke his reader to grasp their new, speculative reapplication. Parmenides uses the mythical motifs and images not to refer to the old realities, but *as* images and motifs to say something new. The metaphor of the route or quest, and the signposts along the way which the goddess reveals, are not metaphors with religious content: they do not assert that there is somewhere such a goddess, or a divine realm hidden behind great doors, etc. Rather, they are precisely metaphors for the *formal* character of his deductions: they do not say what reality is, only what criteria candidates for reality must satisfy.

However incapable Parmenides or other philosophers may have been to take man further into the mystery of that metaphysical transcendence, it was clear that the gods of popular religion did not qualify for residence in that realm. Indeed, those gods became logically irrelevant in the quest for transcendent reality; the question of their existence became demoted to a very secondary, peripheral concern. It was thus, by the new conception of *reality* and its new epistemological criteria, that natural philosophy effected, for the minority that pursued it, a radical undermining of popular religious beliefs.

Socrates, as we have seen, studied natural philosophy and rejected it. But it is clear that in the essential regard just discussed Socrates had been deeply influenced. It is not that he examined the theories and, having found them wanting, turned back to uncritical, popular ways of thinking. On the contrary, Socrates fully absorbed the critical *form of thought*. His personal philosophical stance was thoroughly rationalist insofar as he had become sensitive to the epistemological credentials of various opinions. Indeed, we may go further in identifying the epistemological criteria that informed Socrates' "critical" ignorance. It was Parmenides who, working in the tradition of *a priori* speculation on the nature of πάντα, all reality, drew the necessary formal limits to thinking about reality. It was through Parmenides that the lasting influence of natural philosophy made itself felt on Socrates. Socratic dialectic preserved key features of the Parmenidean quest for ἐόν: first, the οὐσία which Socrates sought to define was the objective τέλος of dialectic; it was the real object of the dialectical quest. Second, Socrates refused to countenance predication of contraries to real being. Much of the Socratic ἔλεγχος was a demonstration that the proffered definition entailed the attribution of the contrary character, not-x, to the *definiendum*, X. (Socrates assumed that the character or quality could be predicated of the Form, for example, "Justice is just." Ἔλεγχος, then, was frequently a test of the proffered *definiens* of X to see if it entailed the predication of some character which was equivalent to not-x.) To show this was for Socrates equivalent to refuting the proffered definition, for he assumed with Parmenides that whatever X really is, it is what it is, and is in no sense what it is not (that is, not-x). But above all Socrates accepted Parmenides' criteria of real being. For Parmenides being was "the same and in the same" and "by itself"; for Socrates it was "itself by itself." For Parmenides it was "equal to itself"; for Socrates it was "like itself." For Parmenides it was "now, all at once, *one*, continuous"; Socrates sought the *single* character (μία ἰδέα) by which the many instances were what they were.[64]

The Parmenidean concept of absolute being, with its correlate notion, absolute truth, figured in another, most important feature of Socratic philosophy. Socrates' insistence on his own ignorance presupposed a standard of absolute being and truth which stood as the measure of his own failure. The most he could do, in accordance with the Parmenidean analysis, was to set himself in *quest* of what really was. That meant dialectical inquiry departing from human δόξα (opinion, seeming) and following out one line of argument at a time. Of necessity a full grasp of reality in all its systematic ramifications eluded mere mortal intelligence. The foremost result of dialectic was the elimination of misconceptions, the breaking down of the hold of δόξα on the mind; only rarely did one arrive at a truth, a piecemeal, tentative grasp of the (Absolute) Truth.

Parmenides, as we have seen, made conscious use of religious metaphors to elaborate his metaphysical concept of being. In a similar vein Plato used current religious metaphors to interpret the Socratic philosophical way as the highest form of the divine πάθος of love. In the *Phaedrus* myth of the ascent of the winged charioteer and steeds to the vision, in the company of the gods, of the holy mysteries, Plato has blended Homeric imagery with that of the religious mysteries. In addition to the presence of the Homeric gods by explicit mention (Zeus, 246e, 250b, 252e; Hera, 253b; Apollo, 253b; Ares, 252c) or allusion ("for the rest, all such as are ranked in the number of the twelve as ruler gods lead their several companies, each according to his rank," 247a), there is mention of heavenly feasting and banqueting (247a), chariot driving by Zeus and other gods, ambrosia and nectar (247e), and the brilliant, pure light of the divine realm (250b-c). And the attainment of the vision of the Forms is likened to initiation into sacred, purifying mysteries in terms strongly redolent of the Eleusinian mysteries: εἶδόν τε καὶ ἐτελοῦντο τῶν τελετῶν, sight of and initiation into the mystery rites, 250b8; μακάριαι θέαι, spectacles of bliss, 247a4; τελέους ἀεὶ τελετὰς τελούμενος, the full vision of the perfect mysteries, 249c7-8; τελετή, mystery rite, 253c3. At *Symposium* 210e ff. Diotima speaks of the final phase of Socrates' initiation into the mysteries of Love as a sudden *beholding* of something wonderful, that is, divine Beauty itself—which again suggests a comparison with the ἐποπτεία of the Eleusinian mysteries.

Through such religious metaphors of the great dialogues of the middle period Plato has given expression to the truth which Socratic irony concealed: *the Socratic way was a religious initiation or passage through the philosophical* λόγος *to the vision of the Forms as a sublime mystery.*[65] Indeed, it was precisely because the philosophical λόγος functioned as a rite of passage that irony was demanded: to be in the Socratic way (as opposed to merely discussing some topic philosophically with Socrates) meant to have attained a personal vision of the Form in and through the philosophical λόγος of which the "uninitiated" outside was incapable. To one not in the Socratic way the λόγοι yielded purely negative results: there was no admittance to the realm of divine realities beyond the λόγοι to such as had not attained that sublime intellectual breakthrough. Thus *Socratic irony was a function of the Socratic philosophical way as religious mystery*. Irony was required because, though the only approach to divine realities was necessarily *in and through* λόγοι, the divine εἴδη or Forms were not in themselves something λεγόμενον, something uttered. Though they were utterable, a distinction remained between the εἶδος itself and the word which referred to it. And though a mortal human being necessarily made his approach to divine reality through the λόγος, the divine Forms in themselves transcended human, linguistic grasp. Let us examine this seeming paradox in the Socratic way at further length.

For Socrates the Forms were the divine paradigms of the various ἀρεταί which humans exemplified. Socratic philosophy was an attempt to develop one's powers of discerning intellectually those universal Forms common to all the various instances and to fix habitually one's vision on them as the firm foundation for the life of ἀρετή. The means of accomplishing this was διαλέγειν, discussion, but of a certain rigorous sort: logical dialectic and ἔλεγχος. This was to come to an apprehension of the Forms through λόγοι, which can mean words, discourse, accounts, arguments, definitions, all of which maintain their tie to the basic verb, λέγειν, to say or talk. But the Forms were not *linguistic entities* (nor were they concepts, which exist only in human thinking). They were the non-linguistic (or at least extra-linguistic) entities which words ultimately named. The εἶδος or Form, which was a reality in its own right independent of the contingencies of human thinking and discourse, was only *linguistically and discursively displayed* by a λόγος. This λόγος was the constitutive feature of knowledge: it was that which distinguished ἐπιστήμη, knowledge, from δόξα, opinion, what seemed to be true. A thing was known only if a λόγος could be given of it. It was this ability to produce a λόγος, a definition which would stand up to dialectical ἔλεγχος, which Socrates scrutinized his contemporaries for and which he claimed he himself did not possess. Indeed, successful definitions are rare in the Socratic dialogues.[66] Socrates generally took all claims to knowledge in propositional form back to their basic constitutive elements, the Forms, which, once defined, would become the principle of true and authentic knowledge. Thus it was *in terms of* the Forms that real knowledge was produced, but the Forms themselves could not, evidently, be made the objects of scientific *knowledge*. But though the εἶδος resisted every effort to give it linguistic, definitional form, and so enter the body of *knowledge*, the enterprise of Socratic philosophy still stood on firm ground: for beyond the λόγος, and indeed given in the very effort to achieve a λόγος, there was that intuitive vision of the Forms which was given as the end of the dialectical quest and the criterion of its success or failure.

The culminating expression of this truth implicit in Socratic philosophy is to be found in the dialogue of Plato's middle period, the *Symposium*. There it is said that the ultimate vision of the Form of Beauty is neither λόγος nor ἐπιστήμη (211a). Beauty is apprehended in a direct, face to face, quasi-mystical, but nonetheless intellectual, vision which is beyond all language and discursive thought. Thus, though the vision of the Form is attained only *through* words, it is not *simply* conveyed *in* words. Words are at the same time the necessary *means* whereby the vision of the Forms is attained and, as it were, the *limit* or *barrier* which needs to be transcended in vision. Socratic negativity and silence, then, guard what is unsayable in the Socratic philosophical way. It is a principle upon which Socrates insists on pedagogical grounds: what could not be put into words was best left to the initiate to discern for himself in the conduct of dialectical inquiry.[67]

The Socratic-Platonic concept of the philosophical λόγος rested on a logically prior assumption about the nature of language and its relationship to reality—an assumption common to Greek culture generally—namely, that words (that is, language) were names (or signs), and that their function was to name or signify some non-linguistic reality. This very conception of words as names implied that realities were intelligible for *what they were* independent of human language. Language was not viewed as essential and necessary to, and indeed constitutive of, the intelligibility of things. This is evident from the then current νόμος-φύσις debate on "names" (ὀνόματα). Given the conception of language as a system of names, the question naturally arose whether the word signified a thing by a natural rightness or appropriateness (φύσις, ὀρθότης), or whether it did so simply as a matter of arbitrary convention (νόμος). But to ask whether the name aptly fitted or matched the nature of the thing presupposed that the nature was already intelligible in itself. The *Cratylus*, Plato's discussion of "names", is instructive in this regard. In the dialogue both nature and convention theories of words are explored dialectically to the limits of reason, and even beyond, until each theory breaks down into intolerable absurdities. Having reached the conclusion that neither theory is evidently sufficient by itself to account for the relation of words to the objects they named or signified, Socrates states his firm conviction that, whichever theory (or complementary combination thereof) is ultimately true, things may be known in and by themselves (αὐτὰ δι' αὐτῶν, 438e7; δι' αὐτῶν,

439a6) without names; names are no sure guide to "the truth of things" (τὴν ἀλήθειαν τῶν ὄντων, 438d7-8); names are ultimately irrelevant to inquiry into "real things" (τὰ ὄντα, 439b5), into "absolute beauty or good, or any other absolute existences" (αὐτὸ καλὸν καὶ ἀγαθὸν καὶ ἓν ἕκαστον τῶν ὄντων οὕτω, 439c8-d1). Thus for Plato and Socrates human λόγοι (or more properly, ὀνόματα) referred to (named, signified) the Forms, yet at the same time the Forms transcended human language. They were what they were purely, simply, and absolutely, independent of human thought and language.

Socrates proclaimed to the jury at his trial that his conduct of philosophy was his service of the God. Indeed, he claimed that he was the only true practitioner of the religion of the Athenian πόλις. Herein lay the profound tragedy and irony of Socrates' trial and death. Socrates could do no more than heroically confront the jury with his claim to be the purest expression of service of the God: consistent with his ironic life-stance, Socrates refused to explain the positivity of his religious way, yet he stood steadfast before the orthodoxy of his day and submitted to their condemnation of him.

After the death of his mentor, Plato ventured to illuminate the dark, mysterious interior of the Socratic way which had remained hidden behind Socrates' outward, ironic, negative face. Through the metaphorical use of mythical imagery, which yielded a full measure of insight only to those with eyes to see, to those who had gained admittance to the sublime mysteries of the philosophical way, Plato interpreted the positivity of the Socratic way while protecting its secret. Yet implicit in Plato's vision of the Socratic philosophical way was a truth which Socrates' jury rightly suspected: Socrates rejected the *self-understanding* of traditional religion. Socrates rejected the orthodox understanding of the gods and man's relationship to them. In the spirit of Greek philosophical rationalism generally, Socrates looked upon the traditional pantheon, and the arcana of mythical tales about them, as works of imaginative fancy. Of a similar fanciful character was the popular concept of religion: religious rites and customs were a commerce between men and putative beings in another, celestial compartment of the cosmos. The relationship was characterized on direct analogy with the human, secular relationship between the strong, powerful noble and those over whom he held power—that is, honor-tribute rendered to the divine ἄριστοι was exchanged for boons for earthly life. In the *Phaedrus*, however, by confining the gods to the region inside the heavens, and ceding them only a *relatively* superior footing to men, and by assigning the vision of the Forms to "that place beyond the heavens [which] none of our earthly poets [that is, Homer, Hesiod, and all the succeeding generations of poets] has yet sung," Plato relegated all of traditional religion to a level inferior to that of philosophy. Religion became a lower metaphor for the philosophical life. Religion was supplanted by philosophy; its truth was appropriated and fulfilled on a higher level. All talk of gods in their Olympian heaven and human commerce with them gave way to the view of their common beatific contemplation of truly divine reality which transcended both classes of beings.

Yet Socratic philosophy was not merely a rationalistic agnosticism; nor was it a theological criticism, after the fashion of Xenophanes. Rather, the Socratic way was a radical recasting of the essential Greek world-view, an inherently religious world-view. In the Socratic way the central features of that world-view were isolated and given new expression. The gods and traditional religion were not taken into account in the Socratic way simply because they were not logically necessary to that religious experience of life. The gods were divine because they possessed certain divine characteristics and powers: it was those characteristics and powers—in general terms, the ἀρεταί—which represented the primary objects of religious valuation in the old synthesis. They were experienced as divine, lovely, awesome, good and desirable: they were the absolute, unquestioned values of the Greek experience of life.

But the old religious synthesis was also a *world-view*. That is, these primary modes of religious experience were fashioned together into a set of attitudes, assumptions, and convictions about life, a total *Weltanschauung* characterized by an openness of human life to experienced transcendence, an acceptance of the limits of the human condition, and a dynamic recognition of the dialectical tension of man's longing to possess the divine. As we have seen, Socrates' radical recasting of the tradition had two main thrusts. First, to resolve an inherent antinomy in the old synthesis, and second, to sublimate it from the level of mere experience (on which level there was clearly a religious crisis in late fifth-century Athens) to the level of philosophical insight. Divine transcendence was reinterpreted in terms of the pure, divine, eternal reality of the Forms, which represented at once the metaphysical essence or reality of the world and the ideal end or goal of human activity. The same profound attitudes of traditional religion were translated to these objects of philosophical inquiry. They constituted the supreme access given to a mortal human being to that realm of open, transcendent mystery within which human life was lived.[68]

Through the metaphor of possession by the deity Plato acknowledged that Socrates' conduct of philosophy constituted a religious way, an authentic mode of religious self-transcendence and self-transformation, for those who by personal insight penetrated beyond merely negative, logical disputation. The philosophical life was an ultimate personal, religious posture in the universe, a way of salvation through intellectual enlightenment. Possession by divine ἀρετή became a metaphor for that gradual process whereby the Good and the Right became *absolute* values transcending and supplanting all the narrow, self-centered values of the individual. Through the myth of the face to face vision of the heavenly Form in the train of the gods Plato referred to that growing certainty of the Form that eluded explicit knowledge and definition. Through prolonged practice of philosophical inquiry there was cultivated within, an inner, spiritual, intuitive "eye" for an objective, inherently right and good order of things that transcended human subjectivity. (In this fundamental respect Socrates came down squarely on the side of φύσις in the νόμος-φύσις debate of the fifth century.) This vision beyond logical disputation, but somehow inherently implicit in it, of the divine, lovely, ideal right order of things—above all in the human, social order—for those who had attained to a godlike condition of philosophical contemplation, represented an absolute claim on the individual. There was no question of submission to divine ἀρετή as an egoistic, purely private good. Socrates did not seek ἀρετή *in order to be virtuous or superior*, that is, for his own self-esteem and the esteem of others. To perform virtuous acts in order to obtain the esteem that accrued from them would be to make ἀρετή secondary and relative to the ego—for the claim of ἀρετή as a value would in that case be subordinate to the good esteem of the self. The supreme value in such a scheme of things would not be ἀρετή but self-aggrandizement (as indeed was the tendency in the old cultural order of Greece).[69] But in Socrates there was no such "odor" of virtue: Socrates always and everywhere, that is, absolutely, submitted his own interests to the judgment of what was the Right and the Good. Through the practice of philosophical reflection the Form of the Good had come to exert a permanent, habitual hold on his ψυχή. Socrates had died to his own self-interests—even his instinct for self-preservation yielded to the claim of ἀρετή. He had transcended the self and become possessed by love for divine ἀρετή.[70] Though the efforts of his will were involved, Socrates had passed over into a more than human state in which his will had become permanently, habitually oriented to divine ἀρετή. His continuance in the philosophical way was not the simple result of acts of his own will: he suffered the vision of divine ἀρετή as a divine erotic πάθος, and not simply as a momentary, fleeting act of seeing, but as a permanent condition of life. Socrates thus spoke a profound truth when he said to his jury that his conduct of philosophy was his service of the God, for through the life of philosophy Socrates had attained a godlike condition, and was actively engaged in leading men to that same sublime vision of the divinely beautiful Good wherein they too would become possessed and in their own measure godlike.

> Therefore is it meet and right that the soul of the philosopher alone should recover her wings, for she, so far as may be, is ever near in memory to those things a god's nearness whereunto makes him truly god. Wherefore if a man makes right use of such means of remembrance, and ever approaches to the full vision of the perfect mysteries, he and he alone becomes truly perfect. Standing aside from the busy doings of mankind, and drawing nigh to the divine, he is rebuked by the multitude as being out of his wits, for they know not that he is possessed by a deity. (*Phaedrus* 249c-d)

1 The English word "irony" as it is commonly used has lost the implication of feigned *ignorance*, and accordingly, of refusing to offer an opinion of one's own. Rather, when one speaks ironically one is making a positive statement, but it is the *opposite* of the *prima facie* meaning of one's words. The *Oxford English Dictionary* defines "irony":

> A figure of speech in which the intended meaning is the opposite of that expressed by the words used; usually taking the form of sarcasm or ridicule in which laudatory expressions are used to imply condemnation or contempt.

2 Though the famous passage on Socrates' art of philosophical midwifery stands in so late a dialogue as the *Theaetetus*, it nonetheless is in full accord with the early characterization of Socrates:

> My art of midwifery is in general like theirs; the only difference is that my patients are men, not women, and my concern is not with the body but with the soul that is in travail of birth. And the highest point of my art is the power to prove by every test whether the offspring of a young man's thought is a false phantom or instinct with life and truth. I am so far like the midwife that I cannot myself give birth to wisdom, and the common reproach is true, that though I question others, I can myself bring nothing to light because there is no wisdom in me. The reason is this. Heaven constrains me to serve as a midwife, but has debarred me from giving birth. So of myself I have no sort of wisdom, nor has any discovery ever been born to me as the child of my soul. Those who frequent my company at first appear, some of them, quite unintelligent, but, as we go further with our discussions, all who are favored by heaven make progress at a rate that seems surprising to others as well as to themselves, although it is clear that they have never learned anything from me. The many admirable truths they bring to birth have been discovered by themselves from within. But the delivery is heaven's work and mine. (150b-d)

3 One thinks, for example, of Callicles' begrudging, perfunctory participation in Socratic ἔλεγχος in the *Gorgias* (see 489 ff., esp. 499b, 501c, 506c, 516c, 519d).

4 See *Symposium* 202 ff., esp. 204b-c.

5 At *Phaedrus* 247a there is mention of spectacles of bliss along the heavenly roads in addition to the final sublime vision in the region outside the heavens. The point of these heavenly wayside spectacles seems to be that the gods keep the Forms in view as they go about their worldly activity. Their work is

governed by a constant vision of the divine paradigms.

6 Socrates may also be seen as an image or human embodiment of the δαίμων Eros: the mythological description at *Symposium* 203c-e of Eros, the offspring of Resource and Need, would seem to be intended as a disguised description of Socrates. Cf. Thomas Gould, *Platonic Love* (New York, 1963), 57: "[Socrates] is not beauty, he is merely the personification of the love of beauty; not the desirable, but the *daemon* Desire at its best."

7 Trans. Lee M. Capel (Bloomington, 1968).

8 See Georg Wilhelm Friedrich Hegel, *The History of Philosophy*, trans. E.S. Haldane (1892; rpt. London, 1963), 384-448, for Hegel's discussion of Socrates. Cf. also Hegel's discussion of Greek civilization in *The Philosophy of History*, trans. J. Sibree (New York, 1956), 225-77; and J. Glenn Gray, *Hegel and Greek Thought* (1941; rpt. New York, 1968).

9 E.R. Dodds, *The Greeks and the Irrational* (Berkeley, 1966), 2.

10 U. von Wilamowitz-Moellendorff, *Der Glaube der Hellenen* (Darmstadt, 1959), Bd. I, 17. In thus interpreting Wilamowitz' famous phrase we do not intend to suggest that Wilamowitz is an example of a scholar who adopted a non-religious reading of Homer.

11 Trans. Moses Hadas (1954; rpt. Boston, 1964), 4.

12 Cf. also *Iliad* 2.166 ff. where Athene appears to Odysseus to convey a similar message.

13 English translations of Homer are those of Richmond Lattimore: *Iliad* (Chicago, 1951) and *Odyssey* (New York, 1968).

14 Cf. also 13.155, 15.667, 16.210, 16.275 for additional examples of μένος inspiration by humans.

15 She is a bird at *Odyssey* 1.319, a vulture at 3.371, a swallow at 22.238.

16 Cf. also *Odyssey* 16.449-51; 17.36-37; 19.53, 604; 21.358.

17 As Albert Camus observed in *The Plague*, it is times of crisis that bring out what is truest and deepest about a person's character.

18 *The Greeks and the Irrational*, 11.

19 See *Ibid.*, 2 ff. for examples.

20 Martin Nilsson, "Götter und Psychologie bei Homer," *Archiv für Religionswissenschaft*, 22(1923-24), 365.

21 If not in the fields, at least on the battlefield. But it is noteworthy in this regard that Odysseus is skilled in all the pastoral and agricultural tasks connected with his holdings (see M.I. Finley, *The World of Odysseus* [New York, 1954], 70-71).

22 Cf. A.W.H. Adkins, *Merit and Responsibility: A Study in Greek Values* (Oxford, 1960), 63:

> The maintenance of his *time* is the chief aim of Homeric man and Homeric god; and god, like man, ever fears that it may be diminished: for it depends on others, and on their acts, not their intentions. Accordingly, it is acts, not intentions, of which gods take account, spurred on by a scale of values in which one's position is so precarious. In a sense, the gods must be even more touchy than men. That they have more *arete* and *time* than men is, apart from their immortality, the only clear distinction between the lesser Homeric gods and mankind. Indeed, it is by an excess of *arete* that men become gods; an excellent reason why the gods should not only resent slights upon their *time*, but should also be jealous of human success, which constitutes so large a part of *arete*.

Cf. also A.W.H. Adkins, "Homeric Gods and the Values of Homeric Society," *Journal of Hellenic Studies*, 92(1972), 3-11; and E.R. Dodds, *The Greeks and the Irrational*, 32.

23 Though this truth was qualified by the need to recognize the social hierarchy in the divine sphere.

24 Though perhaps it falls short for suggesting a purely business transaction and omits the connotations of a quasi-feudal relationship.

25 See for example, *Iliad* 9.98-99.

26 M.I. Finley, *The World of Odysseus*, 83-84, lists as equivalents of θέμις: "custom, tradition, folkways, mores, whatever we may call it, the enormous power of 'it is (or is not) done'."

27 For a similar view of Zeus' justice in Homer see H. Lloyd-Jones, *The Justice of Zeus* (Berkeley, 1971), chap. 1 and 2, and cf. esp. his statement on page 49:

> Our examination of the *Iliad* has shown that it is from this very notion that a god is affronted by any infringement of his rights within a particular sphere that the concept of Zeus as the champion of justice first developed.

28 George M. Calhoun, "Polity and Society," in A.J.B. Wace and F.H. Stubbings, *A Companion to Homer* (London, 1962), 450.

29 Compare E.R. Dodds, *The Greeks and the Irrational*, 52, note 18:

> Those who argue otherwise [than that there is "no indication in the narrative of the *Iliad* that Zeus is concerned with justice as such"] seem to me to confuse the punishment of perjury as an offence against the divine τιμή (4.158 ff.), and the punishment of offences against hospitality by Zeus Xeinios (13.623 ff.), with a concern for justice as such.

It will be seen that if the view of the justice of Zeus argued above is correct, then there is no "confusion". The justice of Zeus in both the *Iliad* and the *Odyssey* is grounded on his τιμή. There is no question of any "justice as such," if by that is meant "what is right as such" outside of "what is done," or what is enforced by individual moral conscience, in either the *Iliad* or the *Odyssey*. The increased "moral" sensitivity (or fair play) of the gods, and Zeus in particular, in the *Odyssey*, noted by Dodds (32) and Lloyd-Jones (28) should not be taken as a matter of "justice" in the Homeric sense. Despite the departure of the gods in the *Odyssey* from the *Iliad* pattern of positively conniving to bring misfortune and disaster on men, the gods still exact "justice", that is, vengeance, retribution, for offenses against their τιμή. So the gods in the *Odyssey* are more "just" from our point of view, but are not measurably more just from the Homeric point of view.

30 *Merit and Responsibility: A Study in Greek Values*, 31.

31 *Ibid.*, 32-35.

32 While the term does not occur in the *Iliad*, it occurs with some frequency in the *Odyssey*.

33 Cf. A.W.H. Adkins, *Merit and Responsibility*, 24: "Now *kaka* denotes things which are unpleasant, without any moral connotation."

34 *Ibid.*, 42.

35 *Ibid.*, 10-11.

36 *Ibid.*, 48-49.

37 *The World of Odysseus*, 66.

38 *Merit and Responsibility*, 58-59.

39 *Ibid.*, 59.

40 The original distinction between shame and guilt cultures was made by the anthropologist, Ruth Benedict. Adkins follows E.R. Dodds in viewing Homeric society as a shame-culture. Cf. esp. E.R. Dodds, *The Greeks and the Irrational*, 17 and 26 (note 106).

41 *Merit and Responsibility*, 37-38, 50-52.

42 *Ibid.*, 51-52.

43 For further discussion of Adkins' analysis of the value-scheme of Homeric society see A.A. Long, "Morals and Values in Homer," *Journal of Hellenic Studies*, 90(1970), 122-39, and Adkins' response to Long's criticisms, "Homeric Values and Homeric Society," *Journal of Hellenic Studies*, 91(1971), 1-13.

44 Cf. M. Nilsson, *Greek Piety* (New York, 1969), 8: "it was not the communal religion, but only poetry and myth which described the gods' appearance and activity."

45 If the transcendent power be perceived as the result of a personal being's willed act, it is but a short step to the conviction that the being can be persuaded by prayer and offerings. Thus all religion as "commerce" with the gods is generated simply and naturally from Homeric man's basic apperception.

46 Lines 1-7 (trans. Richmond Lattimore).

47 To reinterpret the φύσις of line 5, which Richmond Lattimore has translated as "strength".

48 *Third Pythian Ode* 61-62. Cf. also *Fifth Isthmian Ode* 14-16: "Strive not to be a Zeus; all things are thine, should a share of these boons fall to thy lot. Mortal aims befit mortal men."

49 See R. Lattimore, *Greek Lyrics*, (1949; rpt. Chicago, 1960), 14-16.

50 This suggests that Greek philosophy and the other more obvious forms of rationalism should be seen as a function of the wider self-confident, self-reliant creative activity of the Greeks.

51 In this respect they were basically politically neutral.

52 In Xenophon's *Symposium* one Niceratus says, "My father, wishing me to become an accomplished man [ἀνήρ ἀγαθός] made me learn the whole of Homer, so that even today I can still recite the *Iliad* and the *Odyssey* by heart." At *Phaedrus* 245a Plato speaks of lyric poetry "glorifying the countless mighty deeds of ancient times for the instruction of posterity."

53 See Henri Marrou, *Education in Antiquity* (New York, 1956), 71.

54 To which might be added the obligation to return a gift or favor.

55 To be more precise, it was not every faction that displayed

this spirit; it was in the first instance the Periclean party, the party that controlled Athenian politics.

56 *The Peloponnesian War*, trans. Rex Warner (Harmondsworth, 1954), I.76.

57 In this sense they differ profoundly from a true aristocrat.

58 *Republic* II.366-67; cf. also Glaucon at II.358.

59 For this and the following points see *Gorgias* 501 ff.

60 In their study, *Who Was Socrates?* (New York, 1960), Alban D. Winspear and Tom Silverberg observe that Socratic philosophy undermined the cause of the democratic party by questioning the right of "the man in the street" to rule (70-71). Hence, they simply conclude, Socrates necessarily served the anti-democratic aristocratic party. But this is to impose a straightjacket on Socrates: he must be either for or against the people's party. Winspear and Silverberg do not countenance the possibility that Socratic ἔλεγχος constituted a fundamental critique undercutting both political factions.

61 See G.S. Kirk and J.E. Raven, *The Presocratic Philosophers* (Cambridge, 1963), 176. (Cf. also the *Genesis* account of creation from slime.)

62 That is, the four elements, earth, air, fire and water. It also follows from this that Xenophanes and Empedocles in some sense represent reversions to old ways of thinking.

63 New Haven, 1970.

64 Of course Parmenides sought an absolute One, while Socrates sought, with respect to *each* virtue he attempted to define, the one Form in the many instances. On this difference see Plato's account in the *Parmenides*, 128e-130a.

65 In the *Seventh Letter* (340b-341d) Plato states that the philosophy he sought to teach others was not a doctrine which could be put into words and handed over as though it were a special area of study. Rather, after a long period of apprenticeship to instruction, and the more subtle, prolonged influence of close companionship, there came about a sudden, inner, intellectual and personal transformation (341d)(which Plato likens to a spark catching hold and leaping up into a blaze). That is, the only passage to the authentic life of philosophy was through the λόγος, but such dialectical ἔλεγχος by itself was mere sophistic logic-chopping, mere eristic without positive fruit or point. Thus, in the Platonic philosophical way the λόγος needed to be completed by an inner seeing, specifically

of the Forms, as a matter of practice, as a "habit of daily life" (340d).

66 The definitions of shape (σχῆμα) as the limit of a solid at *Meno* 76a and of quickness (τάχος) as the quality which accomplishes much in little time at *Laches* 192a-b are notable exceptions.

67 In another fundamental respect, however, this characterization of the Socratic way as the face to face vision of a single, sublime object is misleading. For the knowledge of the Good, for example, the highest Form, is also a *synoptic* vision, a seeing how the various specific goods of life are to be ordered hierarchically into a harmonious whole. In the developed Platonic concept of the soul—which can in this respect hardly be considered as contrary to Socratic thought—the three parts, emotion, appetite, and reason, each performs its own function without encroaching upon or interfering with the function of the other parts—the highest, ruling function, of course, belonging to the reasoning part. The vision of the Good is precisely the seeing of all the separate goods of life together in one single, systematic, integral vision. To (be able to) see the ideal order of all facets, ends and values of human existence *is* to have attained "the face to face vision of the Good."

68 They were not, however, the *sole* modes of human access to the divine: Socrates still recognized many of the traditional modes of the irruption of the divine into human *experience*. He frequently gave expression to his awe at the divine beauty of some youth, or occasionally at the inspired character of someone's speech (not always ironically). He no doubt saw something divine in the works of the sculptors, architects, painters and poets who had adorned the civilized life of Periclean Athens so splendidly. And there was of course his own "divine sign". And according to *Phaedo* 60c ff. Socrates spent his last few days in prison before his death composing a hymn to Apollo and setting the fables of Aesop to verse in obedience to a command received in a dream to "practice and cultivate the arts."

69 This constitutes the most fundamental respect in which Xenophon's Socrates is to be marked off from Plato's. Xenophon's Socrates gives off a distinct odor of virtue, out of his complacent self-esteem at his own virtue.

70 At *Laws* 731d-732b Plato warns against self-love as the gravest obstacle to the attainment of ἀρετή in the soul.

Appendix I

Aristophanes' Portrait of Socrates in the 'Clouds'

As might be expected, quite a variety of attitudes have been taken towards the value of Aristophanes' testimony. Burnet and Taylor were inclined to take a relatively positive attitude. They took the *Clouds* to be a caricature of basic fact. And they attempted to vindicate through detailed historical criticism the fundamental historicity of Aristophanes' portrait at a number of subtle points. Their general attitude is perhaps best expressed in Taylor's words:

> When Aristophanes makes it the main point of his play to represent Socrates as the head of something like a regular "school" who combine physical science with what we should call "spiritualism", though we should be very foolish if we took his representations at anything like their "face value", we should be equally foolish not to ask ourselves what are the real facts which explain the caricature, and whether we cannot discern them reappearing from a different angle of vision in what we are told by Plato or Xenophon.[1]

There have been other scholars as well who have assumed this positive attitude, though, unhappily, they have not always exercised the same restraint over their scholarly ingenuity as Burnet and Taylor. They have seen definite references to the historical Socrates in the most passing allusions and the vaguest, loosest terminology in Aristophanes. A very different attitude has been taken by two recent scholars. Kenneth Dover and A.R. Lacey have in their studies minimized the historical value of many of the passages in the *Clouds* wherein scholars have most often seen allusions to the historical Socrates.[2] Yet even so, they recognize the probability that there is some vague correspondence of the Socrates of the *Clouds* to the historical Socrates: they accept the general bearing of Taylor's remarks above,[3] while rejecting most of their particular identifications of Socratic elements. The outcome of their account is, as Gregory Vlastos puts it, that "the Aristophanic portrait, though composed much earlier than either Plato's or Xenophon's, offers no basis for correcting Plato's."[4] Yet for all their impressive, and, indeed, ultimately persuasive, scholarly arguments at particular points, they leave relatively untouched the central claim in Burnet's position. Burnet astutely noticed that *Phaedo* 96a ff. assigns to the early Socrates an interest in a number of topics which read like a list of the diverse intellectual currents at Athens at very nearly the time of the play (423 B.C.).[5] Burnet also pointed out that there is a sound, independent historical tradition that Socrates was the pupil of Archelaus, the disciple and successor of Anaxagoras.[6] Lacey suggests, "As for his long association with Archelaus, it may well be, as Hackforth says, that 'what kept him was his teacher's lectures on ethics and politics'."[7] But even if we suppose that Socrates was chiefly interested in these, it is hardly plausible to suppose that he was not acquainted with Archelaus' physical theories.

These two observations taken together seem to indicate that Aristophanes' account of the principal features of Socrates' σοφία (skill, expertise, wisdom), namely, physical speculation on the nature of the heavens and its implied atheism with regard to the traditional gods, accurately reflects the philosophical interests of the real Socrates.[8] This apparent convergence of Plato and Aristophanes on the central feature of Aristophanes' portrait has of course impelled scholars to look for further correspondences, to take seriously the possibility that other features of his caricature derive from otherwise unattested fact. The answer to that question, to whatever extent an answer is possible, must rest on an examination of the play itself. We shall therefore postpone the special problem of the precise meaning of *Phaedo* 96a ff. and its relation to the *Clouds* until we have submitted the play as a whole to internal criticism.

In Aristophanes' comedy Socrates and his disciples live in a small house (οἰκίδιον, 92) which serves as their φροντιστήριον (94), a "thinkery" (or as we might say today, "think tank") for "clever and accomplished souls" (ψυχῶν σοφῶν, 94).[9] There, as Strepsiades (the old fool from the country who is the main character in the comedy) understands it, two things are taught: the sky is a hemispherical lid (πνιγεύς, choker) over the earth and we men are the charcoals (ἄνθρακες, 96-97); and how to win any case (once money is paid for the instruction) whether right or wrong (98-99). Strepsiades seems to have only a vague idea of these men and their teachings, but he clearly looks on them with respectful deference. To him they are "deep thinkers" (μεριμνοφροντισταί, 101) and "fine, distinguished men of character and accomplishment" (καλοί τε κἀγαθοί).[10] Pheidippides, his son, has a different opinion of them. To him they are scurrilous scoundrels full of vanity and pretension. They have dirty feet from wearing no shoes and are sickly and pallid in complexion from their self-confinement indoors (102-04).

The two items which Strepsiades names as topics of instruction at the "Thinkery" are really quite distinct kinds of philosophical interests. Though we are introduced in the play to the whole gamut of Socrates' wisdom,[11] it might be pointed out that Strepsiades is interested only in the two Logics (see 112 ff.), or more particularly, the "worse" Logic. For he hopes that by learning that Logic he will be able to defeat those who argue from what is generally accepted to be right and proper and decent. Strepsiades has incurred heavy debts. He thus hopes the "wrong" Logic will free him from his debts.

The Socrates of the *Clouds* is the master of every knowledge high and low. Nothing is too grand or too minute for the wisdom of Socrates. Geometry and astronomy are studied at the school, as well as "things under the earth," searching out even the regions below Tartarus (188 ff.). Among other things Socrates is expert in the solution of problems requiring practical ingenuity. He devises a way to measure the length of a flea's foot and thus to measure the length of a flea's jump in terms of flea's feet (144 ff.). The example ridicules Socrates in much the same way as the familiar caricature of medieval theology: how many angels can fit on the head of a pin? Ridicule is poked at what seems to be a degraded intellectualism poring over irrelevant minutiae. Similarly, Socrates' astuteness in the physiology of gnats is enthusiastically praised. Aristophanes seizes an opportunity to mock intellectuals while drawing, no doubt, some loud guffaws from the audience by his indelicate explanation of how gnats hum (indeed blast away as with a trumpet) through their butt-end (156 ff.).

Socrates is also accomplished in what we would consider more properly the "sophistical" arts—rhetorical eloquence and logical disputation. He offers to teach Strepsiades measures (or meters, περὶ μέτρων), rhythms (περὶ ῥυθμῶν), and words (περὶ ἐπῶν) (636 ff.). By "words" he seems to mean a kind of speculative grammar; in it is included the knowledge of whether a word is rightly (ὀρθῶς) the gender commonly given it. We learn from Plato that ὀρθοέπεια (correct language) and περὶ ὀνομάτων ὀρθότητος (on the correctness of names, or words) were favorite topics of the sophists (see *Phaedrus* 267c, *Protagoras* 338e ff., *Euthydemus* 277e, *Cratylus* 384d). Now, all of this Socrates considers to be propaedeutic to the learning of the one thing Strepsiades wants—the "wrong" Logic. But Socrates eventually gives up in exasperation at the ignorant, forgetful[12] old dolt (see 783 ff.). At 476 Socrates was commissioned by the Clouds to "try to instruct the old man and stir up his mind and test his intelligence."[13] Most of Socrates' attempts to instruct Strepsiades take place inside the φροντιστήριον (that is, off-stage), but we do get a few glimpses of his pedagogical technique. At 700 ff. Socrates is coaching Strepsiades how to "think through for [him]self some of [his] own problems" (695):

Consider and scrutinize in every which way
and whirl yourself about once you have packed it together tight.
But whenever you fall into a difficulty
quick, latch on to some other thought. (700-05)

And as if that were not vague, worthless enough instruction he follows up with this advice:

Come now, cover yourself up and give your mind free play
for subtleties; think over things in detail making right
distinctions and observations.
If you have any difficulty with any of your ideas
put it aside for a while
and then bring it back before the mind anew and weigh it
up. (740-45)

At 762 Socrates says the idea is to "let out the slack on your mind and let it range about in the air." On this evidence Socratic pedagogy was merely handing out ambiguous intellectual tricks. It is no wonder it was of no use to Strepsiades—his attempts to satisfy his teacher grew more and more absurd until Socrates finally had him thrown out.

The climax of sophistical education was the "wrong" Logic (or Argument, λόγος). Now, Socrates does not teach the Logic in the play. He leaves the stage as soon as the two personified Logics appear for their extended debate. Socrates says, strangely, "Pheidippides will learn from the Logics in person, but I shall not be present" (886-87). But it is clear elsewhere that the "wrong" Logic is part of Socrates' σοφία. At 1106 the "wrong" (or "worse") Logic offers to teach Pheidippides to speak (διδάσκω σοι λέγειν). This is evidently equivalent to making him "a clever sophist" (1111). At 1146 ff. it is Socrates who is recognized as the young man's teacher, the one to whom credit is due for the successful education of Pheidippides in the "wrong" Logic. And though at 1465-67 it is recognized that Pheidippides had more than one teacher (Chaerephon is mentioned),[14] at 1403 it is Socrates himself (αὐτός; cf. 195, 219) whom Pheidippides credits with turning him from his dissolute ways to logical subtleties. He then proceeds to demonstrate by means of the newly learned Logic that it is right for him to beat up his father. At 1448 ff. Strepsiades damns his son, Socrates, and the Logic he has learned to hell.[15] In short, though the "wrong" Logic is not put in Socrates' mouth in the play, it is nonetheless recognized to be part of his wisdom. (We shall discuss the character of this new Logic below.)

We have not so far mentioned the most distinctive aspect of Socrates' philosophical teaching in the *Clouds*—and the aspect which reveals his religion. Socrates spends much of his time aloft in a basket[16] contemplating heavenly or "lofty" things (τὰ μετέωρα πράγματα, 228). He explains what he is doing in these terms:

> Never could I have rightly discerned matters celestial
> Did I not suspend my judgment and mingle my intellect
> With its kindred air. If I gazed upward from below, nothing
> Could I find. Earth's force draws intellect's sap to itself
> And so it is with watercress too.[17]

Kirk and Raven are surely right in thinking that Aristophanes has used the philosophy of Diogenes of Apollonia for his model here.[18] According to Theophrastus, Diogenes held that Air was the φύσις, the substance or basic "stuff", of the universe.[19] Simplicius reports Diogenes' novel argument in support of the view:

> My opinion, in sum, is that all existing things are differentiated from the same thing, and are the same thing. And this is manifest: for if the things that exist at present in this world-order—earth and water and air and fire and all the other things apparent in this world-order—if any of these were different from the other (different, that is, in its own proper nature), and did not retain an essential identity while undergoing many changes and differentiations, it would be in no way possible for them to mix with each other, or for one to help or harm the other, or for a growing plant to grow out of the earth or for a living creature or anything else to come into being, unless they were so composed as to be the same thing. But all these things, being differentiated from the same thing, become of different kinds at different times and return into the same thing.[20]

Diogenes thus formulated a new argument in support of the reductionistic physical monism of the cosmological philosophers. Everything was basically "just", or "merely", air. Now, this kind of rationalistic materialism was reductionistic with regard to religion as well. There was no room left for the gods and goddesses of popular tradition in the universe of the φυσικοί. But what is especially interesting to us is that Diogenes' philosophical ἀρχή (origin, first principle) was also divine. He says,

> Men and the other living creatures live by means of air, through breathing it. And this is for them both soul (i.e. life-principle) and intelligence . . . and if this is removed, then they die and intelligence fails.[21] And it seems to me that that which has

> intelligence is what men call air, and that all men are steered by this and that it has power over all things. For this very thing seems to me to be a god and to have reached everywhere and to dispose all things and to be in everything. And there is no single thing that does not have a share of this; but there are many fashions both of air itself and of intelligence.[22]

> And this very thing (Air) is both eternal and immortal body, but of the rest some come into being, some pass away.[23]

By calling Air a "god" Diogenes did not conceive it theistically. The divinity of the basic material stuff of the universe consisted *simply* in its being eternal, immortal, the principle of motion and life in a body, and the principle of intelligent order in the cosmos.

Socrates' peculiar brand of heavenly wisdom in the *Clouds* certainly depends on suppositions such as the above. Contemplation consists of lifting one's airy mind into more direct physical proximity with the airy divinities of the heavens. By thus suspending oneself one overcomes the weighing-down of the intelligence by the moisture in it. Intelligence is apparently a quasi-vaporous substance and thus can become more or less moist (which would suggest in turn some sort of equivalence between stupidity and water on the brain).[24] The manner of conceptualization here is the same as Diogenes' brand of physical speculation.

To some extent what Socrates has to say about religious matters would seem to be very much in the spirit of Diogenes' pronouncements. Socrates says he does not accept the traditional gods. At 247-248 he says, "The gods aren't current coin with us." And at 367 he explicitly maintains, "There is no Zeus." Yet he looks upon Air and Breath and Ether, etc. as divine. But apart from these non-theistic divine principles, and unlike Diogenes, there stand the Clouds, which are clearly conceived to be goddesses. At 253 they are referred to as "our household goddesses" (ταῖς ἡμετέραισι δαίμοσιν)—they are evidently the patronesses of the φροντιστήριον. They are called "great goddesses" (μεγάλαι θεαὶ) at 316. At 365 Socrates asserts, "these [Clouds] are the only gods [θεαί]; all the others are nonsense." The fact that Socrates treats only the Clouds as *personal* deities does not prevent him from blurring the difference between them and the other, non-personal divinities. The truth is that he frequently brings them into uneasy juxtaposition. Such, for example, is 423-24, "Surely you won't believe any more in any god except the ones we believe in—Chaos and Clouds and Tongue, these three." If we look at all the other "gods" besides the Clouds (air and ether at 253, chaos and tongue at 423, breath, chaos and air at 627) we note that they form a "family" of deities having a common airy, vaporous, gaseous nature. Since Socrates can claim that the Clouds are the *only* gods (365) it must be the case that they can stand for all the rest. They are somehow simultaneously identical with the other "gods" they represent; yet they also stand apart as the only personal deities. "Tongue" is the obvious exception to this family.[25] But this has to do with Aristophanes' comic purposes. It is the deity Tongue which best incarnates his reason for designating this set of airy deities as the patrons of Socrates' religious-philosophical school. For the Clouds are the patronesses of "battles of the tongue" (419). It is precisely because they are by nature airy, vague, obscure, ever in flux, ambiguous, elusive, that they are the perfect sponsors of sophistry, the art of being able to bring out any argument the victor in discussion. (We should note that mist and cloud were Homeric devices used by the gods to confuse and obfuscate and hide things from human minds, a kind of negative revelation.) "Tongue" seems to be intended to stand for the speaking aspect of the airy deities; it refers to the goddesses under their aspect of heavenly windbags. At 292 Socrates takes thunder to be the "voice" (φωνή) of the Clouds; they are answering his plea to make themselves manifest to the high-priest (Socrates) and the new initiate (Strepsiades). Socrates explains to his prospective disciple all the wondrous benefits of the Clouds' patronage:

> [T]he heavenly Clouds [are] great gods for men who don't work. It is they who grant us judgment [γνώμη], disputation [διάλεξις], and intelligence [νοῦς], as well as dealing in the marvelous [τερατεία], circumlocution [περίλεξις], and striking and checking one's opponent in argument [κροῦσις καὶ κατάληψις]. (316-18)

At 331 ff. the fruits of their patronage are described:

> By Zeus, you don't realize that these [mist and dew and smoke] watch over sophists—
> soothsayers, healers, fashionable men who have nothing better to do than sit around all day wearing their bejewelled signet rings, songsters in the dithyrambic contests, astrological quacks. They support any old idler doing nothing at all so long as he sings their praises in poetry. (331-34)

Socrates is of course the "priest of all this most subtle, frivolous talk" (359).[26] But what is especially interesting in this regard is that Aristophanes insinuates a comparison of Socrates with Pythagoras. Socrates is presented as the master of a religious-philosophical community sworn to secrecy about its doctrines. At 219 the student answers Strepsiades' inquiry about who the creature aloft in the basket is with the simple reply, αὐτός, "It is *he*." There is here the same tone of hushed reverence for the Master discernible in the familiar Pythagorean expression, αὐτὸς ἔφα, "he himself said it."[27] Similarly at 195 a student is anxious for all members of the party to move inside lest "he" (literally, 'κεῖνος, "that one") catch them exposing themselves too long in the open air. Though the Master himself is absent his authority is palpable. At 143 we are told that the teachings handed down in the Thinkery were to be held as "mysteries" (μυστήρια).[28] It was "not allowed" (οὐ θέμις, 140) to divulge the teachings to any outsider.[29]

Aristophanes goes beyond what is known about Pythagoreanism in his staging of Strepsiades' initiation into the cult of the Clouds and their manifestation to him. But if Aristophanes did not draw on Pythagoreanism for his depiction of the initiation ceremony he need not have had any other particular religious cult in mind as a model.[30] For the general procedure of special cults (enthronement, coronation with a chaplet, anointing), which is all Aristophanes has borrowed, would have been common knowledge.[31]

The patient and close examination of all the features of Aristophanes' Socrates makes the task of critical evaluation almost superfluous. For it becomes immediately obvious that the portrait is a crude, superficial conflation of every intellectual tendency of the day. Physical speculation was distinct from the sophistical arts that taught the ability to talk and argue persuasively in public. And neither of these was, so far as we know, set up after the pattern of Pythagorean communities.[32] Further, there is the intrinsic incompatibility between Socrates' teaching that the Air (in its many forms) was divine and preaching that the Clouds were the only gods man was to worship and honor. The bearing of physical speculation was atheistic—it was a way of thinking which undermined traditionally conceived religious cult. Socrates' cult of Clouds may have been directed to new, untraditional gods, but the conception was quite traditional and orthodox. Aristophanes no doubt had added this element for its dramatic value. It is to be observed that abstract physical concepts like Air, Ether, Vortex, etc. have little dramatic value. But a concrete personification as goddesses provides distinct advantages to the dramatic staging of the play. At 252 ff. where the Clouds are being "revealed" to Strepsiades Aristophanes even seems to mock his own staging of their appearance. Strepsiades, who is having difficulty perceiving the goddesses (see 322, 324, 328; at 330 he apologizes that he always thought of them as just mist and dew and smoke), finally perceives them in the form of women (they were dramatically represented by a chorus of women). "But how can the Clouds be women," he says (340 ff.), "—look, they even have noses!" There remains the possibility, however, that Aristophanes' cloud-goddesses allude to a real facet of Socrates' thought. The personal δαίμονες may ultimately be an allusion to Socrates' δαιμόνιον, the well-known, but non-theistically conceived, divine inspiration which Plato and Xenophon inform us about.

When one considers to what extent the *Clouds* is given over to high buffoonery (there is considerable preoccupation with man-eating bugs and vermin, the penis, and gassy discharges from human digestion) it is very likely that Aristophanes has simply rummaged indiscriminately through the "modern" intellectual trends for whatever might be successfully burlesqued. There are two general characteristics of Socrates' teachings that support this view: first, they are vague and imprecise, suggesting that Aristophanes had no more than the layman's understanding of these schools; second, they are related in a facetious tone—the choice of words, for instance, hardly promotes taking the teachings seriously. But there are more specific reasons for doubting that the historical Socrates taught this hodge-podge of philosophical wisdom.

At 358 ff. the chorus addresses Socrates:

> Greetings, old man, who seek the science of subtle speech!
> And you too, priest of cobweb folly; say what you wish.
> No sophist high-flown would we rather oblige, Prodicus excepted;
> He for his mind and wit, but you because you strut in the streets
> And roll your eyes and go barefoot and take abuse and walk in pride
> Confident in our patronage.[33]

What is curious here is the distinction between Prodicus and Socrates. Prodicus is to be preferred for his σοφία and γνώμη, terms which are indicative of sophistical learning in general. But Socrates is acclaimed for quite other reasons—he goes about in the streets pompous and grave, exposing himself to frequent abuse from the populace. The distinctive thing about Socrates seems to be not his sophistical learning, but the disdain and scorn his physical appearance evokes in public. The Socrates who is supposed to be the representative *par excellence* of the new intellectual trends is nonetheless curiously atypical. The truth is that there are a number of internal discrepancies and inconsistencies in Aristophanes' portrait of Socrates. Some of the details of his account show Socrates to be distinctly out of step with the "sophists" of the day.

In the argument between the Right and Wrong Logic the παιδεία (education) of days gone by is contrasted with the "new-fangled" teaching. The Wrong Logic is the dramatic personification of the new iconoclastic intellectualism. The Right Logic sings the praises of the good old days, the days when the traditional virtues were valued and sought by all. The old παιδεία emphasized propriety, simplicity, martial discipline, physical toughness, conformity to tradition, respect and reverence for authority, sexual decorum and continence. Right Logic accuses the young men of the day of being shameless "softies". They indulge themselves in every sort of dainty luxury and pleasure. Instead of accomplishment in athletics they care only for endless chatter and idle debate; the courtroom and the public gathering have supplanted the gymnasium as the scene of their sport. But far from living the "good life" of the sophisticated idlers of the day, according to the *Clouds* the Socratic philosophical way entailed rigorous asceticism.[34] And far from frequenting the luxuries of the bath, the Socrates of the *Clouds* is represented as dirty, vermin-ridden, indolent, and thus poor. But the sophists earned healthy fees and maintained themselves in a certain amount of style. Further, from the testimony of Plato's *Symposium* (219e ff.) we know that Socrates must have been extraordinarily physically tough. He endured the hardships of the campaign so well that he aroused the resentment and animosity of his fellow soldiers out of jealousy and a sense of inferiority. And under fire of battle Socrates single-handedly saved the wounded Alcibiades. Then at the retreat from Delium Socrates again distinguished himself for coolness under fire and valor.[35] So Socrates was a skilled, tough soldier, and his reputation as such had no doubt reached the populace.

The conclusion is evident: as an independent historical document Aristophanes' *Clouds* is thoroughly unreliable. No doubt there is some grain of truth in the portrait of Socrates, but it remains indistinguishable to us now from the "nonsense" (as Plato calls it in the *Apology*[36]). Fact could hardly be differentiated from fiction at all without using control sources such as Plato and Xenophon. But their accounts differ sharply from Aristophanes'. In fact Plato is acquainted with his play and flatly contradicts some of its main allegations (in particular, that Socrates "searches into the things under the earth and the things in the sky, and makes the weaker argument defeat the stronger," *Apology* 19b). Their own accounts make quite clear what Aristophanes' account implies: that there were some very important differences between Socrates' own mode of philosophizing and that of the other intellectuals of the day. In all probability, then, the *Clouds* was conceived as an attack on Socrates principally because he was the most conspicuous and notorious intellectual figure of the day. Aristophanes, whether out of ignorance or as a crude polemic, has suppressed the differences and added extraneous elements, all to his own end: the presentation of an uproarious, rollicking comedy.

APPENDIX I

1 *Socrates* (1933; rpt. Garden City, 1953), 21.

2 A.R. Lacey, "Our Knowledge of Socrates," *The Philosophy of Socrates*, ed. Gregory Vlastos (Garden City, 1971), 28-29; Kenneth Dover, "Socrates", *Aristophanes: Clouds* (Oxford, 1968), xl-xliv (rpt. as "Socrates in the *Clouds*" in *The Philosophy of Socrates*, ed. Vlastos, 58-63).

3 As does W.K.C. Guthrie, *A History of Greek Philosophy* (Cambridge, 1969), III, 422.

4 Gregory Vlastos, "The Paradox of Socrates," in *The Philosophy of Socrates*, ed. Vlastos, 1.

5 J. Burnet, *Plato's Phaedo* (Oxford, 1911), xxxviii-xlii, 99-109.

6 *Ibid.*, 100.

7 A.R. Lacey, "Our Knowledge of Socrates," 27.

8 A.D. Winspear and T. Silverberg, for example, in their study, *Who Was Socrates?* (New York, 1960), see an "inescapable contradiction" between the Aristophanic representation and the Platonic idealization of Socrates (vi). Though recognizing that the Socrates of the *Clouds* is a caricature, they nonetheless think it necessary to accept its general features in entirety: "The *Clouds* clearly is an attack by an essentially conservative playwright on the foremost and best-known exponents of popular materialism and radical skepticism at Athens" (43).

9 Burnet sees in the "souls" an allusion to the Socratic doctrine of immortality and the practice of death (care of the soul) (see his *Plato's Phaedo*, liv). But this is to ask the word to bear a considerable weight. In the context of the play the word points to the half-dead, half-alive state of the φροντισταί—they are pale and sickly (features frequently mentioned in the *Clouds*; see K. Dover, "Socrates", xxxiii for references). Thus the primary level of meaning—they are "ghostly" figures—actually draws upon the traditional meaning of the word, and not the new religious use of the word (whence Burnet sees Socrates deriving the above doctrines). The point is a good example of the tenuous "identifications" scholars have made of fleeting mentions of terms familiar to us from Plato.

10 The adjectival formula of course stands for the ideal of personal excellence, ἀρετή, which implies all of the following: nobility and strength of character, physical prowess (particularly in battle) and beauty, ability to lead and influence others, success and the renown that accrues from it.

11 See K. Dover's remarks on the meaning of σοφιστής and σοφία in the late fifth century, "Socrates in the *Clouds*," 54, note 12:

> Since Plato we have been accustomed to distinguish between the sophist and the philosopher, and therefore lack a word to cover both. The distinction was not made in the language of Aristophanes' time, nor was the word σοφιστής so narrowly confined as later.

And in *Aristophanes: Clouds*, 106, ad 94:

> σοφία in Aristophanes, and in the fifth century generally, most commonly denoted an active, creative skill or artistry, for which knowledge, practice, and native wit are all required.

12 It is interesting that the testing of Strepsiades is understood to be a test of his *memory* (482-83). And when Socrates' patience is finally exhausted, he exclaims, "To the devil with you, you most *forgetful*, inept old crony" (789-90). A reverse allusion to Socrates' doctrine of recollection? Perhaps, but still, like the mention of the "miscarriage of thoughts" (an allusion to Socrates as mid-wife?) at 137, it is only fuel for idle speculation. They remain only possible, fleeting allusions.

13 My translation, as are the following, unless otherwise indicated.

14 See K. Dover's remarks on Chaerephon, *Aristophanes: Clouds*, xcv-xcvii.

15 By mentioning Socrates and the Logic separately it is not implied that the Logic was distinct from Socrates' own personal wisdom. Aristophanes has merely made a comprehensive statement of the evil Strepsiades wishes to damn: teacher, teaching, person taught.

16 Or mat suspended by its corners sling-like; cf. K. Dover, *Aristophanes: Clouds*, 126, ad 226.

17 The translation is Moses Hadas' from *The Complete Plays of Aristophanes*, ed. M. Hadas (New York, 1962), 108.

18 G.S. Kirk and J.E. Raven, *The Presocratic Philosophers* (Cambridge, 1963), 443, note 2.

19 *Ibid.*, 429-30.

20 *Ibid.*, 431, no. 602 (fr. 2).

21 *Ibid.*, 434-35, no. 605 (fr. 4).

22 *Ibid.*, 435, no. 606 (fr. 5).

23 *Ibid.*, 436, no. 607 (fr. 7).

24 Cf. Heraclitus, fr. 118: "A dry soul is wisest and best."

25 χάος does not here mean a disordered, shapeless mass, nor does it likely mean space or void. Rather it refers to the expanse of airy sky between the heaven (firmament) and earth. Cf. Kirk and Raven, *The Presocratic Philosophers*, 27.

26 At 436 Socrates is termed a πρόπολος, a priest or minister.

27 See Kirk and Raven, *The Presocratic Philosophers*, 221, note 4.

28 The secrecy of the Pythagoreans with regard to their doctrines was legendary; see Kirk and Raven, *The Presocratic Philosophers*, 221, nos. 265-66.

29 Cf. K. Dover's observation, *Aristophanes: Clouds*, 112, ad 140:

> The expressions οὐ θεμις and οὐ θεμιτον are particularly used of divulging secrets to those who have not gone through rites of initiation or do not belong to a given sex, family, or nationality.

Also on this topic see the interesting paper by A.W.H. Adkins, "Clouds, Mysteries, Socrates and Plato," *Antichthon, Journal of the Australian Society for Classical Studies*, 4(1970), 13-24, and the reply to it by G.J. de Vries, "Mystery Terminology in Aristophanes and Plato," *Mnemosyne*, 26(1973), 1-8.

30 Taylor's opinion that Socrates was probably initiated in the Orphic religion in childhood and remained permanently impressed by it (*Socrates*, 51) has few supporters today.

31 See K. Dover, *Aristophanes: Clouds*, 130, ad 254.

32 See K. Dover's comment, *Ibid.*, xli; W.K.C. Guthrie (*History*, III, 372) relates an observation of F.M. Cornford's:

> [T]here is something in a claim once made by Cornford, that we can recognize in the Socrates of the *Clouds* at least three different types which were never united to perfection in any single person: first the Sophist, who teaches the art of making a good case out of a bad one; secondly the atheistic natural philosopher like Anaxagoras; and thirdly the ascetic moral teacher, ragged and starving through his own indifference to worldly interests.

33 Moses Hadas' translation, *Complete Plays*, 112.

34 See 412 ff.

35 Cf. also *Laches* 181b.

36 φλυαρία, 19c4.

Appendix II

Plato's Intellectual Biography of Socrates: '*Phaedo*' 96a ff.

We turn now to the special problem presented by *Phaedo* 96a ff. The account there departs from the usual Platonic (and Aristotelian) picture of the Socrates who was concerned only with ethics and politics. None of the other Socratic dialogues ever represents Socrates as showing the slightest interest in natural philosophy. It comes as something of a surprise, then, when in the *Phaedo* Socrates embarks on a lengthy excursus to tell us of all the physical matters he speculated about in his early days. The argument from silence, of course, is never a strong one, but the overall impression of the early, Socratic dialogues in this regard is unequivocally confirmed in so many words by the *Apology*. For at 19b ff. we have not only an unequivocal statement that he neither has any knowledge with respect to the nature of physical reality nor takes any interest in it, but we even have an explicit rejection of Aristophanes' representations:

> Very well, what did my critics say in attacking my character? I must read out their affidavit, so to speak, as though they were my legal accusers: Socrates is guilty of criminal meddling, in that he inquires into things below the earth and in the sky, and makes the weaker argument defeat the stronger, and teaches others to follow his example. It runs something like that. You have seen it for yourselves in the play by Aristophanes, where Socrates goes whirling round, proclaiming that he is walking on air, and uttering a great deal of other nonsense about things of which I know nothing whatsoever. I mean no disrespect for such knowledge, if any one really is versed in it—I do not want any more lawsuits brought against me by Meletus—but the fact is, gentlemen, that I take no interest in it. What is more, I call upon the greater part of you as witnesses to my statement, and I appeal to all of you who have ever listened to me talking—and there are a great many to whom this applies—to clear your neighbour's minds on this point. Tell one another whether any one of you has ever heard me discuss such questions briefly or at length, and then you will realize that the other popular reports about me are equally unreliable.
>
> The fact is that there is nothing in any of these charges. . . .
>
> (*Apology* 19b-d)

In this light it is no wonder that many scholars find *Phaedo* 96a ff.

rather unsettling in its admissions, for it seems to fly directly in the face of the overall portrait of Socrates in the Platonic dialogues.

In this as in all matters of Platonic scholarship there has been no lack of varying interpretations. Some, notably Zeller and Bonitz, have seen no historical value in the autobiographical form of the *Phaedo* account; they see it rather as a general, impersonal sketch of the stages of philosophical development leading up to Plato's own theory of Forms.[1] And more recently A.R. Lacey has argued that Plato's attribution of an early, scientific period and an interest in teleological explanation to Socrates has no more historical value than his attribution of the theory of Forms (attributed by most scholars to Plato, and not, at least in its fully mature form, to Socrates).[2] On the other hand, there is the opinion of Kenneth Dover: "It is quite possible for both [*Apology* 19c-d and *Phaedo* 96a ff.] to be true, if we take them as meaning just what they say; if we read more into *Phaedo* 96a ff. than it says, reconciliation becomes impossible."[3] The compatibility of the two passages rests, according to him, on the distinction between Socrates' early period of *interest* and *inquiry* into natural science and the assertion that Socrates professed to *teach* scientific doctrines: "It is plain that this account of a metaphysical curiosity which the scientific speculations of others failed to satisfy is separated by a very wide gulf from Aristophanes' portrayal of a Socrates who professed to teach scientific doctrine in mechanistic terms."[4] W.K.C. Guthrie's opinion is similar:

> Plato uses this narrative [*Phaedo* 96a ff.] for his own purposes, but it would be strange indeed if it had no basis in fact. To the inherent improbability may be added the congruence of the account with information from Xenophon, and with the equally reasonable supposition that the representation of Socrates in the *Clouds* is a farcical exaggeration of certain known trends of his thought rather than based on nothing at all.[5]

Speaking to the apparent contradiction between *Apology* 19 and *Phaedo* 96, Guthrie argues:

> Assuming that [*Apology* 19 was] actually used by him in his defense, we need not accuse him of 'lying for the sake of saving his skin' [referring to a phrase used by Hackforth in his discussion of the *Apology*]. His study of the natural world may have ended forty years before, and was in any case an inquiry undertaken to satisfy himself. He never taught it publicly nor promulgated any theories of his own, though no doubt he would eagerly debate the current theories with a few chosen friends.[6]

Though the basic terms of this interpretation are acceptable,[7] there is an inadequacy in it which needs to be shored up by further argument. It minimizes the sharpness of the conflict between the two passages on the plain sense of the words. *Phaedo* 96a 6-8 says, "When I was young, Cebes, I had a remarkable enthusiasm for the kind of wisdom known as natural science."[8] *Apology* 19d 4-5 says, "Tell one another whether any one of you has *ever* (πώποτε) heard me discussing (διαλεγομένου) such questions [things below the earth and in the sky and how to make the weaker, or wrong, argument defeat the stronger, or right, argument] briefly or at length." We cannot suppose that Socrates' early inquiry into natural philosophy did not entail *discussion*. In *Phaedo* 96a ff. we find a list of questions in which Socrates was interested that is fairly representative of the philosophical currents of the day. These philosophical questions were openly debated and discussed. We can hardly suppose that *if* Socrates became acquainted with all these current theories he did so privately. But the *Apology* says that Socrates could never be found discussing such questions. In what follows, then, an attempt will be made to buttress Guthrie's and Dover's basic interpretation by supplying specific considerations that remove the *prima facie* conflict.

Let us consider Burnet's attempted way through the impasse. Since he accepted the complete historicity of both the *Phaedo* and the *Apology*, he was of course committed to solving the above difficulties. His tack was to appeal to Socratic irony. When Socrates *says* he does not "know" any of the scientific wisdom attributed to him by Aristophanes and others, what he *means* is that although he is acquainted with all there was currently to be known of these things, he does not consider that "knowledge" because "in the simplicity of his heart, he cannot refrain from asking more ultimate questions."[9] Thus, on Burnet's interpretation Socrates uttered the statement at *Apology* 19 at his trial concealing his own real mind. His utterance was true only by virtue of a mental reservation made privately. But on the plain sense of his words one would have to incline more towards Hackforth's objection that this is plain deception: "If Socrates did know all there was to be known about such things, he is not being ironical, but is lying, and that too to save his own skin, to influence the court in his favour: for the rebuttal of the old accuser's charge of μετεωροσοφία is designed to remove the popular misconceptions which he feels to be the real present danger."[10] And this is a disturbing suggestion in its own right, since it is difficult to think that Socrates would lie to save his skin if he was prepared to be martyred for his views. Burnet hopes to slide by the crucial point of conflict in the two accounts by suggesting that Socrates "never talked about these matters *in public*."[11] But Hackforth astutely points out that in a later passage Socrates refuses to allow the suggestion that there was any distinction between his private and public teaching: "if anyone asserts that he has ever learned or heard from me privately anything which was not open to everyone else, you may be quite sure that he is not telling the truth" (*Apology* 33b). There is, then, a serious clash between the *Apology* and the *Phaedo* which is not evaded by an appeal to the distinction between private and public, or between professing to teach and inquiring (because Socrates says he never even discussed such topics).

The truth of the matter is that Plato's account at *Phaedo* 96a ff. provides extraordinary difficulties. Let us approach the matter step by step. Socrates begins by telling us of his extraordinary enthusiasm for the wisdom called natural science. Generally he understood this natural science to be the explanation of things in three respects: through what does a thing (literally, "each thing," ἑκάστου) come to be, through what is it destroyed, and through what is it (διὰ τί ἔστι, in the *prima facie* sense, in the context of physical speculation, "through what [physical cause] does a thing [continue to] exist"—or, as Socrates will implicitly interpret it in his "simple", "ignorant" αἰτία in *Phaedo* 99c-103c, after becoming disenchanted with physical speculation and frustrated in his quest of an Anaxagorean-style teleological account, "through what is it what it is").[12] He relates two different phases or "moments" (if we are not to take the division chronologically, as we shall argue below we should not) of his scientific investigations.[13] First, he says he "often [πολλάκις] twisted this way and that to answer certain questions."[14] Burnet has made some extremely pertinent historical identifications of the questions that Socrates says he investigated. The results of his researches are as follows.

96b2-3: "Is it when the conjunction of the hot and the cold results in putrefaction, as some say, that living creatures develop?" This was the doctrine of Archelaus, who was an eclectic philosopher known principally as a disciple and successor of Anaxagoras.[15] Let us note Kirk and Raven's judgment of Archelaus:

> [I]t is hard to resist the conclusion that Archelaus was a second-rate thinker, motivated by the desire to revise the system of Anaxagoras by the inclusion of as many as possible of the doctrines of his most eminent predecessors. From Anaximander he borrowed, besides his biological theories, the primacy of the hot and the cold; from Anaximenes he apparently borrowed the doctrine of the condensation and rarefaction of air; from Empedocles he seems to have taken the four 'elements'; and from Anaxagoras he inherited, with a number of modifications of

> detail such as that concerning the shape of the earth, almost everything else. It is hardly surprising that the resulting synthesis is lacking in great interest or importance.[16]

So we see that Archelaus' philosophy was an unimaginative conflation of various features of the natural philosophy of the day. Now, Burnet has produced evidence of a sound historical tradition that Archelaus was Socrates' teacher.[17] This means that we have good independent historical evidence that Socrates was exposed to all the major currents in the natural philosophy of the day early in his career. As we look to the other questions that held Socrates' interest, we find this borne out.

96b4: "Is it blood that we think with, or air or fire?" Burnet observes:

> The question of the 'seat of the soul' or sensorium was keenly debated in the first half of the fifth century B.C. The views that the soul is blood or breath are primitive, but both had just been revived as scientific theories. Empedocles had said αἷμα γὰρ ἀνθρώποις περικάρδιόν ἐστι νόημα, and he was the founder of the Sicilian school of medicine. . . . The doctrine that the soul is air was as old as Anaximenes, but had just been revived by Diogenes of Apollonia . . ., and is attributed in the *Clouds* (230) to Socrates. The Heracliteans at Ephesus of course maintained their master's view that the soul was fire.[18]

96b5-8: "Is it blood that we think with, or air or fire? Or is thought due to something else, namely the brain's providing our senses of hearing, sight and smell, which give rise to memory and judgment, and ultimately, when memory and judgment have acquired stability, to knowledge." Burnet observes: "The credit of being the first to see that the brain was the seat of consciousness belongs to Alcmaeon of Croton . . ., and the same view was upheld in the fifth century B.C. by Hippocrates and his school."[19]

Burnet argues that this curious mixture of Ionian and Italian philosophical views points to a date in the middle of the fifth century B.C. and no other time.[20] It would be an anachronism to date such a confluence of ideas earlier or later. Further, Burnet has argued persuasively that Plato repeatedly and consistently evidences real genius at being able to recreate bygone historical periods in his dialogues, periods such as the later fifth century which was so different from the post-Periclean age in which Plato grew up.[21] All of this is strong evidence that there is indeed some degree of truth to Aristophanes' depiction of Socrates in the *Clouds* as a natural philosopher. And though some scholars may take Plato to be creating a literary fiction in the *Phaedo* when he sets forth the theory of Forms, and the "make-shift" method of explaining reality in terms of the Forms, as belonging to Socrates (points which we shall have reason to examine more closely in Appendix IV), they are not similarly warranted to take the account of Socrates' early natural scientific interests as a literary fiction.

However, caution is required. For Socrates reports that he "had simply no gift whatever for this sort of investigation" (96c). Far from advancing in wisdom in these matters, his end-state was worse than the beginning. He ended even unlearning certain axioms of common-sense which were fundamental to such scientific accounts of nature (such as, that a human being came to be what he was through adding particles of flesh to flesh and bone to bone by eating). It appears on the basis of such experiences he could hardly claim to be himself a natural philosopher. In general the passage gives the impression of being an ironic account of Socrates' learned ignorance: he was awed at all the fine knowledge to which physical speculators pretended and submitted their theories to scrutiny. The considerations (96c-97b) which contributed to the complete undermining of his confidence in the project of natural philosophy are very significant in this regard. They are not considerations which stem from physical speculation itself. They are rather logical considerations, specifically of an Eleatic character. That is, they are examples of pure *a priori* reasoning not unlike, for instance, Zeno's arguments against plurality. The scientific theories supposed that one could explain the coming to be of a thing by the addition of one thing to another; scientific explanation consisted of an identification of the constituent elements of a thing and an account of how they were put together to form the new thing. But what confounds Socrates is a logical paradox in the very *idea* of addition (taken as an adding of things). We commonly suppose that when we add one to one we obtain something else than what we had before the addition, namely two. That is, we take two as that which (or, the thing which) results from adding one thing and one thing. But the operation of adding the one thing to the other thing does not add anything to either thing: each remains simply the single thing it is. What then accounts for that which results from the operation of addition, namely the two? Is it possible that the bringing together (adding) works this change? But if we suppose that the operation of adding performed on one thing changes it somehow into two, then how can we explain how the opposite operation, dividing, also works the same result, namely yields two? Because of this *logical* paradox Socrates no longer accepts the "old method" of explaining how natural things come to be.

We are not told by Plato how or when Socrates came to this Eleatic philosophical point of view; as the tale is told by Plato,

Socrates' thinking is already informed by it as he encounters the various physical theories of the day. It is true, of course, that the so-called "mature" theory of Forms, which most scholars take to have been formulated for the first time in clear, unequivocal language by Plato at *Phaedo* 99d ff., constitutes the solution to the original Eleatic perplexities raised at 96d-97b. For example, the new αἰτία of 10 being 2 more than 8 is not 2 (or the addition of 2) but the Form, (greater) "numerousness."22 To some the natural complementarity of the original Eleatic objections to natural philosophy and their solution by the new αἰτία in terms of the Forms is cause for suspecting the historical veracity of Plato's account. They would see the Eleatic considerations, along with the entire autobiography, as Plato's attempt to set the stage for the exposition of his own theory of Forms at 99d ff. However this might be (and we shall consider the question at greater length in Appendix IV), for the moment it will suffice to observe that the manifest, *prima facie* understanding of the passage indicates that Socrates inquired into physical speculation and formulated his criticism of it from wholly different premises from those of the physical speculators—thus a major obstacle to the compatibility interpretation (of *Apology* 19b ff. and *Phaedo* 96a ff.) is removed. Let us turn now to the second phase or "moment" of Socrates' scientific investigations.

In relating the episode of his becoming acquainted with Anaxagoras' philosophy (97b8-99c6) Socrates speaks as if he was already persuaded that an explanation of things in terms of Mind (as the principle ordering and arranging everything in the universe in the way that was best for each individual thing and for the universe as a whole) was right and proper and good. It was not that Anaxagoras had persuaded him of this. It was the promise of such an account that had aroused Socrates' interest; Anaxagoras had not been able, as it were, to produce the goods. Socrates says such an explanation was "after my own heart." It was *already* Socrates' distinctive philosophical attitude to demand an explanation of the universe in terms of the good. Because natural philosophy could not supply such an explanation he turned to the moral and political sphere. Mechanical, reductionistic and materialistic explanations of the universe were completely unsatisfactory to him. Socrates expected an αἰτία of the universe that was intelligible to ordinary human experience—that is, an explanation in terms of categories taken from everyday human experience, and not in terms of some non-evident physical "stuff" or principle. Plato thus represents Socrates' moral humanism in philosophy, at least in some of its basic pre-suppositions, as pre-dating his acquaintance with Anaxagoras.

But that is not all. As Plato represents it, Socrates turned to

Anaxagoras' philosophy only after he became disenchanted with other speculative theories. However, if Socrates became acquainted with the former set of physical theories through Archelaus, *the disciple of Anaxagoras*, the basis for the division into chronological phases collapses: we cannot plausibly suppose that Socrates did not become acquainted with Anaxagoras under Archelaus.

This conclusion carries a significant implication: that the distinctive perspective revealed in the Anaxagoras episode at *Phaedo* 97c ff. was not the chronological consequence of the first episode. (There is, after all, no connection drawn between the considerations which undermined the first phase and the convictions Socrates evidences in the second.) We are thus unavoidably led to the new, however surprising, conclusion that, as Plato relates it, *both* Eleatic logic and an inclination towards explanation in moral, humanistic terms (particularly teleological explanation in terms of the good) were features of his thought from the very first, and that they antedated even his youthful inquiry into natural philosophy.[23]

On the basis of the foregoing arguments we may conclude that Socrates was at no time satisfied with the scientific theories of the day, and that he inquired into such matters from wholly different premises. He was never in any real sense a natural philosopher, for he never became convinced that the basic enterprise was valid. Thus he never taught such doctrines. He must have "discussed" such theories in the minimal sense entailed by mere acquaintance with them. But he did not "discuss" them in the sense that he participated with other committed and professed natural philosophers on their terms in the search for "scientific" truths about nature. With this qualification, the *Apology* and the *Phaedo* must be said to be, as Guthrie and Dover maintained, compatible.

1 See R. Hackforth, *Plato's Phaedo* (Indianapolis, 1955), 130.

2 A.R. Lacey, "Our Knowledge of Socrates," *The Philosophy of Socrates*, ed. Gregory Vlastos (Garden City, 1971), 43-44.

3 K. Dover, "Socrates in the *Clouds*," *The Philosophy of Socrates*, 68.

4 *Ibid.*.

5 W.K.C. Guthrie, *A History of Greek Philosophy* (Cambridge, 1969), III, 422.

6 *Ibid.*, 423.

7 To which may be added R. Hackforth (see his *Plato's Phaedo*, 130-31).

8 For translations of the *Phaedo* I have used R. Hackforth, *Plato's Phaedo*.

9 J. Burnet, *Plato's Euthyphro, Apology of Socrates and Crito* (Oxford, 1924), 82, ad 19c4.

10 R. Hackforth, *The Composition of Plato's Apology* (Cambridge, 1933), 148.

11 J. Burnet, *Plato's Euthyphro*, 83, ad 19d5. So also does W.K.C. Guthrie, in the quote at the bottom of page 204 above.

12 *Phaedo* 96a8-10. Gregory Vlastos, in his brilliant paper, "Reasons and Causes in the *Phaedo*" (in G. Vlastos, ed., *Plato, I: Metaphysics and Epistemology* [Garden City, 1971], 132-66, esp. pages 155-58; originally published in *Philosophical Review* 78[1969], 291-325), argues that it was precisely the achievement of Socrates' "simple" or "ignorant" αἰτία in *Phaedo* 99c-103c to see the ambiguity of the basic questions which natural philosophers were addressing, and to distinguish physical αἰτίαι, or explanations, from logical ones: positing the Forms as metaphysical first principles, Socrates (that is, Plato) proceeded to deduce *a priori logical* truths about the physical world.

13 See 97c-d, where the second, Anaxagoran phase is conceived to be a teleological approach *to supplying the same three* αἰτίαι.

14 Or, "I went through all sorts of contortions to answer certain questions"—both are my paraphrases of 96a10-b1.

15 See J. Burnet, *Plato's Phaedo*, 96, ad 96b3. Archelaus was also known as an elegiac poet.

16 G.S. Kirk and J.E. Raven, *The Presocratic Philosophers*

(Cambridge, 1963), 398-99.

17 J. Burnet, "Socrates", in Hastings' *Encyclopedia of Religion and Ethics* (Edinburgh, 1920), XI, 665. Cf. also Kirk and Raven, *The Presocratic Philosophers*, 395: "[T]he tradition that Archelaus was a pupil of Anaxagoras and teacher of Socrates is too well attested to be doubted."

18 J. Burnet, *Plato's Phaedo*, 101, ad 96b4. The quote from Empedocles is from fr. 105 Diels.

19 *Ibid.*, ad 96b5. R. Hackforth (*Plato's Phaedo*, 123, notes 1 ff.) and W.K.C. Guthrie (*History*, III, 423, note 2) concur in Burnet's identifications.

20 J. Burnet, *Plato's Phaedo*, 102, ad 96b9.

21 *Ibid.*, xxx-xxxvii.

22 See G. Vlastos, "Reasons and Causes in the *Phaedo*," 156-57, note 64.

23 These findings undermine the interpretation of Socrates by A.D. Winspear and T. Silverberg in their study, *Who Was Socrates?* (New York, 1960). In their view the historical Socrates has been appropriated by the newly emergent idealist philosophy (of Plato) and interpreted one-sidedly as "a kind of disembodied mind" (vi). They seek to reverse the process of idealization, and indeed virtual canonization (85), of Socrates and bring him back down to earth by viewing him in his concrete historical context amidst the political factionalism and strife of the Athens of his day (on the principle that "thought always is consciously or unconsciously a reflection of social forces," 26). They differentiate two radically different phases of Socrates' career separated by a period of transition or conversion. In his early phase Socrates was a proponent of materialistic speculation with its attendant ethical relativism and atheistic skepticism; he was a member of the left-wing democratic party and stood for νόμος (that the morally right and good was but a matter of convention or might) in the νόμος-φύσις debate of the day. The later Socrates, however, was converted to the other side of the struggle: intellectually he now stood for φύσις (that the morally right and good was eternally grounded in the nature of things and divinely sanctioned), and politically he threw in his lot with the conservative, aristocratic party.
The crux of their view of Socrates, however, is an interpretation of *Phaedo* 96a ff.:

From the passage in the *Phaedo* just quoted one or two

> points arise in fairly clear outline. Socrates went through a philosophical conversion; this conversion was a turning-away from materialism and a concept of material causation to idealism and a belief in teleological causation. (35-36)

It is interesting to observe their tergiversations with respect to Plato's *Apology*: having posited this radical cleavage between the early and late Socrates they find it necessary to accuse Plato of "deliberately confound[ing] two quite separate things; the accusations that Aristophanes had made against him—based on the intellectual interests of his early manhood—with the distrust that had arisen much later" (77). Similarly they find it "obviously ridiculous" that their later conservative, aristocratic Socrates should be accused of atheism (79). (We have argued above, in Chapter Two, that the charge brought against Socrates was atheism [that he had to prove he was orthodox in his thinking], that in this respect Socrates gave no defense in the sense of a positive denial of the charge, and that he was in fact *legally* an atheist.)

Appendix III

Xenophon's Portrait of Socrates: An Overall Evaluation

Hegel stands at the head of a long line of scholars who saw in Xenophon their most reliable guide to the historical Socrates. For our knowledge of Socrates, he said, "[W]e must hold chiefly to Xenophon in regard to the content of his knowledge, and degree in which his thought was developed."[1] Their position, essentially, is that because Xenophon was a man of ordinary intellect and had no special interest or ability in philosophical matters we can be fairly certain that his Socratica are the most accurate and impartial testimony we have. A recent exponent of this general position is Leo Strauss:

> For our precise knowledge of Socrates' thought we depend on Plato's dialogues, Xenophon's Socratic writings, Aristophanes' *Clouds*, and some remarks of Aristotle. Of these four men Xenophon is the only one who, while knowing Socrates himself, showed by deed that he was willing to be a historian. Hence it would appear that the primary source for our knowledge of Socrates should be the Socratic writings of Xenophon.[2]

But a closer look at Xenophon's works shakes one's confidence in their historical value. Burnet sagely advises that "in estimating Xenophon's claim to be regarded as a historian, we must never forget that he was the author of the *Cyropaedia*."[3] G.C. Field's comments on the *Cyropaedia* shed light on what Burnet must have had in mind:

> This is the famous *Cyropaedia* of Xenophon. In form a biography of Cyrus, the first king of Persia, it is in fact an attempt to draw a picture of Xenophon's ideal ruler and of the kind of training that might produce him. With an undisguised openness, which cannot have been meant to deceive, Xenophon departs, on occasion, widely from the known historical truth. The work is, indeed, frankly a historical novel, though written for purposes of edification rather than amusement, and it can never have been meant to be taken for anything else.[4]

Further, we know that it was not beyond Xenophon to deliberately misrepresent the facts on occasion, especially when it came to vindicating his own historical credentials. In the *Oeconomicus* and in the *Symposium* Xenophon claims to have been a first-hand witness of the conversation he relates, when it is certain that this was impossible (in the latter case Xenophon was an infant at the dramatic date of the dialogue).[5]

Field has argued that the *Memorabilia* is on a different footing from the above works, as well as other Socratic λόγοι such as the dialogues of Plato and Aeschines:

> It is not primarily presented, like these works, as a dramatic composition, but as an attempt to answer a series of charges actually made against a historical personage. As such it would have no point unless it was true to the facts. It is presented to us as history.[6]

Actually the same argument has been forcefully advanced by Gregory Vlastos with respect to Plato's *Apology* (an argument that once established serves as "a touchstone of the like veracity of the thought and character of Socrates depicted in Plato's other early dialogues").[7] In any event, it may be said that Field's argument stands. Arguing against the "literary fiction" view of the *Memorabilia*, Field says,

> But this does not mean that Xenophon invented the whole thing from beginning to end. The simple and natural supposition —much too simple and natural for some of our more ingenious scholars—is that he collected his material in the same manner as he would collect material for his history. The *Hellenica* and *Agesilaus* give us the true standard by which to judge of the *Memorabilia*, not the *Oeconomicus* nor yet the *Cyropaedia*.[8]

There are, however, difficulties with Field's view. First, we cannot be sure that Plato was not one of Xenophon's historical sources. As Field maintains, "In general there is not the slightest real evidence that Plato was a principal or even an important source for Xenophon's picture of Socrates."[9] The emphasis here must fall on the word "real"—Field is talking, evidently, of positive proof. Doubtless there can be no such positive proof. But that there is real cause for suspicion and doubt regarding the independent historical value of Xenophon is clear from the following considerations.

First, Xenophon was in a much poorer position than Plato to know Socrates. Plato was his disciple over a considerable period of time. Xenophon seems only to have made Socrates' acquaintance and not to have submitted himself in a serious and prolonged way to the Socratic way. Plato was present in Athens for the events of Socrates' last days (though at *Phaedo* 59b Plato tells us he was ill and thus absent from Socrates' last conversation). Xenophon was quite young—hardly more than twenty-five when he saw Socrates for the last time. He was not present in Athens for Socrates' trial and death—he had left on a military expedition never to return (he spent the rest of his life in exile from Athens). Thus Xenophon did not have the same close or continuous contact with the circle of Socrates' followers that Plato had. He may well have, as Field urges, researched his Socratica, and in particular the *Memorabilia*, but for the most part his sources were likely to have been other literary defenses (he quite certainly used Polycrates' pamphlet attacking Socrates in the composition of his *Memorabilia*[10]) supplemented by the oral testimony of a few disciples to whom he had access while living in exile.

Second, Xenophon gives us on the whole much less information about Socrates than Plato. We could hardly construct a biography out of his Socratica as we can with Plato's. And what Xenophon does tell us about Socrates confirms Plato on numerous points —there are relatively few, and unimportant, discrepancies on points of fact.

Third, Greek historians generally allowed themselves considerable latitude in relating speeches or conversations,[11] and Xenophon has evidently on numerous occasions projected his own interests into his historical reporting (especially in making his Socrates proclaim the virtues of the country gentleman and in the proportionate importance of the martial arts and virtues in his Socrates' scheme of values). Xenophon is certainly no less "interested" than Plato.

Nonetheless, in the last analysis the historical dependence of Xenophon on Plato cannot be demonstrated. Once this is recognized, many have urged, we must in turn recognize the basic historicity of his account *despite* any preference we may have for Plato's more interesting and profound depiction of Socrates. Accordingly, Field concludes that "there are not likely to be any intentional misstatements in it, and the general picture conveyed by it is probably correct, as far as it goes."[12]

But this will not really do. Taylor and others have viewed Xenophon's Socrates as a kind of "lower key" Platonic Socrates. He is Plato's Socrates with the paradox, irony, and individual character and genius taken out of him. Cornelia de Vogel, for instance, advocates this common view of Xenophon:

> In short, [Xenophon's Socrates is] a man who shares the character and hobbies of the Platonic Socrates—only *not* an ironist. Xenophon represents him as giving good advice in all kinds of situations and never makes him the strange fellow he is in Plato's dialogues.[13]
>
> In considering the essential features of Socrates according to the Socratic dialogues of Plato, we found a remarkable

> correspondence between Plato's description and Xenophon's testimony in the *Memorabilia*. Observing that the note of irony, not-knowing and embarrassment, though not absent from Xenophon if one knows how to read him, was much more strongly stressed by Plato, we found a Socrates discussing the same kind of subjects and in the same manner in both authors. The features of soberness and hardiness which are so prominent in the Socrates of Xenophon appeared to be not lacking in Plato's Socrates either; so that, on the whole, we could state that our most important contemporary sources do not contradict but confirm one another.[14]

And Taylor, as we have seen, emphasizes that "[e]xcept on one or two points of detail, Xenophon does not formally contradict anything which Plato tells us about Socrates."[15] But this manner of looking to the particular facts obscures the general fact that Xenophon's Socrates is a *profoundly* and even, we would go so far as to say, *fundamentally* a different person from Plato's Socrates. The overall impression given by the one is markedly different from that given by the other. This is not to say we should turn our view from particular facts to "generalities" and "impressions". It only means that we should notice the radical differences of their presentation of essentially the same facts. We now turn to an examination of some of those facts.

Let us begin with the *Oeconomicus*. It may of course be noted that we have already argued that this work is not a dependable historical document. The views about the virtues of farming put in Socrates' mouth are pretty certainly Xenophon's own, and not Socrates'. However, Xenophon urges the virtues of farming because it is supremely fitted to produce the ἀνήρ καλός τε κἀγαθός. And the definition of "the man of noble character," of which Socrates is the ideal model, is the same in the *Oeconomicus* as it is in every one of Xenophon's other Socratic works.

The *Oeconomicus* is a work devoted to the praise of the virtues of running a farm or country estate. It does not represent Socrates as a farmer; it only represents him as inquiring of Ischomachus, who runs a farm, why he is called "a distinguished man of nobility" (καλός τε κἀγαθός). Ischomachus exemplifies all the virtues of the country gentleman of fine character. Socrates' inquiry is nothing like a Platonic ἔλεγχος. Far from testing this claim to be a gentleman by the rigors of dialectic, Socrates meekly and respectfully submits himself to Ischomachus as a man who truly possesses wisdom and virtue (11.1).

Guthrie has argued that it is entirely plausible that Socrates knew something of farming: since one of the distinctive features of the Platonic Socrates was his use of homely examples drawn from observation of the various crafts and skills, why not also, Guthrie urges, farmers and estate owners?[16] It is of course true that the Socrates of Plato is a sophisticated city-dweller consumed by a passion for philosophical discussion. In the *Crito* (52a–c, 55c) Socrates is said to be such a lover of the cultured life of Athens that he never leaves the city, except for military service—not even for religious festivals. In the *Phaedrus* (230d) Socrates describes himself, "I'm a lover of learning, and trees and open country won't teach me anything." But actually very little special knowledge of farming is implied in the *Oeconomicus*. Indeed, the most interesting and significant part of the work is a question and answer discussion where Ischomachus attempts to show Socrates that the science of running a farm can be recollected from knowledge gained by casual observation and everyday practical common sense. Xenophon is showing in his own distinctive way that the doctrine of recollection so forcefully dramatized by Plato in the *Meno* is part of his own memory of Socrates. The differences, however, are revealing.

Socrates asks to know the art (τέχνη) of farming (15.3). Ischomachus replies that well he might, for there is no art kindlier to man and none easier to learn (15.4). A little later (15.10) he encourages Socrates saying,

> Why, Socrates, farming is not troublesome to learn, like other arts, which the pupil must study till he is worn out before he can earn his keep by his work. Some things you can understand by watching men at work, others by just being told, well enough to teach another if you wish. And I believe that you know a good deal about it yourself, without being aware of the fact.[17]

One can easily learn farming by observing and by listening to what farmers egregiously tell of their art. But there is the curious reference to knowledge already possessed, though unconsciously. At 16.8 Ischomachus terms his teaching "reminding" (ὑπομιμνήσκειν) Socrates what he already knows about farming. At 18.9 Socrates realizes he knew about reaping and threshing and winnowing without being aware of it. But the chief statement is at 19.14-15 where Socrates reflects back on the discussion with Ischomachus:

> Of course there is nothing in what you have said that I don't know, Ischomachus. But I am again set thinking what can have made me answer 'No' to the question you put to me a while ago, when you asked me briefly, Did I understand planting? For I thought I should have nothing to say about the right method of planting. But now that you have undertaken to question me in particular, my answers, you tell me, agree exactly with the views of a farmer so famous for his skill as yourself! Can it

> be that questioning is a kind of teaching, Ischomachus? The fact is, I have just discovered the plan of your series of questions! You lead me by paths of knowledge familiar to me, point out things like what I know, and bring me to think that I really know things that I thought I had no knowledge of.

Commentators who see here a confirmation of Plato's doctrine of Recollection overlook that Ischomachus goes on to explain that the art of farming is exceptional in being learned so easily ("without wearing oneself out") by *seeing* and *hearing* (καὶ ὁρῶντας καὶ ἀκούοντας, 19.17). Socrates here has been easily "reminded" about the art of farming on the basis of what he has already seen and heard. Nothing more than the most superficial acquaintance with farming as well as a bit of practical sense is necessary to be so "reminded". The method of question and answer then draws from one's *practical experience*. It is not an instance of logical dialectic. It does not recollect truths of reason. It does not probe the true nature of ἀρετή or similar "high" concerns. It is engaged simply in laying bare practical knowledge already acquired.

There is an even more profound difference between Plato's and Xenophon's presentations of Socrates' method of using questions in philosophical investigation. In Plato the questioning is engaged in radical pursuit of ἀρετή and σοφία—philosophical ἔλεγχος is a ruthless, relentless questioning of values and opinions. It is no respecter of persons or of social classes. Gregory Vlastos calls our attention to Socrates' questioning of the traditional class-morality of the Greeks:

> The conviction that high-grade moral virtue was possible only for a man who was well born or, at least, moderately well off, ran wide and deep. The disinheritance of a majority of the urban population . . . from the life of virtue is a reasoned belief in Aristotle. Even that radical remolder of the social fabric, Plato, did not reject the dogma; he only sublimated it. Socrates did reject it. He expunged it from the universe of moral discourse when he made the improvement of the soul as mandatory, and as possible, for the manual worker as for the gentleman of leisure, when he redefined all the virtues, and virtue itself, in such a way as to make of them, not class attributes, but human qualities.[18]

Xenophon's Socrates on the other hand sings the praises of the wealthy landed aristocracy. Ischomachus is set up as a paradigm of nobility and virtue (to use Xenophon's phrase, καλός τε κἀγαθός). He stands for completely conventional and "established" virtues: "This manner of living is, as a result, held in highest repute by the cities, for it seems to provide the best and best-willed citizens to the community" (6.10). Ischomachus defends his wealth (we recall Plato's Socrates was impoverished by his practice of philosophy) on thoroughly unexceptional grounds: it is to offer munificent sacrifices and thus to ensure continued prosperity (5.3); to help his friends in need (11.9); and to see that the city is properly adorned (11.9). The life of farming is prized by the πόλις because it produces physically tough and skilled soldiers and generals for its defense in time of war (5.4-7, 13-16; 11.12-18). And none may be expected to be more loyal in time of war than farmers (6.6-7). Finally, the way of life is praised as the easiest, most pleasant and most gentle to man (15.4). (We note that Plato's Socrates could claim no success at all in his conduct of philosophy and that it was a supremely difficult, arduous path to follow.)

Xenophon's *Symposium* provides a good example of how he could confirm Plato on basic features of Socrates' philosophy while at the same time presenting them in such a fashion that they had the opposite effect and significance. At 4.56 ff. he resorts to the technique of conversation so familiar to us from Plato—he begins plying his companion with questions.[19]

> Let us first, said [Socrates], come to an understanding on the functions that belong to the procurer. Do not hesitate to answer all the questions I ask you, so that we may know our points of agreement. (4.56)

This is, of course, an essential feature of the Platonic Socrates. He does not "know" anything, and so cannot presume to teach any positive doctrine. He must then inquire into and test for himself and others the things that they think they know. Questioning is an essential ingredient in the search for real knowledge, as opposed to opinion, about human virtue and excellence.

Now, the questioning of Xenophon's Socrates leads to a definition of the ideal procurer, or pimp (which Socrates believes himself to be, 3.10): he is the man who can make his clients physically and personally attractive to the many, to the whole πόλις. He accomplishes this principally by teaching them λόγοι that will make them attractive and likeable. He teaches them how to speak so that they will win the affections of the people. But this is a good statement of what the sophist attempts to do. Socratic questioning is engaged not in the search for real knowledge and virtue, but in the enterprise of making young men *appear* beautiful and lovable to the masses. For the Platonic Socrates it was just the opposite—he did not care a whit what the many thought was good and beautiful and lovely, but only what the *man who knew* thought.

It may be that this passage should be interpreted as ironic

humor. The general tone of the discussion at the symposium is rather light and jocular. It rambles on pointlessly for the most part—so much idle talk and friendly banter. As has often been pointed out, it is no doubt a more typical example of that Greek social institution than Plato's *Symposium*. We cannot realistically suppose that speeches of the sophistication and polish that Plato presented were within the capabilities of the typical banquet-goer (especially, perhaps, under the circumstances). What Xenophon said at the outset is a good indication of how his account should be taken: "To my mind it is worth while to relate not only the serious acts of great and good men but also what they do in their *lighter* moods" (1.1). Accordingly, it is possible that Socrates means no more seriously to suggest that he does successfully produce attractive young men for the πόλις than that he really is more beautiful than Critobulus. (Socrates attempts to defeat Critobulus, a real beauty, in a beauty-match by adducing specious but ironic arguments that prove that he, Socrates, is in fact the more beautiful.) But if this ambiguity remains with regard to the *Symposium*, this problem does not present itself with regard to the *Memorabilia*.

At the end of his *Memorabilia* Xenophon provides us with a summary of all the features of his Socrates:

> For myself, I have described him as he was: so religious that he did nothing without counsel from the gods; so just that he did no injury, however small, to any man, but conferred the greatest benefits on all who dealt with him; so self-controlled that he never chose the pleasanter rather than the better course; so wise that he was unerring in his judgment of the better and the worse, and needed no counsellor, but relied on himself for his knowledge of them; masterly in expounding and defining such things; no less masterly in putting others to the test, and convincing them of error and exhorting them to follow virtue and gentleness. To me then he seemed to be all that a truly good and happy man must be. But if there is any doubter, let him set the character of other men beside these things; then let him judge. (IV.8.11)

That the person described in this summary is a very different person from the one described in Plato's Socratic dialogues is apparent even to the casual observer. Plato's Socrates defends himself against the charge of atheism brought against him, but it never becomes clear precisely how orthodox his own religious views are. And the fact that Socrates consistently claims ignorance in all "higher" matters, and specifically the myths of the gods (in the *Euthyphro*), makes it at least plausible that he was brought to trial and executed for atheism. But Xenophon's Socrates is a model of conventional piety—he in no way falls short in the fulfillment of his religious obligations. He not only believes in the traditional gods, but he even develops theological arguments for a divine Mind who providently guides and directs the course of events in the cosmos at large. So plausible is Xenophon's Socrates that the very thing he would defend Socrates against—the charge of atheism—becomes radically implausible. It can only have been a colossal mistake, a bizarre case of misunderstanding. As Vlastos forcefully argues,

> Plato, and he alone, gives us a Socrates who could have plausibly been indicted for subversion of faith and morals. Xenophon's account of Socrates, apologetic from beginning to end, refutes itself: had the facts been as he tells them, the indictment would not have been made in the first place.[20]

The fundamental discrepancy between Plato's and Xenophon's Socrates is not confined to the question of religion. Xenophon's Socrates is *wise*. He possesses *knowledge* in moral matters and assumes the role of the master instructing his associates in moral right and defining the virtues. He tests and refutes those who err and exhorts them to virtue, nobility and moral character. The essential features of Plato's Socrates, on the other hand, are familiar. He is ignorant, and for that reason does not teach wisdom or virtue. He only tests the claim of those who think they possess them, and leads his companions on the disinterested and never-ending search for them. He keeps bringing philosophical inquiry back to definitions, but cannot offer successful ones of his own. Further, Plato's Socrates is paradoxical, for he also maintains that virtue is knowledge. And it is clear from the *Apology* and *Crito* that Socrates believes most sincerely that his present stance before the jury, and indeed his whole career (wherein rests his defense), are just and righteous. How can he believe he is right without also claiming knowledge? Further, Plato's Socrates is ironic. Xenophon's Socrates glibly, inoffensively expounds his wisdom. Plato's Socrates begins in exaggerated deference to the wisdom of those with whom he converses, and ends with biting, provoking cross-examinations that totally collapse his opponents' wisdom. Can he really have been sincere in assuming the posture of the total ignoramus, anxious to glean a morsel of his companion's wisdom?

It can hardly be contested that, as Vlastos puts it, "[Plato's] Socrates is incomparably the more interesting of the two figures."[21] Vlastos has further argued that this very fascination, the very fact that he eludes our sure and confident grasp, is really another argument in favor of Plato's Socrates:

> Plato accounts, while Xenophon does not, for facts affirmed by

> both and also attested by others. For example: that Critias and Alcibiades had been companions of Socrates . . . for his Socrates could not have attracted men like Critias and Alcibiades, haughty aristocrats both of them, and as brilliant intellectually as they were morally unprincipled. Xenophon's Socrates, pious reciter of moral commonplaces, would have elicited nothing but a sneer from Critias and a yawn from Alcibiades, while Plato's Socrates is just the man who could have gotten under their skin.[22]

There is yet another respect in which Xenophon's portrait is radically inconsistent and self-refuting. Xenophon testifies, despite his general characterization of Socrates, to all the essential ingredients of Plato's paradoxical, "ignorant" Socrates, but they are related as marginal, miscellaneous features of his portrait. That is, many of the pieces of Plato's Socrates are in Xenophon's, but Xenophon fails to show how they fit together into a coherent whole. The central features of Plato's Socrates have become non-essential marginalia in Xenophon. At *Memorabilia* I.2.3 Xenophon recognizes in passing that Socrates did not profess to teach virtue:

> To be sure he never professed to teach this [οὐδεπώποτε ὑπέσχετο διδάσκαλος εἶναι τούτου, referring to the virtue and nobility of character in I.2.2]; but, by letting his own light shine, he led his disciples to hope that they through imitation of him would attain to such excellence.

But everywhere in the *Memorabilia* Socrates exhorts and instructs his companions in the life of virtue. We recall first of all Xenophon's unequivocal statement in his final summary. And at I.6.13-14 Socrates and his companions are made out to be a mutual exhortation society, a group of friends intent on encouraging and assisting one another in the moral life.

> [W]e think that he who makes a friend of one whom he knows to be gifted by nature, and *teaches him all the good he can*, fulfills the duty of a citizen and a gentleman. That is my own view, Antiphon. . . . *I teach* [*my friends*] *all the good I can*, and recommend them to others from whom I think they will get some moral benefit. And the treasures that the wise men of old have left us in their writings I open and explore with my friends. If we come on any good thing, we extract it, and we set much store on being useful to one another.

At IV.4.9 Xenophon makes an admission about Socrates which in terms of his own general picture comes as a surprise. Hippias says:

> But I vow you shall not hear unless you first declare your own opinion about the nature of Justice; for it's enough that you mock at others, questioning and examining everybody, and never

> willing to render an account yourself or to state an opinion about anything.

This is clearly reminiscent of the Platonic Socrates who resorts to ἔλεγχος by means of question and answer out of his own lack of knowledge. Actually Xenophon relates a few examples of Socratic ἔλεγχος in his *Memorabilia.* At I.2.47 it is said that those who came to Socrates for instruction were "cross-examined for their errors." But the examples of ἔλεγχος which Xenophon relates differ greatly from the Platonic variety. In III.6 Socrates shows a young upstart with pretensions of becoming a politician that he really knows none of the things requisite for that position. But the youth's ignorance is merely on points of fact which could be remedied by better information or simply experience. And Socrates' argument nowhere questions that there are some politicains (presumably with the requisite experience) that do possess real and thorough knowledge of these matters. At IV.2.8-40 Xenophon relates what is perhaps his best example of Socratic ἔλεγχος.[23] Euthydemus' opinion is resoundingly defeated, whereupon he dutifully admits he has been brought to utter confusion about his own views. But the ἔλεγχος is barren of rigorous logical dialectic and argument from logical contraries (a hallmark of Platonic ἔλεγχος). Socrates merely adduces counter-instances. And neither here nor anywhere else does Xenophon furnish us with an example of philosophical inquiry of the "What is *X*?" type.

But, to return to Hippias' charge against Socrates, what comes so much as a surprise is the suggestion that Socrates typically had no views of his own to expound when it is the *central* feature of Xenophon's Socrates that he is a moral teacher and paradigm. Xenophon makes a neat distinction that would seem to solve this contradiction: on the one hand, "the searching cross-examination with which he chastised those who thought themselves omniscient," and on the other hand, "his daily talks with his familiar friends." He is arguing that one must look to the latter if one is properly to judge of Socrates' competence in teaching virtue. And at IV.2.40 Euthydemus, having been convinced of his ignorance, turns to Socrates as his only hope to attain virtue of knowledge:

> Socrates, for his part, seeing how it was with him, avoided worrying him, and began *to expound very plainly and clearly the knowledge* that he thought most needful and the practices that he held to be most excellent.

A very neat distinction indeed, for now Xenophon can, and does, insinuate himself as a authority to that inner circle of plain and clear wisdom that Socrates expounded. Ἔλεγχος and questioning *were* part of the Socratic way, only they were the face he showed to the public, to those who thought they were omniscient.

The consequences of this distinction should, however, be noted. It means that the rigorous logical dialectic was not an essential part of Socrates' philosophy. The *real* philosophy of Socrates was the plain, conventional, moral truisms he expounded in clear language to his friends. On Xenophon's account ἔλεγχος, questioning and ignorance were all non-essential features. In fact, on his account Socrates is really no philosopher at all; he is a *moralizer*. He is a fine, upright citizen, and teaches others how to become the same. He teaches them how "to do their duty by house and household, and relatives and friends, and city and citizens" (I.2.48). He teaches them to be active and energetic in practical affairs (IV.5.1). He teaches them, so far as he can, everything they need to know to succeed in the work they are fitted for (IV.7.1). And he emphasizes over and over the crucial importance of self-discipline (ἐγκράτεια) for the life of virtue.[24] (At I.5.4 it is called the κρηπίς, "foundation", of virtue.) The values which Socratic philosophy stands for are well summarized by a passage from Prodicus' *On Heracles* which Xenophon has Socrates approvingly relate at II.1.28:

> For of all things good and fair, the gods give nothing to man without toil and effort. If you want the favour of the gods, you must worship the gods: if you desire the love of friends, you must do good to your friends: if you covet honour from a city, you must aid that city: if you are fain to win the admiration of all Hellas for virtue, you must strive to do good to Hellas: if you want land to yield you fruits in abundance, you must cultivate that land: if you are resolved to get wealth from flocks, you must care for those flocks: if you essay to grow great through war and want power to liberate your friends and subdue your foes, you must learn the arts of war from those who know them and must practise their right use: and if you want your body to be strong, you must accustom your body to be the servant of your mind, and train it with toil and sweat.

Perhaps the most remarkable bit of self-refuting testimony in Xenophon's portrait of Socrates is an isolated and exceptional passage at *Memorabilia* IV.5.12-6.1. Socrates, Xenophon says, never ceased investigating with his companions what each thing is (σκοπῶν τί ἕκαστον εἴη τῶν ὄντων). He made them skilled in logical discussion (διαλεκτικωτέρους) which entailed distinguishing things according to kind (κατὰ γένη). (At I.2.31 Xenophon denies that Socrates taught the philosopher's art, λόγων τέχνη, "the art of words.") He also tells us (what is surely a Platonic feature) that Socrates took his dialectical opponent back to the definition of whatever they were discussing (IV.6.13).

One could hardly have derived this view of Socratic philosophy from reading the *Memorabilia*. As has been pointed out, one looks in vain for any examples of the rigorous logical dialectic, or inquiry into the essential character of a thing, such as we find in Plato's Socratic dialogues. Indeed, Xenophon's Socrates is downright obtuse when it comes to such things. At III.8.1 ff. Aristippus, who is doing the questioning here, asks Socrates, "How then can that which is unlike the beautiful (τὸ τῷ καλῷ ἀνόμοιον) be beautiful?" Aristippus' reasoning seems to be: you say beautiful things are often quite dissimilar; but a thing is beautiful by virtue of its likeness to the Beautiful; how then can beautiful things be unlike each other if all of them are alike in being like the Beautiful? Socrates, however, fails to pick up the abstract, logical force of Aristippus' objection. Like so many of his slow-witted partners in the dialogues of Plato, Socrates here replies that the objection does not hold because this beautiful thing is different from that beautiful thing. Logical dialectic seems to be a dark secret to Xenophon's Socrates.

The conclusion may be stated briefly. While all the principal elements of the Platonic Socrates are evidenced in Xenophon's Socrates, in Xenophon they do not form a coherent, self-consistent whole. From an examination of the many points at which Xenophon and Plato at least partially parallel and corroborate each other, it is Xenophon who manifests a relatively superficial grasp of Socrates' life and career. Xenophon, then, can hardly be taken as an alternative or corrective account to Plato's in the respects they diverge, for his account stems from basic misapprehension.[25]

1 Quoted from Hegel's *Geschichte der Philosophie*, ii, 69 in J. Burnet's *Plato's Phaedo* (Oxford, 1911), xiii.

2 *Xenophon's Socratic Discourse: An Interpretation of the Oeconomicus* (Ithaca, 1970), 83. See also his *Xenophon's Socrates* (Ithaca, 1972).

3 *Plato's Phaedo*, xiii.

4 *Plato and his Contemporaries* (1930; rpt. London, 1967), 135.

5 *Ibid.*, 138; J. Burnet, *Plato's Phaedo*, xxii; W.K.C. Guthrie, *A History of Greek Philosophy* (Cambridge, 1969), III, 343.

6 *Plato and his Contemporaries*, 140.

7 "The Paradox of Socrates," *The Philosophy of Socrates*, ed. G. Vlastos (Garden City, 1971), 3-4.

8 *Plato and his Contemporaries*, 142.

9 *Ibid.*, 141. Chroust, however, takes Xenophon's dependence on numerous other Σωκρατικοὶ λόγοι, including Plato's, as "commonly accepted" and "need[ing] no further elaboration" (*Socrates, Man and Myth* [London, 1957], 8). See his documentation in the accompanying notes, 229-30.

10 See for instance, G.C. Field, *Plato and his Contemporaries*, 139.

11 See G.C. Field's comments on Thucydides and comparison with Xenophon, *Ibid.*, 142-43.

12 *Ibid.*, 144.

13 "Who Was Socrates?" *Journal of the History of Philosophy*, I (1963), 151. Through most of her essay she emphasizes that irony is the distinguishing feature, but on page 156 she recognizes, rightfully, that "not-knowing" and "embarrassment" (which Socrates causes his partners in conversation) are also distinguishing features.

14 *Ibid.*, 156-57.

15 A.E. Taylor, *Socrates* (1933; rpt. Garden City, 1953), 22.

16 W.K.C. Guthrie, *History*, III, 336, n. 1.

17 The translations from the *Oeconomicus* and the *Memorabilia* (discussed below) are from E.C. Marchant, *Xenophon: Memorabilia and Oeconomicus* (London, 1923). For translations of Xenophon's *Symposium* and *Apology* (or *Defense*, as we choose to call it to avoid confusion with Plato's *Apology*) we have used O.J. Todd, *Xenophon: Symposium and Apology* (published in one volume with

Carleton L. Brownson, *Anabasis*, Books IV-VII)(London, 1922).

18 "The Paradox of Socrates," 19.

19 For other, less important points of convergence, see W.K.C. Guthrie, *History*, III, 344.

20 G. Vlastos, "The Paradox of Socrates," 3.

21 *Ibid.*, 2.

22 *Ibid.*, 2-3. Vlastos' interpretation here follows basically in the footsteps of Kierkegaard's in *The Concept of Irony* (trans. Lee M. Capel [Bloomington, 1968], 53-54):

> We must first bear in mind that Xenophon had a purpose . . . namely, to show what a monstrous injustice it was of the Athenians to condemn Socrates to death. Xenophon has been so successful at this, moreover, that one more readily believes his purpose was to prove it was an absurdity or mistake. Indeed, he defends Socrates in a manner whereby he is rendered not only innocent but utterly harmless. Thus one falls into the deepest wonder as to what kind of demon must have bewitched the Athenians to such an extent that they were able to see more in Socrates than in any other good-natured, garrulous, and ludicrous old geezer who does neither good nor evil, who opposes no one, and who is so amiably disposed toward the whole world if it would only listen to his chatter. And what pre-established harmony in folly, what higher unity in madness could be imagined than that Plato and the Athenians should join hands in killing and immortalizing such a proper old Philistine? This would surely be an irony upon the world without parallel. As in a dispute it occasionally happens that when the crux of the argument is brought to a head and begins to be interesting, some well-meaning third party takes it upon himself to reconcile the warring powers and leads the whole affair back to a triviality, just so much Plato and the Athenians have felt out of sorts with Xenophon's irenic interpolation. In fact, Xenophon, by cutting away all that was dangerous in Socrates, has finally reduced him to utter absurdity—compensation, no doubt, for his having done this so often to others.

23 In the opinion of Robert Wellman in his study, "Socratic Method in Xenophon," *Journal of the History of Ideas*, 37(1976), 307, this is the only clear-cut instance of ἔλεγχος in Xenophon.

24 Norman Gulley, in *The Philosophy of Socrates* (London, 1968), 197, observes: "Self-control (σωφροσύνη, ἐγκράτεια) is, indeed, the key moral concept for Socrates in the *Memorabilia*."

25 In his interpretation of Xenophon's *Hiero* (*On Tyranny* [New York, 1963], 109) Leo Strauss remarks: "What the attitude of the citizen-philosopher Socrates was can be ascertained only by a comprehensive and detailed analysis of Xenophon's Socratic writings." In terms of Strauss's works on Xenophon's Socratica (*Xenophon's Socratic Discourse: An Interpretation of the Oeconomicus* and *Xenophon's Socrates*) this must be taken to be a statement of intent, conviction and belief, and not a conclusion based on argument. For, having defined his frame of reference in terms of the detailed analysis, exegesis and commentary on the text of Xenophon before him, Strauss systematically ignores both the question of the fundamental and systematic incompatibility of Plato's and Xenophon's Socrates, as well as the body of critical argument against the reliability of Xenophon's Socratic writings. So far as we can see Strauss simply *declares* that Xenophon is the key to an understanding of Socrates and then proceeds to confine his vision to the detailed exegesis of the text.

Appendix IV

Socrates and Plato in the Early Platonic Dialogues

As has been indicated in Chapter One, we have confined our discussion to Plato's early dialogues, commonly called the Socratic dialogues, in order to reconstruct Socrates' religious thought. The assignment of Plato's dialogues to early, middle and later groups or periods is fundamental, then, to the distinction we would make between Socrates' thought and that of the mature Plato, and thus demands at least our brief consideration.

The designation of groups is more than chronological: it refers to phases in the development of Plato's thought. The key element, however, in this evolutionary reading of Plato is the stylometric method, a purely technical innovation which yields conclusions as to the relative chronological order of the dialogues. This ingenious scholarly invention was first devised in the last century by Lewis Campbell and perfected in this century by Arnim, Lutoslawski, Raeder, Wilamowitz, and above all by Ritter.[1] W.D. Ross describes this method succinctly in the first chapter of his *Plato's Theory of Ideas*:

> The method that has proved most fruitful, and has led to the most harmonious results when used by different scholars, has been the stylometric method. Starting with the tradition reported by Diogenes Laertius, that Plato left the *Laws* unpublished, and with the universally accepted view that it is the latest of Plato's works (unless the *Epinomis* be accepted as his and dated later), taking the style and vocabulary of the *Laws* as a standard, and testing the affinity of other dialogues to the *Laws* in respect of a large number of independent points (the use of particular particles, the choice of this or that one of two synonyms, the avoidance of hiatus, etc.), different scholars have arrived at results which partly agree and partly disagree, about the order of the dialogues.[2]

Of course, as Ross mentions, the method has yielded somewhat different results in different scholars' hands; it cannot be relied on for the order at precise points in the spectrum. But on the whole a rough order is reasonably clear. When scholars have surveyed from this perspective the movement from the early to the late dialogues a broad shift in the style of thinking has become discernible:

> [T]he early, Socratic dialogues share the following traits which become increasingly faint in the later Platonic dialogues until they completely disappear in the end: artistic unity, dramatic character, presentation of Socrates as a person and an embodiment of his philosophy rather than a mere spokesman for theories, dialectic interchange and real opposition between interlocutors, undogmatic search for definitions and maieutic, aporetic, negative, ironic, elenctic character.[3]

The stylometric method, then, renders the dialogues into a rough chronological continuum; it does not in itself contain the principle of division into the three groups of earlier, middle and later; neither does it in itself provide the basis for characterizing the early group as Socratic as opposed to Platonic. It is a source external to the dialogues, the independent testimony of Aristotle, that has enabled scholars to make these differentiations. This is despite the fact that to do so flies in the face of the explicit view which Plato set forth in the dialogues, that his thought was continuous with and inextricable from that of his great mentor. Where the full-blown theory of Forms is set forth clearly and unequivocally in the person of Socrates at *Phaedo* 100 it is said to be "nothing new, but what I have constantly spoken of both in the talk we have been having and at other times too."[4] But, as we have noted, Aristotle tells us that it was Plato who first separated the Forms. According to Aristotle Socrates' orientation was humanistic and ethical; he was concerned with philosophy as the instrument of the life of ἀρετή. With Plato the perspective shifted. A new metaphysical consideration was adduced, and a new, generalized conclusion about the nature of the universal was drawn:

> Socrates . . . was busying himself about ethical matters and neglecting the world of nature as a whole, but seeking the universal in these ethical matters, and fixed thought for the first time on definitions; Plato accepted his teaching, but held that the problem applied not to sensible things but to entities of another kind—for this reason, that the common definition could not be a definition of any sensible thing, as they were always changing. Things of this other sort, then, he called Ideas, and sensible things, he said, were all named after these, and in virtue of a relation to these; for the many existed by participation in the Ideas that have the same name as they. (*Metaphysics*, I, 987b1-10, trans., W.D. Ross.)

Through Plato the universal came to be conceived metaphysically. Further, and most important, the universals that Socrates sought to define were "*in*" sensible things; they did not "exist apart" from the things they were common to. The *distinguishing feature* of Plato's metaphysicizing of Socratic moral inquiry, according to

Aristotle, was that Plato set the Forms apart (separated them) as "of another sort," as "something different" from individuals.[5]

With Aristotle's testimony in mind, the attention of scholars was turned to a set of four dialogues (the *Phaedo, Symposium, Republic* and *Phaedrus*) about which two special facts were evident: first, they formed an intermediate group between two other sets of dialogues (whatever their internal chronological orders).[6] Second, this middle group of dialogues evidenced a distinctive characterization of the Forms. This view of the Forms, scattered throughout the middle dialogues, may be summarized as follows: the Forms reside in an empyrean realm of eternity, purity and light, utterly separate from the world in which mere mortal souls, weighed down by the dross of their bodies, grope their way amidst shadowy half-realities, in ignorance, error and delusion. The soul's true destiny is to free itself, to separate itself off from its impure condition and rise into that region of divine light, beauty and truth.

One will look in vain for such a two-world ontology, with its accompanying view of the soul, in the earlier group of dialogues; and the later group probes problems and weak points in the middle theory of Forms, and examines special cases of Forms which behave inconsistently with the expectations of that theory (such as Forms that seem to "mix", to have necessary, internal connections, with one another). The *Timaeus* and the *Laws* are somewhat special cases: the former, though it appears to assume a two-world ontology, attempts ultimately to cancel out sensible individuals by a radical idealism, that is, to replace participation and imitation (logically, relationships between two classes of things) with the imaging of the Form in the indeterminate Receptacle; the *Laws*, despite the fact that it is a recasting on another level of the *Republic*, makes scant mention of the Forms and even this does not presuppose a two-world ontology. It was natural, then, for scholars to conclude that it was this theory of Forms, formulated in terms of two separate worlds, to which Aristotle was referring. The middle dialogues were thus authentic Platonic philosophy, and the earlier dialogues were representative of Plato's thought when it was still dominated by his great teacher.

This Aristotelian view of the origin of the theory of Forms is frequently echoed in modern commentators. G.M.A. Grube, for instance, following Wilamowitz and Ritter, holds that the language of Forms in the Socratic dialogues refers only to the common quality of particular things which receive the same predicate, "these common qualities being considered not as transcendentally existing but as immanent in the particulars."[7]

This distinction between transcendent and immanent Forms is central to two other notable interpretations of the origin of the theory of Forms. It becomes the principal feature of W.D. Ross' work, *Plato's Theory of Ideas*. Actually, Ross discusses the Socratic dialogues only as the early stage of *Plato's* thought, and does not broach the topic of the historical Socrates—which is, of course, just as it should be in a study of *Plato's* theory of Ideas. It might be pointed out, however, that Ross considers the interests of Socrates and Plato to have been identical on several fundamental points.[8] Nevertheless, it suffices that his view of the early stages of the Platonic theory of Forms is obviously problematic for anyone taking, as we do, the "Socratic" dialogues to be basically true representations of Socrates' philosophy.

Ross looks upon Socratic definition as the attempt to define the universal common to and immanent in particulars which bear its name. But evidently he thinks that the Socratic "What is (the Form) *X*?" question only *implies* (or, as he puts it, contains "in germ", contains "the seed of", the view) that "to every common name there answers a single entity which is referred to in every occurrence of the name," a view which is tantamount to the theory of Ideas.[9] In the early dialogues the interest is practical: the definition of virtues is a means of becoming virtuous. Because of this the metaphysical implications of the "What is *X*?" question are not seen. Ross paints a picture of how the metaphysical implications came to be gradually realized. Little by little the language of the theory as well as the awareness of its implications appear. He ventures so far as to range the Socratic dialogues in chronological order according to the degree of development of thought. The *Charmides* must be earliest because it shows the least signs of the theory. The *Laches* seeks to define the virtue courage, which is the same in all courageous things—thus, Plato has arrived at the notion of the universal. The *Euthyphro* advances things further, Ross argues, by contributing the terms ἰδέα and εἶδος used "in their special Platonic sense," though Ross does not specify here what this is.[10] The *Hippias Major* adds the phrase αὐτὸ τό, "the *X* itself." Having discussed the development of thought in these dialogues Ross observes:

> At this stage the relation of the Idea to the particular is thought of simply as that of universal to particular; there is as yet no mention of the failure of the particular to be a true instance of the Idea. . . . [T]he point is not made that no particular is ever a true instance of an Idea, that the Idea is a standard or limit rather than a universal,[11] and the relation of the individual to it that of imitation, not of participation.[12]

Later, in summarizing the early dialogues he remarks:

> [This] whole group of early dialogues treats the Ideas as being immanent in particular things. It is 'present' in them; it is placed 'in them' by the craftsman; it comes to be 'in them'; it is 'common' to them; the particulars, in turn, 'possess' it or 'share in' it.[13]

In the last analysis the difference for Ross between the philosophy of the early and the middle dialogues comes down to one thing: in the early dialogues the Forms are immanent, in the middle dialogues they are transcendent.[14] The other features of the mature theory—deficient realization, paradeigmatism, imitation and participation—are all merely derivative notions; they are consequences of the metaphysically transcendent conception of the Forms.

As we noted, Ross does not concern himself with the question of the historicity of the portrait of Socrates in the early dialogues: he is only concerned with the philosophical views there propounded. Yet the implications are clear: if the early dialogues are basically historical, as we have maintained, then Socrates must be refused the credit for having arrived at the theory of Forms. His philosophy was practical and moral in orientation. His perspective was not at all metaphysical; he was interested only in the particular questions, "What is courage?", "What is justice?", etc. It may be that the language in which his philosophy was couched had, *in potentia* as it were, certain metaphysical implications, but it would be no metaphysical theory until those implications were explicitly realized and drawn out. The absence of the theory of Forms in the early dialogues, then, becomes, in Ross' account, a means of differentiating Socrates from Plato.

J.E. Raven holds Aristotle's testimony in similar high regard. He finds it "inconceivable" that Aristotle was wrong in assigning the theory of Forms to Plato and not to Socrates.[15] When Aristotle says that Socrates did not regard his universals as separables he is uttering "a bald statement of fact, not a prejudiced criticism." In other words, the *Euthyphro cannot* mean what it appears to mean: that the use of ἰδέα and εἶδος to indicate the Form X by which individual x's are x, as well as the reference to the Form as the παράδειγμα by which one can judge particular instances, indicate that Socrates had already arrived at the conception of the Forms as independent entities. Raven is confident that the frequently propounded explanation suffices to explain the undeniable language of the Forms in the Socratic dialogues. It is the "common characteristic" Socrates is asking for. And that, he asserts, is "something wholly different" from the celestial Form which we gazed upon before we were born into our bodies. Raven projects the image of Socrates as the ethical humanist struggling to defend the objectivity of moral values against the relativism of the sophists. "He knew *by instinct* that there are eternally and universally valid ethical standards."[16] As Plato grew older, however, he came to see that Socrates' quest for moral absolutes could not be divorced from ontological questions, questions about the nature of the physical world: "Platonism is essentially a metaphysical or ontological theory of nature which grew gradually out of the prior Socratic problem of how we ought to live our lives."[17] It is not until *Phaedo* 95e-102a that that theory is fully formulated. Raven sees this passage as setting forth *both* a new metaphysic *and* a new method. The new method, of course, marks Plato's abandonment (presaged in the *Meno*) of Socratic ἔλεγχος for positive, constructive teaching: the Forms become premises for deducing *a priori* conclusions. But the new metaphysic seems to include a *set* of features (which Raven is not careful to distinguish): the Forms have become intelligible, immutable, eternal realities in another world utterly discontinuous with the realm of sensible things; the Forms have become metaphysical causes of sensible things; and the Forms are said to be in things by "presence" and "communion".[18]

As we have just seen, the *Euthyphro* contains much of the key terminology of the Forms. The terms ἰδέα and εἶδος are both used. At 5d the Form Holy is referred to as "the Holy itself by itself" (τὸ ὅσιον αὐτὸ αὑτῷ); it is said to be "like itself" (αὐτὸ δὲ αὑτῷ ὅμοιον) and "having a certain single character (ἔχον μίαν τινὰ ἰδέαν). At 6d the Form Holy is referred to as the εἶδος itself *by which* holy things are holy. And at 6e the Form is said to be a παράδειγμα. Yet most have failed to see any theory of Forms here. And well they might, if it is the theory of Forms of the middle dialogues they are thinking of. One will look in vain in the early, Socratic dialogues for the most characteristic feature of that theory as it is enunciated in say the *Phaedo* or the *Republic*. There the Forms are conceptualized in terms of what we have called the metaphor of two worlds. R.E. Allen characterizes the main features of this middle theory of Forms in his study, *Plato's 'Euthyphro' and the Earlier Theory of Forms*:

> For all its likenesses, the theory of Forms assumed in the *Euthyphro* is not to be identified with the theory found in Plato's middle dialogues. Burke once remarked that 'though no man can draw a stroke between the confines of night and day, yet light and darkness are upon the whole tolerably distinguishable.' It is so with the early and the middle dialogues. The difference between the *Euthyphro* on the one hand, and the *Phaedo* and *Republic* on the other, is perhaps not the difference of light and darkness. But it is tolerably plain. The philosophy

of the middle dialogues is a nest of coupled contrasts: Being and Becoming, Appearance and Reality, Permanence and Flux, Reason and Sense, Body and Soul, Flesh and Spirit. Those contrasts are rooted in an ontology of Two Worlds, separated by a gulf of deficiency. The World of Knowledge, whose contents are the eternal Forms, stands to the World of Opinion, whose contents are sensible and changing, as the more real stands to the less real, as originals stand to shadows and reflections. The visible world is an image, unknowable in its deficiency, of an intelligible world apprehended by reason alone. If the seeds of this view are sown in early dialogues such as the *Euthyphro*, they have not there yet been brought to harvest.[19]

However true this general contrast may be, Allen has shown that close attention to the assumptions on which Socratic dialectic works yields surprising results. In his study of the *Euthyphro* and the other early dialogues Allen has identified an "earlier" or "Socratic" theory of Forms specified in the following way: there are real, objectively existing Forms which are universals, are παραδείγματα, are the οὐσία by which things are what they are, and are the objects of real definitions. This constitutes a *metaphysical* theory—not *the* (Platonic) metaphysical theory of Forms, but *a* metaphysical theory of Forms that is similar, though with subtle, important differences. In the following several pages let us review Allen's findings with regard to this Socratic theory of Forms.

The Form has objective existence; the Form is the object of real definition. The best way to show that the Socratic Form is a real, metaphysical entity is to examine the Socratic concept of definition. Socratic dialectic entails "real definition": that is, it presumes the existence of what it attempts to define:

> The kind of definition here in view is, of course, real definition, not nominal definition; it is definition not of words which are true of things, but of the nature of those things of which words are true. Real definition is analysis of essence, rather than stipulation as to how words shall be used or a report as to how they are in fact used. Because it is analysis of essence, real definition is, as stipulation is not, either true or false.[20]

Definition is conceived as an attempt to capture in a λόγος the οὐσία in reality, the οὐσία by which real things (and actions) in the world are what they are. The *definiendum* is an extra-linguistic reality (though it is never explicitly placed by Socrates "in the world," or anywhere else for that matter). Its existence does not have to be proved once the meaning is clarified by definition—Socratic dialectic is already committed to the existence of whatever εἶδος it strives to define. This "striving" alludes to the teleological dimension of Socratic dialectic:

> For Socratic dialectic, existence is, so to speak, a given: the aim is to penetrate its nature, and that penetration will be expressed in a definition. . . . In the early dialogues, real definition is an account of an object—an object which serves as the goal of inquiry. And in this connection it is perhaps worth observing that if such definition is not definition of a word, neither is it definition of a 'concept'. Euthyphro's conception of holiness, or what the ordinary Athenian ordinarily understood by the word 'holiness', is inadequate to the nature and essence of holiness; this is shown by *elenchus*, dialectical refutation. The relation of our ordinary concepts to Forms is in some sense teleological: the Form of holiness is presumably what Euthyphro would understand by the word 'holiness' if he fully understood the meaning of his words.[21]

And that is a comment not about the ability fully to use the word in the language, but about the reality which the word in the language signifies.

The readiness with which Socrates' opponents agree that there is Justice, Courage, Holiness, etc., that they are "things", indicates that the use of ordinary language commits one to the existence of these virtues in some sense. But that is not to say that ordinary language commits one to the special, metaphysical conceptualization as universals, standards and essences such as Socrates leads men to. Socrates' questioning reveals that ordinary language-users do not really know the things they are talking about. And in the process of dialectic Socrates urges on his partner that there is an objective reality, Justice, Courage, Holiness, etc., which evades his grasp, but which he must enter into the rigors of logical dialectic to grasp. It will only render itself up to one in the effort to mark off its boundaries, to delineate it just in and by itself and from the other virtues. Socrates suggests that it is *because* the peculiar metaphysical status of the object is ignored in ordinary talking and thinking that the ordinary, uncritical person is ignorant of what the virtues are.[22]

Yet the metaphysical theory is continuous with ordinary language in the sense that it is inferred from a concept of language implicit in the ordinary use of language.

> If the meaning of the word 'holiness' is holiness, and if holiness is a Form or essence, it is reasonable to suppose that the relation holding between the word and the thing is one of designation or naming. The early dialogues support this view.

> In the *Protagoras*, Socrates asks whether the thing (πρᾶγμα) which Protagoras has just named (ὠνομάσατε) is just or unjust (330c); and later, the question of whether virtue is one or many takes the form of an inquiry whether 'wisdom', 'justice', 'temperance', 'courage', and 'holiness' are names (ὀνόματα) for different things or names for the same thing. The early dialogues assume a referential theory of meaning: they assume that abstract nouns, or some of them, are names.[23]

The persons Socrates engages in dialectic already know quite well how to use the word in the language. Consider in this connection Meno's reply to the question, "What is virtue?":

> Meno: But there is no difficulty about it. First of all, if it is manly virtue you are after, it is easy to see that the virtue of a man consists in managing the city's affairs capably, and so that he will help his friends and injure his foes while taking care to come to no harm himself. Or if you want a woman's virtue, that is easily described. She must be a good housewife, careful with her stores and obedient to her husband. Then there is another virtue for a child, male or female, and another for an old man, free or slave as you like, and a great many more kinds of virtue, so that no one need be at a loss to say what it is. For every act and every time of life, with reference to each separate function, there is a virtue for each one of us, and similarly, I should say, a vice. (*Meno* 71e-72a)

Socratic dialectic defines not the way words are *in fact* used, but the way they *ought* to be used as determined by the objective essence which the word is meant to name.

The Form is a universal. Socratic dialectic, and in particular the "What is *X*?" question, asks for the εἶδος or ἰδέα which (1) is the *same* in all *x*'s, that is, all instances of *X*, (2) all *x*'s *have*, (3) is *common to* all *x*'s.

The Form is a paradeigma. Socrates supposes that the *x*'s are of "the same sort" (τοιοῦτος, οἷος) as the Form *X*, and thus the Form becomes a παράδειγμα, a model or standard by which one might judge questionable instances of *x*'s. Logically and epistemologically the *X* is prior to *x*'s. Logically, because to talk of *x*'s implies knowledge of what the *X* is. Epistemologically, because to know that something or other is an *x* one must know what the *X* is. The Form is always the same by itself; and it is never qualified by its opposite—two features necessary to the Form to be a παράδειγμα. Anything which is not always *x* or can be qualified by not-*x* cannot be an answer to the question, "What is *X*?"

The Form is an οὐσία, *an essence.* In asking "What is *X*?" Socrates is asking for the essence and not a mark distinguishing particular instances.[24] Knowledge of οὐσία is prior to knowledge of πάθος. One must know the "what-ness" of a thing before one knows whether a,b,c, etc., are necessary (or, for that matter, non-necessary) properties of *X*. Further, it is important to realize in what sense the Form is the "being" (οὐσία) of things.

> [I]n Plato's early dialogues Forms are not the being of that which they are Forms. A universal, being one, cannot constitute the being of a plurality—precisely why Aristotle was led to distinguish substantial form from universal. The *Euthyphro* does not imply that holiness is the being of any given holy thing or action as holy; it implies only that holiness is that *by* which holy things are holy. It implies, to borrow another bit of Aristotelian vocabulary, that holiness is a cause.[25]

By "being" Allen seems to mean *individual* being, or existence; in this sense the Form does *not* constitute the being of things. That is, it is not an immanent substantial form. Nonetheless, the Form is a metaphysical reality.

> Metaphysically, Forms affect the career of the world: they are the real natures of things, and the world is what it is because they are what they are.[26] If Forms are to exist, we might expect them, not as it were to just sit there, but to do honest work, to affect the career of the world. This they do; for we shall find that, in the early dialogues, Forms are causes.[27]

Without the Forms real things in the world would not be *what* they are. The Forms constitute the essence of the (things in the) world. Nonetheless, as Socrates thinks of it, the Form is not simply identical with the being of the thing. It is the οὐσία *by which* (instrumental dative)[28] things are what they are. This way of putting it shows that while it serves as the essence of things the Form is a distinct object or entity in its own right.[29]

> There is an argument in the *Hippias Major* which makes this assumption [that the Form is not the "being" of things but the cause of their οὐσία] explicit. Socrates leads Hippias to agree that justice *is* something (ἔστι τι τοῦτο), and that this is true of wisdom too, for, 'things which are just and wise and so on would not be such *by* them, if they were not something'. Because beautiful things are beautiful by beauty, Hippias is compelled to agree that beauty *is* something too. Socrates then goes on to raise the question: What is it? (*Hippias Major*, 287c-d).
>
> The argument is an excellent one: if beauty is that by which beautiful things are beautiful, and if beautiful things exist, beauty exists. Beauty is not a word, not a thought, not a concept. It is an existing thing, for the things it makes beautiful are existing things, and they are not made beautiful by our words or thoughts or concepts.[30]

This is the precise sense in which the Form is a cause—it is, to use Aristotle's terminology, an essential or formal cause.

The recognition of such a theory of Forms in the Socratic dialogues forces us to conclude that Aristotle is mistaken in claiming that Socrates did not "separate" the Forms.[31] The truth lies rather with Plato (and Burnet and Taylor who took him at his word) in the *Phaedo* (100) where he maintains that there is "nothing new" to the simple-minded αἰτία he there sets forth. This αἰτία, which he "has constantly spoken of," consists of positing the Form in and by itself separate from particular instances and then explaining the instances in terms of the Form:

> *Phaedo* 100d6-8: for I won't go so far as to dogmatize about the right term to describe how the Form comes to be in the thing, but merely affirm that *all beautiful things are beautiful because of the beautiful itself* [τῷ καλῷ πάντα τὰ καλὰ (γίγνεται) καλά].

In a word, the Form is the *formal cause* of its instances. As we have seen, this is precisely the view of the Form in the Socratic dialogues.[32] Indeed, the very language of the *Hippias Major* forms a striking comparison:

> Socrates: Then are not all beautiful things beautiful by beauty [τὰ καλὰ πάντα τῷ καλῷ ἐστι καλά]?
> Hippias: Yes, by beauty.
> Socrates: Which has real existence [Ὄντι γέ τινι τούτῳ]?
> Hippias: Yes, what else do you think? (287c8-d2)

In short, the separateness of Form from particular is not the distinctive new feature of the Platonic or "middle" theory of Forms. It will not do to conceive the Forms in the early, Socratic dialogues as somehow "immanent" and not metaphysically "separate". Thus they cannot *in this regard* be distinguished from the theory of Forms in the middle dialogues.

1 For brief accounts of the stylometric method and other linguistic research on the dialogues one may consult: J. Burnet, *Platonism* (Berkeley, 1928), 7-17; Raymond Simeterre, "La Chronologie des oeuvres de Platon," *Revue des Études Grecques*, 58(1945), 146-62; W.K.C. Guthrie, *A History of Greek Philosophy* (Cambridge, 1969), III, 48-52.

2 Oxford, 1951, 1.

3 Laszlo Versényi, *Socratic Humanism* (New Haven, 1963), 178.

4 He refers to it also as his "well-worn theme," 100b.

5 *Metaphysics* 1086b2.

6 So that something like the following schema was obtained:

Early dialogues	Middle dialogues	Later dialogues
Hippias Minor	*Phaedo*	*Parmenides*
Charmides	*Symposium*	*Theaetetus*
Laches	*Republic*	*Sophist*
Euthyphro	*Phaedrus*	*Politicus*
Crito		*Timaeus*
Apology		*Critias*
Gorgias		*Philebus*
Protagoras		*Seventh Letter*
Hippias Major		*Laws*
Euthydemus		
Cratylus		
Meno		
Menexenus		
Lysis		

The placement of the *Phaedrus*, however, is somewhat problematic: for some scholars it has strong affinities with the *Theaetetus* and *Parmenides* (see R. Simeterre, "La Chronologie," 151-62. In any case, the same rough, overall chronological scheme obtains.

7 G.M.A. Grube, *Plato's Thought* (1935; rpt. Boston, 1958), 9.

8 *Plato's Theory of Ideas*, 11-12.

9 *Ibid.*, 11.

10 *Ibid.*, 12.

11 Which seems in point of fact to be wrong: observe Socrates at *Euthyphro* 6e:

> Well then, show me what, precisely, this ideal is, so that, with my eye on it, and using it as a standard [παραδείγματι], I can say that any action done by you or anybody else is

holy if it resembles this ideal, or, if it does not, can deny that it is holy.

12 *Plato's Theory of Ideas*, 17.

13 *Ibid.*, 21.

14 For Ross's use of the word "transcendence" with respect to the mature theory of Ideas see *Ibid.*, 19, 21.

15 *Plato's Thought in the Making* (Cambridge, 1965), 39. It is interesting that John Burnet had just the opposite conviction, that Plato could not possibly be distorting the truth when he put the theory of Forms in Socrates' mouth:

> I cannot bring myself to believe that [Plato] falsified the story of his master's last hours on earth by using him as a mere mouthpiece for novel doctrines of his own. That would have been an offence against good taste and an outrage on all natural piety; for if Plato did this thing, he must have done it deliberately. There can be no question here of unconscious development; he must have known quite well whether Socrates held these doctrines or not. I confess that I should regard the *Phaedo* as little better than a heartless mystification if half the things commonly believed about it were true. (*Plato's Phaedo*, xi-xii)

16 *Plato's Thought in the Making*, 9.

17 *Ibid.*, 11.

18 Thus Raven emphasizes essentially the same thing as Ross's imitation and participation, but from the opposite perspective. It might also be noted that Raven does not stress deficient realization or paradeigmatism as distinguishing features of the new metaphysical theory.

19 London, 1970, 68.

20 *Ibid.*, 79.

21 *Ibid.*, 82.

22 It was because A.K. Rogers, in his study, *The Socratic Problem* (New Haven, 1933), failed to grasp what was involved in the Socratic quest for definitions that he could put forward the specious view that Socrates on the one hand was a moral sage and mystic seer, while Plato was a professional scientist, logician and metaphysician. Rogers viewed logical definition as an authentic Socratic element (158), but for Socrates this was "a method of emotional insight" (158) which was ultimately an ineffable moral and religious "experience" of the virtues

of goodness, justice, temperance, etc. (68, 134). It was Plato who logicized and metaphysicized the Socratic way. Following Burnet and Taylor in not differentiating between the dialogues of the early and middle periods for his reconstruction of the historical Socrates, Rogers ranged across the two sets of dialogues to differentiate what he perceived were two quite distinct strains of thinking indicative of two different personality types or temperaments: on the one hand, the moral sage and mystic, on the other, the professional scientist and academician (92, 109, 116, 132).

23 R.E. Allen, *Plato's 'Euthyphro'*, 113.

24 *pace* Richard Robinson, *Plato's Earlier Dialectic* (Oxford, 1953), 54.

25 R.E. Allen, *Plato's 'Euthyphro'*, 121.

26 *Ibid.*, 68.

27 *Ibid.*, 113.

28 *Ibid.*, 123. See also M.F. Burnyeat, "Virtues in Action," in Gregory Vlastos, ed., *The Philosophy of Socrates* (Garden City, 1971), 225-26.

29 Allen calls it an "object" on pages 100 and 101.

30 *Ibid.*, 121.

31 Allen observes, *Ibid.*, 134:

> But Socrates is plainly not defining sensibles in the early dialogues: quite apart from the fact that moral Forms have no sensible instances, the non-identity of Forms and their instances is assumed by the dialectic of every early dialogue which aims at definition, for definition is, as we have seen, an account of an object, and that object is a universal. Non-identity is also implied by the fact that Forms are essences and causes, by which things are what they are, and by the fact that Forms are standards for determining what things have them and what things do not.

Also page 135:

> But the passages in the early dialogues which assume the existence of Forms also customarily assume their numerical oneness . . . . Commitment to the existence of Forms in the early dialogues involves commitment to their individuality.

32 We are making a limited point here: the new, simple αἰτία is to be identified with the Socratic theory of Forms only insofar as the εἶδος, a thing different from any particular instance, is that by which (formal cause) a thing is said to

have the corresponding characteristic. There remain very important differences between the Socratic "theory" of Forms and the αἰτία of *Phaedo* 100 (to which Burnet and Taylor did not give sufficient recognition): in the early, Socratic dialogues the λόγος is the object of ἔλεγχος, usually negative, and the εἶδος is the end of the dialectic. In the *Phaedo*, however, the εἶδος is posited in a λόγος which serves as the premise in a positive, constructive argument. Even more important is the appearance in the *Phaedo* of the distinctive two-world ontology and the metaphysical theory of degrees of reality as a means of characterizing the relationship between the class of the Forms and the class of their corresponding instances.

Appendix V

Two Passages from Xenophon's 'Memorabilia'

There are two passages in Xenophon's *Memorabilia* which, because of their intrinsic importance and interest, ought not be omitted from any discussion of Socrates' religion. They are *Memorabilia* I.4.2-19 and IV.3.2-18.

The first is a discussion which Xenophon claims to have heard between Socrates and a certain Aristodemus. Xenophon relates it as an example of Socrates' "daily talks with his friends" (I.4.1) in which he made them morally better men—in this case more pious towards the gods, more just and stronger in their virtue (I.4.19). Aristodemus does not respect any of the traditional religious νόμοι (laws or customs): he neither sacrifices nor prays to the gods; he does not consult oracles, and indeed he goes so far as to ridicule those who do (I.4.2). In this of course he was ἄθεος, impious towards the gods. But whether Aristodemus is an atheist in the stronger sense of disbelieving in the existence of the gods is an obscure point in Xenophon's account. On the one hand Aristodemus affirms it is not the existence of the gods he is skeptical about:

> Here Aristodemus exclaimed: "Really, Socrates, I don't despise the godhead [τὸ δαιμόνιον, speaking of that which orders the universe!]. But I think it is too great to need my service."
>
> "Then the greater the power that deigns to serve you, the more it demands of you."
>
> "I assure you, that if I believed that the gods pay any heed to man, I would not neglect them." (I.4.10-11)

Aristodemus apparently only holds that traditional religion is empty and futile because the gods have no concern for men. But the difficulty is that Socrates does not argue against Aristodemus as though this were all that was at issue. Socrates produces what may be called the first theistic argument from design (thus Norman Gulley in *The Philosophy of Socrates* [London, 1968], 179-92, esp. 190). Socrates argues that the constitution of the human body indicates marvelous forethought and design, and that it is inconsistent and short-sighted not to see the intelligence (νοῦς) and wisdom (φρόνιμον) behind the material universe (I.4.4-9) as well. But it would make sense for Socrates to argue thus only if he took Aristodemus' impiety to stem from what we might generally term the presuppositions of the natural philosophers. We need not suggest that Aristodemus was a natural philosopher; only that he had, like much of the intelligentsia of the day, come under the influence of natural philosophy. At any rate the practical and theoretical aspects of Aristodemus' impiety are not carefully distinguished in the passage. We might compare it with Plato's discussion in Book 10 of the *Laws*. There Plato is concerned to give religious cult and νόμοι a good foundation in his πόλις. He feels that to ground religious practice properly one must ensure that the proper attitudes towards the gods prevail. In order to achieve this he sets himself the task of first refuting the irreligious, atheistic presuppositions of natural philosophy, in particular the view that matter can serve as the ultimate explanatory principle of things. It is spiritual realities, more precisely soul and intelligence, that are ultimate; they necessarily, logically precede the material factors in the constitution of the universe.

We can look in vain for this kind of careful distinction of the theoretical elements in Socrates' argument in the *Memorabilia*. The argument from design is intended to convince Aristodemus that the wonderful solicitude of the gods in fashioning the human body and the natural cosmos is deserving of man's gratitude. That is, Socrates' demonstration that the world is ordered by some intelligence or wisdom is used to convince Aristodemus that he should accept the gods of the πόλις. The argument from design plays but a subordinate role in an apologetic for conventional piety. The form of the argument at I.4.2 ff. is in effect: "Aristodemus, you are being inconsistent; you admire and honor human artists for their creations; how much more worthy of honor and respect are the creators of living, moving, intelligent beings. (Socrates here seems to assume with Aristodemus that the gods of the πόλις are the creators of men and the universe.) Look for instance to the human body: all of man's faculties and especially the organs of sense betray a marvellous solicitude and forethought (πρόνοια, προνοητικός). But you, ungrateful man, see nothing here for which to give thanks to the gods. With regard to the natural world at large, too, the same thing applies—for only the intellectually obstinate and obtuse will deny that the natural world is ordered and governed by intelligence (γνώμη, 4; φρόνιμον, 8; νοῦς, 8; φρόνησις, 17). There is deliberate conscious forethought, not chance, behind things. But all this order and design in nature, Aristodemus, works to your good as a man. Everything works to man's practical advantage and happiness: the organization of the senses, instincts, organs, even man's soul. The deity was careful to create man's soul so that he could apprehend the gods who made them and thus worship them (cf. 13). And seeing how the gods have outfitted man supremely well for attending to all his own needs and desires, how can you be so ungrateful as not to give them worship?"

The argument from the *practical advantages* that accrue to man from the design in the universe is even more apparent in the second passage, IV.3.2 ff. Socrates encourages Euthydemus to "reflect on the care the gods have taken to furnish man with what he *needs*" (ὧν οἱ ἄνθρωποι δέονται κατεσκευάκασι, 3). The cycle of night and day, the sun and the moon, the seasons, the gift of water, fire, the lower animals—all these things were created "for the sake of men" (ἀνθρώπων ἕνεκα, 8), "not only for our needs, but for our happiness and enjoyment" (εὐφραινόμεθα, 5). Even the faculty of reasoning (λογισμός, 11) was given to man not, evidently, so that he might enjoy truth for its own sake, but so that he might combine it with experience and so learn how to use the things of the world to his own advantage (11). Everywhere the emphasis is on the practical. The supreme good is the worldly satisfaction of man, and everything in the universe is ordered to it.

Xenophon considers the topic of discussion in the first passage to be the δαιμόνιον (περὶ τοῦ δαιμονίου, I.4.2). This is a strange term to use to designate the divine νοῦς which orders the cosmos. There is nothing in Greek literature before Socrates, or for that matter in Plato's Socratic dialogues, to prepare us for such a usage. As the term is used in Plato it always refers to the limited "divine something" peculiar to Socrates; it is never suggested that this personal δαιμόνιον has any connection with the cosmos at large. But what is actually discussed in Xenophon's passage under this rubric? At 7 we find this δαιμόνιον is a wise δημιουργός with the concerns of the living beings he has created at heart (σοφοῦ τινος δημιουροῦ καὶ φιλοζῴου). At 9 this single δημιουρός becomes many δημιουργοί—there are at once one creator and many. At 10 it is clear Aristodemus takes this δημιουργός, whose reality he admits, to be the δαιμόνιον. And in the very next sentence he shows that he takes "gods" (θεοί) to be equivalent to these two notions. And in 13 we find it is "the deity" (ὁ θεός) that has shown such solicitude and concern for the constitution of man's nature. Since we find out further that this God, or more properly the Thought (φρόνησις) dwelling in the universe, sees all that happens at every instant in the entire cosmos (17), we may be warranted in supposing the plural to be only a loose way of referring to the singular—for clearly there is only one omniscient νοῦς that rules the cosmos (otherwise it would not be one ordered cosmos). We are left then with the equivalence between ὁ θεός, ὁ δημιουργός, τὸ δαιμόνιον, and, as we find out at the end of 18, τὸ θεῖον as well. For all the looseness, the lack of discrimination, in the use of these terms, one thing is clear—all these various terms are used to refer to the γνώμη, φρόνιμον, νοῦς, φρόνησις governing the creation of living beings. By implication the deity is the soul (ψυχή) of the universe (9).

There is a great deal in Xenophon's account of Socrates' opinions here that we hear for the first time, yet the nature of his account forces us to choose between him and Plato. True, Plato confirms Xenophon on some fundamental points as far as he goes: in the intellectual biography of *Phaedo* 96a ff. Plato relates that it was Socrates' personal conviction that the entire cosmos was ordered to an end, the Good. And the *Meno*, which we take to be the echo of something authentically Socratic, says that all reality forms a realistic, comprehensive system of truth—"all nature is akin" (τῆς φύσεως ἁπάσης συγγενοῦς οὔσης, 81c9-d1). Xenophon's implausible blurring of the various god-concepts is suspect—the lack of subtlety and precision in all probability hides his failure to penetrate and comprehend the material he grasps—but this is not the crucial consideration. Nor is it the fact that Xenophon has Socrates argue that the gifts of divination, alongside the arguments from nature, are evidence of God's loving concern for mankind. But what does force the choice is the radically different *religious* implications of the respective accounts. For Xenophon's Socrates the τέλος (end) of the intelligent order of the universe is the happiness and good pleasure of man. For Plato's Socrates the end to which human conduct must be ordered, and to which the natural cosmos at large is *believed* to be ordered (though ultimately, according to *Phaedo* 96a ff., Socrates has no confidence, no knowledge in this regard), transcends man. The divine ἀρεταί are not relative to human valuations and desires; they are the absolute values by which human aims are judged and ordered. In Xenophon religion is the thoroughly conventional sort—the heavenly commerce rejected in the *Euthyphro*. The wonderful gifts the gods have given man for his good pleasure obligate man's response. But in Plato conventional piety gives way to higher, philosophical piety, *true* piety.

In the light of the above considerations, then, it is apparent that these two passages give us little reason to alter our previous estimate of Xenophon's testimony.

Glossary of Greek Terms

ἀγαθός (*agathos*): good, noble, excellent

ἀθάνατος (*athanatos*): immortal

αἰτία (*aitia*): cause, ground

ἀρετή (*aretē*): excellence, virtue, nobility

ἄριστος (*aristos*): noblest, most excellent

ἀρχή (*archē*): beginning, cause, first principle

ἀσέβεια (*asebeia*): impiety

βασιλεύς (*basileus*): king, prince

δαιμόνιον (*daimonion*): divine; Socrates' divine sign

δαίμων (*daimōn*): divine being

δημιουργός (*dēmiourgos*): maker; divine maker of the world

δίκαιος (*dikaios*): right(eous), just

δικαιοσύνη (*dikaiosynē*): righteousness, justice

δίκη (*dikē*): judgment, law

δόξα (*doxa*): opinion, seeming

εἶδος (*eidos*): form, visible or intelligible

εἰρωνεία (*eirōneia*): irony

ἔλεγχος (*elenchos*): test, scrutiny

ἐόν (*eon*): being

ἐπιστήμη (*epistēmē*): knowledge

ἔρως (*erōs*): love, desire

εὐδαιμονία (*eudaimonia*): well-being, good fortune

εὐσεβές (*eusebes*): pious, piety

θεῖος (*theios*): divine

θέμις (*themis*): law

θεός (*theos*): god

θεουδής (*theoudēs*): god-fearing

θεραπεία (*therapeia*): care, service

GLOSSARY

ἰδέα (*idea*): form, visible or intelligible

κακός (*kakos*): bad

καλός (*kalos*): good, beautiful

καλός τε κἀγαθός (*kalos te kagathos*): a man of nobility, excellence and virtue

λόγος (*logos*): word, account, argument, dialogue, reason

μεγαληγορία (*megalēgoria*): high-sounding talk

μένος (*menos*): strength, valor

μίμησις (*mimēsis*): imitation

νόμος (*nomos*): law, custom

νοῦς (νόος, archaic form)(*nous*): mind

ὅσιος (*hosios*): observant of divine ordinances, pious

ὁσιότης (*hosiotēs*): observance of divine law, piety

οὐσία (*ousia*): being, substance, reality

πάθος (*pathos*): affection, anything that befalls one

παιδεία (*paideia*): education

παράδειγμα (*paradeigma*): pattern, exemplar

πεπνυμένος (*pepnumenos*): wise, prudent

πινυτός (*pinutos*): wise, understanding

πόλις (*polis*): city-state

πολίτης (*politēs*): citizen

σοφία (*sophia*): skill, expertise, wisdom

σοφιστής, σοφός (*sophistēs*, *sophos*): one who possesses skill, expertise, wisdom

σώφρων (σαόφρων)(*sōphrōn*): self-controlled, moderate

σωφροσύνη (*sōphrosynē*): self-control, temperance

τέλος (*telos*): end, goal

τέχνη (*technē*): skill, know-how

τιμή (*timē*): honor, esteem

ὕβρις (*hybris*): pride, arrogance

φύσις (*physis*): nature

ψυχή (*psychē*): soul

Bibliography

Adkins, Arthur W.H. "Clouds, Mysteries, Socrates and Plato." *Antichthon, Journal of the Australian Society for Classical Studies*, 4(1970), 13-24.

———. "Homeric Gods and the Values of Homeric Society." *Journal of Hellenic Studies*, 92(1972), 1-19

———. "Homeric Values and Homeric Society." *Journal of Hellenic Studies*, 91(1971), 1-13.

———. *Merit and Responsibility: A Study in Greek Values*. Oxford: Clarendon Press, 1960.

Allen, R.E. *Plato's 'Euthyphro' and the Earlier Theory of Forms*. London: Routledge and Kegan Paul, 1970.

Barker, Andrew. "Why did Socrates refuse to escape?" *Phronesis*, 22(1977), 13-28.

Berns, Laurence. "Socratic and Non-Socratic Philosophy: A Note on Xenophon's *Memorabilia*, 1.1.13 and 14." *Review of Metaphysics*, 28(1974-75), 85-88.

Bluck, R.S. "Logos and Forms in Plato: A Reply to Prof. Cross." *Mind*, 65(1956), 522-29.

Bowra, C.M. *Periclean Athens*. New York: Dial, 1971.

———. *Tradition and Design*. Oxford: Oxford University Press, 1930.

Bultmann, Rudolf. "Zur Geschichte der Lichtsymbolik im Altertum." *Philologus*, 97(1948), 1-36.

Burnet, John. *Early Greek Philosophy*. 1892; rpt. 4th ed., Cleveland: World, 1967.

———. *Platonis Opera*. 5 vols. Oxford: Clarendon Press, 1900-07.

———. *Platonism*. Berkeley: University of California Press, 1928.

———. *Plato's Euthyphro, Apology of Socrates and Crito*. Oxford: Clarendon Press, 1924.

_____________. *Plato's Phaedo*. Oxford: Clarendon Press, 1911.

_____________. "The Socratic Doctrine of the Soul." *Proceedings of the British Academy*, VII(1916), 235-59.

Burnyeat, M.F. "Virtues in Action." In *The Philosophy of Socrates*. Ed. G. Vlastos. Garden City: Doubleday, 1971, 209-34.

Calhoun, George M. "Polity and Society." *A Companion to Homer*. Ed. A.J.B. Wace and F.H. Stubbings. London: Macmillan, 1962.

Chamoux, Francois. *The Civilization of Greece*. Trans. B. Arthaud. London: Allen and Unwin, 1965.

Chroust, Anton-Hermann. *Socrates, Man and Myth: The Two Socratic Apologies of Xenophon*. London: Routledge and Kegan Paul, 1957.

Cook, Arthur B. *Zeus*. Cambridge: Cambridge University Press, 1914.

Cornford, F.M. "The Doctrine of Eros in Plato's *Symposium*." In his *The Unwritten Philosophy, and Other Essays*. Ed. W.K.C. Guthrie. 1950; rpt. Cambridge: Cambridge University Press, 1967.

_____________. *Principium Sapientiae*. Ed. W.K.C. Guthrie. 1952; rpt. New York: Harper, 1965.

Coulter, Cornelia. "The Tragic Structure of Plato's *Apology*." *Philological Quarterly*, 12(1933), 137-43.

Coulter, James A. "The Relation of the *Apology of Socrates* to Gorgias' *Defense of Palamades* and Plato's Critique of Gorgianic Rhetoric." *Harvard Studies in Classical Philology*, 68(1964), 269-303.

Cross, R.C. "Logos and Forms in Plato." *Mind*, 63(1954), 433-50.

Deman, Th. *Le Témoignage d'Aristote sur Socrate*. Paris: Les Belles Lettres, 1942.

Dietrich, B.C. *Death, Fate and the Gods*. London: Athlone, 1965.

Dodds, E.R. *The Greeks and the Irrational*. Berkeley: University of California Press, 1966.

Dover, Kenneth. *Aristophanes: Clouds*. Oxford: Clarendon Press, 1968.

Dupréel, Eugene. *La Légende socratique et les sources de Platon*. Brussels: Robert Sand, 1922.

Ehnmark, Erland. *The Idea of God in Homer*. Diss. Uppsala. Uppsala: Almqvist and Wiksells, 1935.

———————. "Socrates and the Immortality of the Soul." *Eranos* (1946), 105-22.

Ehrenberg, Victor. *From Solon to Socrates*. London: Methuen, 1968.

Epp, Ronald H. "Katharsis and the Platonic Reconstruction of Mystical Terminology." Φιλοσοφια, 4(1974), 168-79.

Ferguson, A.S. "The Impiety of Socrates." *Classical Quarterly*, 7(1913), 157-75.

Ferguson, John. "On the Date of Socrates' Conversion." *Eranos* (1964), 70-73.

Field, G.C. *Plato and his Contemporaries*. London: Methuen, 1930.

———————. *Socrates and Plato*. Oxford: Parker, 1913.

Finley, M.I. "Socrates and Athens." In his *Aspects of Antiquity*. London: Chatto and Windus, 1968.

———————. *The World of Odysseus*. New York: Viking, 1954.

Fox, Marvin. "The Trials of Socrates." *Archiv für Philosophie*, 6(1956), 226-61.

Friedländer, Paul. *Plato*. Trans. Hans Meyerhoff. Vol. 1, 1958; rev. ed. Princeton: Bollingen, 1973. Vol. 2, Princeton: Bollingen, 1964.

Fritz, Kurt von. "Nóος and νοεῖν in the Homeric Poems." *Classical Philology*, 38(1943), 79-93.

———————. "Νοῦς, νοεῖν, and their Derivatives in Presocratic Philosophy." Part I, *Classical Philology*, 40(1945), 223-42. Part II, *Classical Philology*, 41(1946), 12-34.

Furley, D.J. "The Early History of the Concept of the Soul." *University of London Institute of Classical Studies Bulletin*, 3(1956), 1-18.

Gagarin, Michael. "Socrates' *Hybris* and Alcibiades' Failure." *Phoenix*, 31(1977), 22-37.

Gigon, Olof. *Sokrates: Sein Bild in Dichtung und Geschichte*. Berne: Francke, 1947.

Gould, Thomas. *Platonic Love*. New York: Free Press, 1963.

Gray, J. Glenn. *Hegel and Greek Thought*. 1941; rpt. New York: Harper, 1968.

Greenberg, N.A. "Socrates' Choice in the *Crito*." *Harvard Studies in Classical Philology*, 70(1965), 45-82.

Greene, William Chase. *Moira: Fate, Good and Evil in Greek Thought.* 1944; rpt. New York: Harper, 1963.

Grote, George. *A History of Greece.* Vol. 9 (chap. 68, Socrates). London: John Murray, 1869.

__________. *Plato and the Other Companions of Socrates.* Vol. 1. London: John Murray, 1867.

Grube, G.M.A. "The Gods of Homer." In *Studies in Honour of Gilbert Norwood.* Ed. Mary E. White. Toronto: University of Toronto Press, 1952, 3-19.

__________. *Plato's Thought.* 1935; rpt. Boston: Beacon, 1958.

Gulley, Norman. *The Philosophy of Socrates.* London: Macmillan, 1968.

Guthrie, W.K.C. *The Greeks and Their Gods.* Boston: Beacon, 1950.

__________. *A History of Greek Philosophy.* Cambridge: Cambridge University Press, 1969 (vol. III) and 1975 (vol. IV).

__________. "Plato's Views on the Nature of the Soul." *Recherches sur la tradition platonicienne.* Fondation Hardt, Entretiens sur l'antiquité classique, tome III. Vandoeuvres-Genève, 1955, 2-19.

Hackforth, R. *The Composition of Plato's Apology.* Cambridge: Cambridge University Press, 1933.

__________. *Plato's Phaedo.* Indianapolis: Bobbs-Merrill, 1955.

__________. "Socrates." *Philosophy*, 11(1933), 259-72.

Hadas, Moses. *The Complete Plays of Aristophanes.* New York: Bantam, 1962.

Hamilton, Edith, and Cairns, Huntington, eds. *The Collected Dialogues of Plato.* New York: Bollingen, 1961.

Harrison, E.L. "Notes on Homeric Psychology." *Phoenix*, 14(1960), 63-80.

Havelock, Eric A. *Preface to Plato.* Cambridge (Mass.): Belknap, 1963.

__________. "The Socratic self as it is parodied in Aristophanes' *Clouds*." *Yale Classical Studies*, 22(1972), 1-18.

__________. "Why Was Socrates Tried?" In *Studies in Honour of Gilbert Norwood.* Ed. Mary E. White. Toronto: University of Toronto Press, 1952, 95-109.

Hegel, G.W.F. *Lectures on the History of Philosophy*. Trans. E.S. Haldane. London: Routledge and Kegan Paul, 1955.

————————. *The Philosophy of History*. Trans. J. Sibree. New York: Dover, 1956.

Hoerber, R.G. "Plato's *Euthyphro*." *Phronesis*, 3(1958), 95-107.

Hyland, Drew A. "Ἔρως, Ἐπιθυμία, and Φιλία in Plato." *Phronesis*, 13(1968), 32-46.

Jaeger, Werner. *Paideia: The Ideals of Greek Culture*. 3 vols. Trans. Gilbert Highet. Oxford: Blackwell, 1945-47.

————————. *The Theology of the Early Greek Philosophers*. 1947; rpt. Oxford: Oxford University Press, 1967.

Kierkegaard, Soren. *The Concept of Irony*. Trans. Lee M. Capel. 1965; rpt. Bloomington: Indiana University Press, 1968.

Kirk, G.S. and Raven, J.E. *The Presocratic Philosophers*. Cambridge: Cambridge University Press, 1963.

Lacey, A.R. "Our Knowledge of Socrates." In *The Philosophy of Socrates*. Ed. G. Vlastos. Garden City: Doubleday, 1971, 22-49.

Laguna, Theodore de. "The Interpretation of the *Apology*." *Philosophical Review*, 18(1909), 23-37.

Lattimore, Richmond. *The Iliad of Homer*. Chicago: University of Chicago Press, 1951.

————————. *The Odyssey of Homer*. 1965; rpt. New York: Harper, 1968.

Lloyd-Jones, Hugh. *The Justice of Zeus*. Berkeley: University of California Press, 1971.

Lofberg, J.O. "The Trial of Socrates." *Classical Journal*, 23 (1928), 601-9.

Long, A.A. "Morals and Values in Homer." *Journal of Hellenic Studies*, 90(1970), 122-29.

Magalhães-Vilhena, V. de. *Le Problème de Socrate: Le Socrate historique et le Socrate de Platon*. Paris: Presses Universitaires, 1952.

Maier, Heinrich. *Sokrates: Sein Werk und seine geschichtliche Stellung*. Tübingen: J.C.B. Mohr, 1913.

Markus, R.A. "The Dialectic of Eros in Plato's *Symposium*." *Downside Review*, 73(1955), 219-30.

McLaughlin, Robert J. "Socrates on Political Disobedience: A Reply to Gary Young." *Phronesis*, 21(1976), 185-97.

Moravcsik, J.M.E. "Reason and Eros in the 'Ascent'-Passage of the *Symposium*." In *Essays in Ancient Greek Philosophy*. Ed. John P. Anton with George L. Kustas. Albany: State University of New York Press, 1971, 285-302.

Mourelatos, A. *The Route of Parmenides: A Study of Word, Image, and Argument in the Fragments*. New Haven: Yale University Press, 1970.

Mylonas, George E. *Eleusis and the Eleusinian Mysteries*. Princeton: Princeton University Press, 1961.

Nilsson, Martin P. "Götter und Psychologie bei Homer." *Archiv für Religionswissenschaft*, 22(1923-24), 363-90.

________________. *Greek Folk Religion*. 1940; rpt. Philadelphia: University of Pennsylvania Press, 1972.

________________. *Greek Piety*. Trans. H.J. Rose. New York: Norton, 1969.

________________. *A History of Greek Religion*. 2nd ed., 1952; rpt. New York: Norton, 1964.

________________. "The Immortality of the Soul." *Eranos*, 39 (1941), 1-16.

Oldfather, W.A. "Socrates in Court." *Classical Weekly*, 31(1938), 203-11.

Onians, Richard B. *The Origins of European Thought*. Cambridge: Cambridge University Press, 1954.

Otto, Walter. *The Homeric Gods*. Trans. Moses Hadas. 1954; rpt. Boston: Beacon, 1964.

Panagiotou, Spiro. "Plato's *Euthyphro* and the Attic Code on Homicide." *Hermes*, 102(1974), 419-37.

Parke, H.W. "Chaerephon's Inquiry about Socrates." *Classical Philology*, 56(1961), 249-50.

__________. *Greek Oracles*. London: Hutchinson University Library, 1967.

__________. *A History of the Delphic Oracle*. Oxford: Blackwell, 1939.

Paxson, Thomas D., Jr. "Plato's *Euthyphro* 10a to 11b." *Phronesis* (1972), 171-90.

Phillipson, Coleman. *The Trial of Socrates*. London: Stevens, 1928.

Rabinowitz, W.G. "Platonic Piety: An Essay Toward the Solution of an Enigma." *Phronesis* (1958), 108-20.

Randall, John Herman, Jr. *Plato: Dramatist of the Life of Reason*. New York: Columbia University Press, 1970.

Raven, J.E. *Plato's Thought in the Making*. Cambridge: Cambridge University Press, 1965.

———, and Kirk, G.S. *The Presocratic Philosophers*. Cambridge: Cambridge University Press, 1963.

Rist, John M. *Eros and Psyche*. Toronto: University of Toronto Press, 1964.

Robin, Leon. "Les 'Mémorables' de Xénophon et notre connaissance de la philosophie de Socrate." *L'Année Philosophique* (1910), 1-47.

Robinson, Richard. *Essays in Greek Philosophy*. Oxford: Clarendon Press, 1969.

———. *Plato's Earlier Dialectic*. Oxford: Clarendon Press, 1953.

Robinson, T.M. *Plato's Psychology*. Toronto: University of Toronto Press, 1970.

Rogers, Arthur Kenyon. *The Socratic Problem*. New Haven: Yale University Press, 1933.

Rohde, Erwin. *Psyche*. 2 vols. Eng. trans. 1925; rpt. New York: Harper, 1966.

Ross, W.D. *Aristotle's Metaphysics*. Oxford: Clarendon Press, 1924.

———. *Plato's Theory of Ideas*. Oxford: Clarendon Press, 1951.

———. "The Problem of Socrates." *Classical Association Proceedings*, 30(1933), 16-21.

Rostovtzeff, M. *Greece*. 1926; rpt. Oxford: Oxford University Press, 1963.

Rudberg, Gunnar. *Platonica Selecta*. Stockholm: Almqvist and Wiksells, 1956.

Schaerer, René. *La Question platonicienne*. Neuchatel: Secretariat de l'Université, 1969.

Schleiermacher, Friedrich. *Introductions to the Dialogues of Plato*. Trans. William Dobson. 1895; rpt. New York: Arno, 1973.

Seeskin, Kenneth R. "Courage and Knowledge: A Perspective on the Socratic Paradox." *Southern Journal of Philosophy*, 14(1976), 511-21.

Silverberg, Tom, and Winspear, Alban D. *Who Was Socrates?* New York: Russell and Russell, 1960.

Simeterre, Raymond. "La Chronologie des oeuvres de Platon." *Revue des Études Grecques*, 58(1945), 146-62.

Snell, Bruno. *The Discovery of the Mind*. Trans. T.G. Rosenmeyer. 1953; rpt. New York: Harper, 1960.

Solmsen, Friedrich. *Plato's Theology*. Ithaca: Cornell University Press, 1942.

Sparshott, F.E. "Socrates and Thrasymachus." *Monist*, 50(1966), 421-59.

Strauss, Leo. *On Tyranny: An Interpretation of Xenophon's Hiero*. 1948; revised and enlarged, New York: Free Press, 1963.

____________. *Xenophon's Socrates*. 1972; rpt. Ithaca: Cornell University Press, 1973.

____________. *Xenophon's Socratic Discourse: An Interpretation of the Oeconomicus*. Ithaca: Cornell University Press, 1970.

Strycker, Émile de. "Le *Criton* de Platon." *Les Études Classiques*, 39(1971), 417-36.

__________________. "The Oracle Given to Chaerephon About Socrates (Plato, *Apology* 20e-21a)." In *Kephalaion: Studies in Greek Philosophy and Its Continuation Offered to Professor C.J. DeVogel*. Ed. J. Mansfeld and L.M. de Rijk. Assen: Van Gorcum, 1975, 39-49.

__________________. "Socrate et l'au-dela d'après l'*Apologie* platonicienne." *Les Études Classiques*, 18(1950), 269-84.

__________________. "The Unity of Knowledge and Love in Socrates' Conception of Virtue." *International Philosophical Quarterly*, 6(1966), 428-44.

Tate, J. "Greek for 'Atheism'." *Classical Review*, 50(1936), 3-5.

______. "More Greek for 'Atheism'." *Classical Review*, 51(1937), 3-6.

Taylor, A.E. *Plato: The Man and His Work*. 1926; rpt. London: Methuen, 1960.

___________. *Socrates*. 1933; rpt. Garden City: Doubleday, 1953.

————————. *Varia Socratica*. Oxford: Parker, 1911.

Van Camp, Jean, and Canart, Paul. *Le Sens du mot θεῖος chez Platon*. Louvain: Université de Louvain, 1956.

Versényi, Laszlo. *Socratic Humanism*. New Haven: Yale University Press, 1963.

Vlastos, Gregory. "The Paradox of Socrates." In *The Philosophy of Socrates*. Ed. G. Vlastos. Garden City: Doubleday, 1971, 1-21.

————————. "Reasons and Causes in the *Phaedo*." *Philosophical Review*, 78(1969), 291-325; rpt. in *Plato, I: Metaphysics and Epistemology*, ed. G. Vlastos, Garden City, 1971, 132-66.

Vogel, Cornelia de. "The Present State of the Socratic Problem." *Phronesis*, 1(1955), 26-35.

————————. "Who Was Socrates?" *Journal of the History of Philosophy*, 1(1963), 143-61.

Vries, G.J. de. "Mystery Terminology in Aristophanes and Plato." *Mnemosyne*, 26(1973), 1-8.

Wellman, Robert R. "Socratic Method in Xenophon." *Journal of the History of Ideas*, 37(1976), 307-18.

Wilamowitz-Moellendorff, Ulrich von. *Der Glaube der Hellenen*. Bd. I. Darmstadt: Wissenschaftliche Buchgesellschaft, 1959.

Winspear, Alban D., and Silverberg, Tom. *Who Was Socrates?* New York: Russell and Russell, 1960.

Woozley, A.D. "Socrates on Disobeying the Law." In *The Philosophy of Socrates*. Ed. G. Vlastos. Garden City: Doubleday, 1971, 299-318.

Xenophon. *Memorabilia and Oeconomicus*. Trans. E.C. Marchant. London: Heinemann, 1923.

————————. *Symposium and Apology*. Trans. O.J. Todd. *Anabasis*, Books IV-VII. Trans. L. Brownson. London: Heinemann, 1922.

Young, Gary. "Socrates and Obedience." *Phronesis*, 19(1974), 1-29.

Zeller, Eduard. *Socrates and the Socratic Schools*. Trans. (from Zeller's *Philosophie der Griechen*) O.J. Reichel. London: Longmans, 1885.

Index

INDEX

INDEX

INDEX

INDEX

SUPPLEMENTS

1. **FOOTNOTES TO A THEOLOGY**
The Karl Barth Colloquium of 1972
Edited and with an Introduction by Martin Rumscheidt
1974 / vii + 149 pp. / $3.50 (paper)
ISBN 0-919812-02-3

2. **MARTIN HEIDEGGER'S PHILOSOPHY OF RELIGION**
John R. Williams
1977 / 188 pp. / $4.00 (paper)
ISBN 0-919812-03-1

3. **MYSTICS AND SCHOLARS**
The Calgary Conference on Mysticism 1976
Edited by Harold Coward and Terence Penelhum
1977 / viii + 118 pp. / $4.00 (paper)
ISBN 0-919812-04-X

4. **GOD'S INTENTION FOR MAN**
Essays in Christian Anthropology
William O. Fennell
1977 / vi + 56 pp. / $2.50 (paper)
ISBN 0-919812-05-8

5. **"LANGUAGE" IN INDIAN PHILOSOPHY AND RELIGION**
Edited and Introduced by Harold G. Coward
1978 / x + 93 pp. / $4.00 (paper)
ISBN 0-919812-07-4

6. **BEYOND MYSTICISM**
James R. Horne
1978 / x + 158 pp. / $4.00 (paper)
ISBN 0-919812-08-2

7. **THE RELIGIOUS DIMENSION OF SOCRATES' THOUGHT**
A Study of the Greek Experience of Life
James Beckman
1978 / xiv + 274 pp. / $5.00 (paper)
ISBN 0-919812-09-0

EDITIONS

1. **LA LANGUE DE YA'UDI**
Description et classement de l'ancien parler de Zencirli dans le cadre des langues sémitiques du nord-ouest
Paul-Eugène Dion, O.P.
1974 / vii + 509 p. / $4.50 (broché)
ISBN 0-919812-01-5

Also published / Avons aussi publié

RELIGION AND CULTURE IN CANADA / religion et culture au canada
Edited by / sous la direction de Peter Slater
1977 / viii + 568 pp. / $7.50 (paper)
ISBN 0-919812-06-6

Available from / en vente chez:
WILFRID LAURIER UNIVERSITY PRESS
Wilfrid Laurier University
Waterloo, Ontario, Canada N2L 3C5

Tout chèque doit être fait à l'ordre de Wilfrid Laurier University Press / Make cheques payable to Wilfrid Laurier University Press